INSIGHT GUIDE

CHICAGO

APA PUBLICATIONS
Part of the Langenscheidt Publishing Group

ABOUT THIS BOOK

Editorial

Project Editor
Kerry MacKenzie
Managing Editor
Cameron Duffy
Editorial Director
Brian Bell

Distribution

UK & Ireland
GeoCenter International Ltd
The Viables Centre , Harrow Way
Basingstoke, Hants RG22 4BJ
Fax: (44) 1256-817988

United States
Langenscheidt Publishers, Inc.
46–35 54th Road, Maspeth, NY 11378
Fax: (718) 784-0640

Australia & New Zealand
Hema Maps Pty. Ltd.
24 Allgas Street, Slacks Creek 4127
Brisbane, Australia
Tel: (61) 7 3290 0322
Fax: (61) 7 3290 0478

Worldwide
APA Publications GmbH & Co.
Verlag KG (Singapore branch)
38 Joo Koon Road, Singapore 628990
Tel: (65) 865-1600
Fax: (65) 861-6438

Printing

Insight Print Services (Pte) Ltd
38 Joo Koon Road, Singapore 628990
Tel: (65) 865-1600
Fax: (65) 861-6438

©1999 **APA Publications GmbH & Co.**
Verlag KG (Singapore branch)
All Rights Reserved
First Edition 1992
Fourth Edition 1999

This guidebook combines the
interests and enthusiasms of
two of the world's best known
information providers: Insight
Guides, whose titles have set
the standard for visual travel
guides since 1970, and Discovery
Channel, the world's premier
source of nonfiction television
programming.

Insight Guides editors provide
both practical advice
and a general under-
standing about a
destination's his-
tory, culture, insti-
tutions and people.
Discovery Channel

and its Web site: www.discovery.com,
help millions of viewers explore their
world from the comfort of their own
home and encourage them to try it
firsthand.

From its lively, lovely lakefront
to its thrilling architecture and
world-class museums, from its
appealing neighborhoods such
as Greek Town and Lakeview to
its out-of-town highlights such
as Oak Park and the
scenic North Shore,
this book will show
you the best of
the captivating
Midwest capital,
Chicago.

How to use this book

The book is carefully structured to convey an understanding of Chicago and its culture and to guide readers through its sights and attractions:

◆ The **Features** section, with a yellow color bar, covers the city's history and culture in lively authoritative essays written by specialists.

◆ The **Places** section, with a blue bar, provides full details of all the sights and areas worth seeing. The chief places of interest are coordinated by number with specially drawn maps.

◆ The **Travel Tips** section, at the back of the book, offers a convenient point of reference for information on travel, accommodations, restaurants and other practical aspects of the city. Information may be located quickly using the index printed on the back cover flap, which also serves as a handy bookmark.

The contributors

This new edition, which builds on the earlier edition edited by **Tim Harper**, was edited by **Kerry MacKenzie**, a Chicago-based British journalist who has written for numerous UK publications, including *The Times,* and has edited for consumer magazines on both sides of the Atlantic; she also updated the *Travel Tips* section, with invaluable help from **Michiko Bickelman**.

Other contributors whose text has been adapted from earlier editions are **Manuel Galvan, Tom Hardy, Pam Hardy, Don Hayner, Tom McNamee, Joseph Epstein, Carol Jouzaitis, Stuart Silverman, Sondra Rosenberg, Eileen Norris, Janet Neiman, Lisa Goff, Fernando Jones** and **Barbara Brotman**.

The updaters who provided material for this latest edition, are: freelance journalist **Bridget McCoy**, University of Illinois research professor and freelance journalist **Mark Alleyne**, native Chicagoan and president of Chicago Walkers Club **Nancy Goldman**, and sports journalist **Pat Fitzmaurice**.

The veteran *Chicago Tribune* photographer **Chuck Berman** is responsible for many of the fine images in the book.

Map Legend

—‒‒‒	International Boundary
‒‒‒‒	State Boundary
⊖	Border Crossing
▬•▬	National Park/Reserve
Ⓜ	El (subway)
✈ ✦	Airport: International/ Regional
🚌	Bus Station
Ⓟ	Parking
❶	Tourist Information
✉	Post Office
✝ ⛪	Church/Ruins
✝	Monastery
☾	Mosque
✡	Synagogue
🏰 ⛫	Castle/Ruins
∴	Archaeological Site
∩	Cave
𝐈	Statue/Monument
★	Place of Interest

The main places of interest in the Places section are coordinated by number with a full-color map (e.g. ❶), and a symbol at the top of every right-hand page tells you where to find the map.

CONTENTS

Apartment
building
designed by
Mies van
der Rohe

Insight on ...

Information panels

Travel Tips

Places

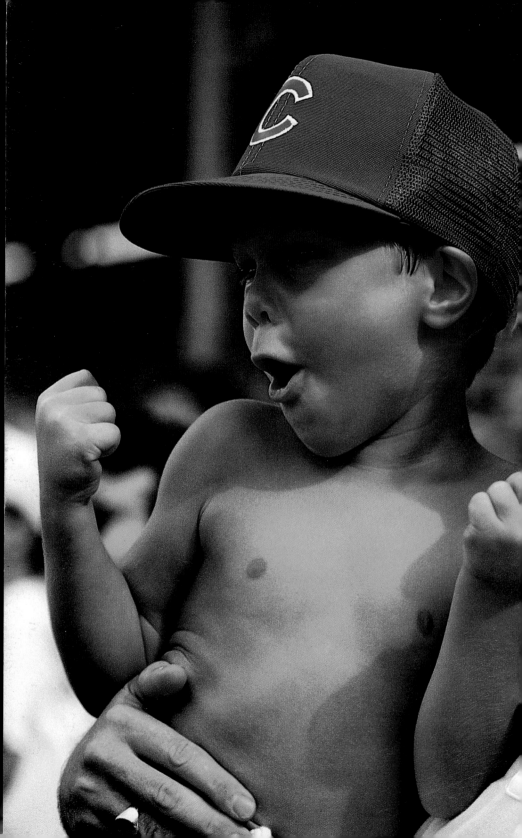

THE CITY OF BROAD SHOULDERS

Chicago, the alluring capital of the Midwest, has world-class museums, glitzy shopping and a magnificent lakefront

Chicago is a blue-collar town with champagne taste. Whether you're having a beer in one of the city's legendary blues bars, delighting in a hot dog at one of the mom-and-pop vending stands, or dining at a four-star restaurant, you will be at ease in Chicago. Chicagoans blaze their own trails. The birthplace of author Ernest Hemingway, who defined a generation of writers, architect Frank Lloyd Wright, who created a new style of architecture, and mobsters such as Al Capone, who modernized organized crime, the city is known for its innovative and often controversial people.

From the industrial giants exploiting Chicago's earliest immigrant workers to the political machines ruling the city with an iron fist, Chicago has always been a bit different. The city that sprang from lakefront swampland, burned in a devastating fire and was rebuilt in steel, has proven to be remarkably resilient. Chicagoans themselves will attest to this remarkable resilience. The proud inhabitants of the Windy City endure bitter winters in anticipation of the thrilling spring and summer seasons to follow.

With miles of open lakefront and parks Chicago is full of scenic points and outdoor activities. Volleyball teams, joggers, rollerbladers, cyclists and strollers crowd the lakefront from April to December. The parks are full of families barbecuing. Some of the world's tallest buildings command views of other states. Chicago, immortalized by Pulitzer Prizewinner Carl Sandburg as "the city of broad shoulders," is poetic in its construction. The lake creates the eastern border of the city from which all things great and small sprawl. At the north end of Michigan Avenue is the Gold Coast with upscale shopping. Further south the museums begin.

But it's the people and the neighborhoods that make the city what it is – ethnically very diverse. Areas such as Bucktown foster Chicago's new artists. Old neighborhoods such as Chinatown and Ukrainian Village are a slice of the homeland.

Trendy Lincoln Park is populated with new families and young professionals. Chicago is spirited. Proud of its world-champion athletic teams Chicagoans are always celebrating some victory. The Cubs won? Party at Wrigley Field! The Bulls did it again? Let's have a rally at Grant Park! The Bears? Well, they haven't done a superbowl shuffle in a while but fans cheer them anyway. With chameleon-like ease Chicagoans can match the pace of the east coast or the laid-back style of the west. Chicago holds the hearts of its people and it will capture the hearts of most visitors too. ❑

PRECEDING PAGES: flipping at the fountain; a chip off the old block; downtown night-clubbers; arriving at O'Hare.
LEFT: tuned-in Cubs fan.

Decisive Dates

PREHISTORIC TIMES

Lake Chicago, which covered much of what is now the American Midwest, receded with the glaciers, leaving swamps separating the prairies and what is now Lake Michigan.

PRE–19TH CENTURY

The Pottawattomie Indians used the swampland linking the Great Lakes and the Mississippi River to trade, and called it "Checagou" in reference to the stink of rotting wild onions.

1673 Louis Jolliet, a gold-seeking explorer, and Father Jacques Marquette, a Jesuit priest, directed by the Indians, canoed into the marshland that would become Chicago.
1779 Jean Baptiste Point DuSable established a trading post on the bank of the river, at what is now Michigan Avenue.

AFTER THE REVOLUTIONARY WAR

1795 General "Mad Anthony" Wayne led troops that overran the Indians and forced them to give up tribal lands, including much of what is now downtown Chicago.
1803 Federal soldiers arrived from Detroit and built Fort Dearborn.

1812 In an Indian insurrection, 52 men, women and children at the fort were slain in the Fort Dearborn Massacre. Troops put down the uprising and rebuilt the fort.
1825 The Erie Canal opened.
1831 The first bridge was built over the river, linking the north and south sides of town.
1833 During the population and property boom, a downtown plot that had sold for $300 in the previous year was resold for $60,000.

CHICAGO INCORPORATED AS A CITY

1837 With a population that had grown to 4,170 from 50 in seven years, Chicago was incorporated as a city. William B. Ogden won the election as Chicago's first mayor.
1848 The Chicago Board of Trade, the world's oldest and largest futures exchange, was formed, launching Chicago as the world center for commodities trading.

AFTER THE GREAT CHICAGO FIRE

1871 The fire killed 300, left 100,000 homeless and destroyed 18,000 buildings.
1886 Discontent among workers culminated in the bombing deaths of seven policemen in the Haymarket Riot. Four anarchists were hanged for the bombing.
1889 Architect Frank Lloyd Wright built his much-admired Home and Studio in Oak Park.
1889 Jane Addams founded Hull House and began the welfare movement based on "settlement houses" serving poor communities.
1890 Chicago's population, heavily bolstered by European immigration, passed one million.
1892 The University of Chicago was founded.
1893 The Columbian Exposition was a world's fair that drew the nation's attention.

START OF A NEW CENTURY

1900 Engineers completed a massive project to reverse the flow of the Chicago River and stop waste running into Lake Michigan.
1906 Upton Sinclair caused an uproar with his book *The Jungle*, an exposé of unsanitary and cruel conditions in the stockyards.
1909 Daniel H. Burnham, the architect, unveiled a city plan calling for preservation of the lakefront for public recreation and culture.
1919 After the drowning of a black boy on a public beach, race riots left 38 dead.
1919 Eight White Sox players, including star slugger Joe Jackson, accepted bribes to lose

baseball's World Series and were subsequently bannedfrom the sport.

1920 The Michigan Avenue Bridge opened.

THE GANGSTER ERA

1929 Seven gangsters were killed in the St Valentine's Day Massacre.

1929 The Wall Street stock market plunged Chicago into the Great Depression.

1931 Tony Cermak put together the first ethnically "balanced" ticket, paving the way for Chicago's Democratic political machine.

1931 Crime boss Al "Scarface" Capone was convicted of federal income tax evasion and sentenced to 11 years in prison.

1934 Bank robber John Dillinger was gunned down at the Biograph Theater by federal agents tipped off by "The Lady in Red."

1942 A group of physicists achieved the first nuclear chain reaction.

1947 Al Capone died of syphilis.

1951 Nelson Algren published the acclaimed prose poem *Chicago: City on The Make.*

1952 Hugh Hefner, circulation director of *Children's Activities* magazine, borrowed $1,600 to start a new publication called *Playboy.*

1955 Richard J. Daley, a.k.a. "Hizzoner" and "Da Boss," was elected mayor.

1960 Mayor Daley's "late" returns swung the presidential election away from Richard Nixon to John F. Kennedy.

BIRTH OF THE CIVIL RIGHTS MOVEMENT

1960 Saul Alinsky formed the Woodlawn Organization, which became a focal point for the Chicago civil rights movement.

1966 The Rev. Martin Luther King Jr founded the Chicago Freedom Movement.

1968 Divisions over the Vietnam War burst into street violence in what investigators later called a "police riot" against demonstrators at the Democratic National Convention.

1969 The Chicago Seven trial riveted the nation's attention, along with the "Days of Rage" campaign by militant antiwar factions.

1971 The Union Stock Yard closed.

1972 The Chicago Mercantile Exchange, begun in 1919 as a tiny butter and egg market, pioneered the financial futures markets.

PRECEDING PAGES: Marc Chagall's *The America Windows,* Art Institute. **LEFT:** Mayor Richard J. Daley in 1975. **RIGHT:** Jesse Jackson.

1974 The world's tallest office building, the 110-story Sears Tower, opened downtown.

1976 Chicagoan Saul Bellow won the Nobel Prize for Literature.

1976 Mayor J. Daley died in office.

1979 Jane Byrne won the mayoral race over Michael Bilandic, Daley's successor, who was blamed for failing to clear the streets of snow.

1987 Harold Washington, Chicago's first black mayor, died after four years in office.

THE REIGN OF DALEY JR

1989 Richard M. Daley Junior became mayor.

1992 Carol Mosely Braun became the first black

woman to be elected to the US Senate.

1992 The Loop was flooded.

1993 The Chicago Bulls won the NBA Basketball Championship for the third year in a row.

1995 Mayor Daley was re-elected.

1995 Basketball star Michael Jordan came out of retirement.

1996 Chicago hosted the Democratic Convention, the first since 1968.

1996 The Sears Tower lost the "world's tallest building" title.

1998 The Bulls won the NBA Basketball Championship for the third year in a row.

1999 Michael Jordan retired again.

1999 Record-breaking blizzards hit the city. ❑

Jacques Marquette

FROM SWAMP TO SKYSCRAPER

With characteristic Midwestern resilience, Chicago rose the first time

from marshland and a second time from the ashes, after the Great Fire of 1871

Two French explorers with very different reasons for being in the New World are given the credit for being the first Europeans to set eyes on what is now Chicago. Louis Jolliet was searching for gold. Father Jacques Marquette was out saving souls. Splashing about in the marshlands together in 1673, they formed Chicago's prototypical dynamic duo: the man of plunder and the man of prayer, the getter and the giver. They represented two strains of men who one day would build this contradictory city, who would nail it together in a greedy man's haste, jack it up out of a prehistoric muck and reshape it like soft putty after it had endured cholera, fire and financial collapse.

Meatpackers and merchants

Jolliet was the forefather who begat meatpacker barons and merchant princes and condominium kings. Marquette was the forefather who begat social workers and community organizers and advocates for the street-curb poor. At worst, they worked at cross purposes, the men on the make trampling all. At best, they joined in common cause, cash and compassion working together. A pretty park, for example, can soothe men's souls – and increase a real estate agent's profits. These are the types who built Chicago, transforming marshland into Big Shoulders.

Chicago is, above all, an American city, a mid-continental Uncle Sam of gold coasts and slums, of babbling tongues, of punch clocks and blues and verve. It owes that verve to generations of strong backs, to its precious few visionaries and to a few scoundrels, too. Lovely on its lakefront, shabby on its back streets, like a rusting Chevy in the alley, Chicago is a cauldron bubbling with contrasts, like the nation itself. It both nurtures and corrupts. Chicago, America's City. Incorporated March 4, 1837.

Twelve thousand years ago, Lake Chicago, a larger version of today's Lake Michigan,

covered much of what is now the Midwest. As the great glacial lake receded, it left behind vast, waving prairies and a shoreline swamp. America's native people – the Indians who were Chicago's first immigrants – embraced the swampland. They called it Checagou or Checaguar, or something close. It meant "wild

onion" or "skunk," apparently a reference to the smell of rotting marshland onions that permeated the entire area. The name implied – and still implies – great strength.

From the beginnings of human inhabitation, the swamp was a place of action, a dealing and swapping ground.

The Pottawattomies, traveling by canoe, traded furs and skins there. The swamp linked North America's two great waterways: the Mississippi to the southwest – via the Des Plaines and Illinois rivers – and the Great Lakes to the north and east.

During spring rains, shallow-bottomed Indian canoes traversed the swamp, traveling

---

LEFT: Father Jacques Marquette.

RIGHT: Pottawattomie chief.

about eight miles from the Des Plaines River to Lake Michigan to deliver their occupants to trading powwows.

Jolliet, the entrepreneur, saw the big town coming. Paddling along, coasting past high prairie grasses, he predicted to Marquette: "Here some day will be found one of the world's great cities." And a later explorer, named Robert Cavalier, Sieur de La Salle, saw the future too. "This will be the gate of an empire," he commented. "The typical man who will grow up here must be

> **DEDICATED TO DUSABLE**
>
> The DuSable Museum of African American History was first sited in the home of its founders, Charles and Margaret Burroughs.

enterprising. Each day, as he rises, he will exclaim, 'I act, I move, I push.'"

America became a land where bustling, sophisticated cities and towns dotted the East Coast. Those cities' paved streets were lined with shops selling imported goods. People read newspapers every day and went to the doctor when they were sick or to the attorney when they had a legal problem. Families attended church together on Sunday.

Trappers and trading posts

Only a few hundred miles to the west, however, were farmers and trappers and hunters who literally lived off the land and might go weeks

without seeing a neighbor. Many believed that the country was getting too crowded if they could see the smoke from the next farm. For what few supplies and little companionship they needed, these self-sufficient frontiersmen depended on the small, scattered settlements and trading posts. There they would swap their vegetables or skins culled from the local animals for food and luxury items that they didn't grow or make for themselves at home.

Chicago was one such gathering place, growing from trading post to settlement to village to city largely because of a geographical location that allowed easy transport in all directions. Many of those who came to Chicago in the early days were not farmers or frontiersmen themselves. Some were misfits drawn by the prospect of fewer social and legal constraints in what was at that time the "Wild West." Many were dreamers who believed the West was going to grow dramatically, and then went west themselves to realize those prophecies. They came to Chicago to be big fish in a little pond, and then to make the pond bigger.

The house that Jean built

It was a black man who led the way. Jean Baptiste Point DuSable, the tall French-speaking son of a Quebec merchant and a black slave, established a trading post in 1779 on the north bank of the Chicago River at what is now Michigan Avenue. He erected Chicago's first permanent house. Later, he sold the house to another trader, John Kinzie.

Meanwhile, the white man's government began to force out the red man – in the name of progress, of course. General "Mad Anthony" Wayne in 1795 overran the Indians and forced the Pottawattomie tribe to cede huge tracts of Midwestern land, including "six miles square at the mouth of the Chickago River." It was prime real estate even then, a speculator's dream as swamps and forestland turned almost overnight into commercial property. The Indians, who had no concept of "owning" the land they lived on, were summarily pushed out as white men sold each other pieces of paper they called

LEFT: Jean Baptiste Point DuSable.
RIGHT: Fort Dearborn, 1803.

"titles." In this way the white man entitled himself at a stroke to control and own the land.

Flight from the fort

Blue-coated US soldiers arrived from Detroit. In 1803, they built Fort Dearborn at what is now Lower Wacker and Michigan. Ordered to evacuate Fort Dearborn during the War of 1812 against the British, settlers and soldiers fleeing the fort were ambushed by Indians allied with the British. Fifty-two men, women and children from the fort were slain in what is now known as the Fort Dearborn Massacre. But the pioneering deluge was checked only briefly:

the soldiers returned, Fort Dearborn was rebuilt, and 5,000 Pottawattomies were booted out for good. Scattered like bungalow dwellers in the path of a coming expressway, some Indians were relocated or drifted to government reservations, often hundreds of miles away; others tried to eke out a living on the edge of the white world, doing menial labor.

A few Indian families and small groups became poor wanderers, seeking but never finding a place where they could carry on their traditional way of life. No matter what the Indians tried, however, Pottawattomie children and grandchildren became more and more absorbed

HISTORY ON THE BRIDGE

The original site of Fort Dearborn is demarcated today at the junction of Michigan Avenue and East Wacker Drive, by the Michigan Avenue Bridge. A visit to the bridge will be rewarded by an excellent view of both the Wrigley and *Chicago Tribune* buildings, especially at nighttime when they are spectacularly floodlit. The bridge's four pillars, each over 10 feet (3 meters) high, were erected in 1928; each features sculptures dedicated to the first Europeans in the area and key moments in the city's history. "The Pioneers," on the northwest pillar in front of the Wrigley Building, is dedicated to all the European pioneers. Across from it is "The Discoverers," featuring a depiction of Jolliet

and Father Marquette. "Regeneration" is the sculpture on the southeast pillar, dedicated to the rebirth of the city after the Great Chicago Fire of 1871, and "Defense," on the southwest pillar, represents the defense of Fort Dearborn.

The glaring public ethnocentrism of the times is reflected in the fact that Chicago's earliest non-native settler, the black man Jean Baptiste Point DuSable, fails to merit a mention on any of the bridge's monuments. Likewise, the Native Americans are represented in the sculptures and inscriptions as either brutal savages or servants to the Europeans. The original Fort Dearborn, beside the southwest pillar, was made a Chicago landmark in 1971.

into the white world. In effect, after the Fort Dearborn Massacre the traditional Pottawattomie tribe ceased to function as it had done for generations.

Boom town

Things happened fast after that. In 1825, the Erie Canal was opened, creating a new water route between Chicago and the East to transport furs, grain, lumber and livestock. The Illinois Legislature plotted a course for the Illinois-Michigan Canal that would connect Lake Michigan and the Mississippi. Federal dollars paid for dredging a harbor. Chicago

tians, Protestants, Catholics and infidels. Among Protestants there were Calvinists and Armenians. Nearly every language was represented. Some people had seen much of the world, and some very little."

Everything was new. Anything was possible. Audacious men blustered like the prairie winds. On March 4, 1837, in Vandalia, the southern Illinois community that was later replaced by Springfield as the state capital, the Legislature approved a charter that formally recognized Chicago, previously a village, as a city. The tallest building in the city was a lofty two stories. Nobody owned a basement. Nobody

boomed, though it was less a town than a real estate lottery. A chunk of Lake Street property bought for $300 in 1833 was sold one year later for $60,000.

New wagons rolled in daily. Settlers from the East swelled the population from 50 in 1830 to 4,170 in 1837. Buoyed by immigrants from Ireland and Germany, within 30 years the population had topped 40,000. Traders and merchants came. So did saloon keepers and prostitutes. As with Jolliet, the lure was money. An early mayor, newspaper publisher "Long John" Wentworth, recalled in the 1880s: "We had people from almost every clime, and almost every opinion. We had Jews and Chris-

had access to gas. Nobody had a paved street.

In New York, the *Chicago American* reported that day, picketers were protesting against bread prices. In Washington, contributions were being accepted for the construction of the Washington National Monument. Out in the brand-new city of Chicago, meanwhile, businessmen were advertising 4,000 pounds of log chains, bushels of garden seed, Brandreth Vegetable Pills ("known to benefit persons of a bilious or costive habit of body") and even promoting smaller Midwestern towns ("Albion – One of the Healthiest Spots in Western America").

Two months later, in an election marred by brawls, a former New York state legislator named William B. Ogden defeated the early settler, John Kinzie, to become Chicago's first mayor. Ogden first stomped into town in the 1830s, steaming mad because one of his relatives had purchased, sight unseen, a muddy tract along State Street for $100,000. All Ogden wanted to do was get rid of the useless land.

But after selling a third of the land for the same amount he had paid for the whole lot, Ogden changed his mind. He stuck around. He got rich. He was made for this town, Chicago. He was part Jolliet and part Marquette, part money man and part civic man, a getter and a giver. In the course of piling up his fortune, he

a posse of 30 cops and hundreds of citizens on a clean-up crusade. They demolished every disreputable house in town.

When Chicagoans tired of slopping around in the mud, a sanitation engineer named Ellis Sylvester Chesbrough proposed raising the level of the entire city. Sidewalks were promptly boosted up, turning ground floors into basements. George Pullman, the railroad man, then used armies of workmen to jack up the buildings themselves. And when Chicagoans tired of contracting cholera and dysentery from foul shoreline drinking water, city workers dug a two-mile tunnel out into the lake to tap clean

built the city's first drawbridge and also its first railroad – which these days is called the Chicago & North Western.

Aspirations and action

Chicago's early history is replete with the doings of men with huge egos and boundless ambition. They left personal imprints (and sometimes skid marks) on an impressionable city. When "Long John" Wentworth, elected mayor in 1857, tired of the dogfights and sex shows in the red-light district, he personally led

LEFT: displaced Indians, *circa* 1907.
ABOVE: the new Chicagoans, *circa* 1907.

water. For good measure, Chicago amazed the world in 1900 by making its river run backward. That feat, aimed at using fresh lake water to flush away the polluted, disease-carrying riverflow, was an engineering marvel of locks and channels that is still often studied today.

Chicago was leaving the provinces behind and emerging as America's crossroads. By 1856, Chicago was the hub of 10 railroad trunk lines. Raw materials brought by wagon, barge, ship and train were turned into products to build and feed the country – lumber from nearby forests, iron ore from Minnesota, livestock and produce from some of the richest farmland in the world. Chicago led the world in the transportation of cattle, grain and lumber. Grain elevators, jabbing the skyline, were the Sears Towers of the day.

As surely as one clever manufacturer knew how to turn out a product, someone else knew how to sell it. The mail-order giants Sears, Roebuck & Co. and Montgomery Ward & Co. were born in Chicago. Legendary merchants, whose names are still in evidence not only on Chicago hotels and department stores but in branches scattered across America's retail landscape, included Marshall Field, William Wieboldt, Potter Palmer, Samuel Carson and John Pirie. And, if the soul of Marquette was sometimes

sweeping in mile-long billows and breakers over the doomed city." Three hundred people were killed; 100,000 were left homeless; 18,000 buildings were destroyed. Chicago's first city was in ashes.

So they built a second:a sturdier town of fireproof brick. Two days after the fire, W.D. Kerfoot, a spunky real estate agent, posted a sign on a shack: "All gone but wife, children and energy." Money was there to be made. No time to mourn. Chicago warn't no sissy town.

A civic ripening emerged out of the great fire's ashes. Architects from all over the world, sensing unlimited creative and financial

conspicuously absent, if the rascals sold spoiled beef and defective weapons to the Union Army, if the political booster boys seemed all too forgiving of City Hall corruption and 400 brothels, well, hell, to quote a future alderman, "Hinky Dink" Kenna: "Chicago ain't no sissy town."

Up in flames

Then came the fire. The Great Chicago Fire of 1871 started, according to the legend, on October 8 in Mrs O'Leary's barn, now the site of the Chicago Fire Department Training Academy. O'Leary's cow got the rap; it kicked a lantern, they said. The fire spread fast, an eyewitness describing it as "a vast ocean of flames,

opportunity, flocked to Chicago. They endowed the city with a touch of New World class, a skyline of state-of-the-art office buildings. Many of the post-fire classics, particularly those in the range of 14 to 18 stories high along South Dearborn Street, remain the relatively earthbound bulwarks of the steel-frame construction process that led to today's skyscrapers.

Because it was continuing to grow so quickly as an industrial and commercial center, downtown Chicago needed big buildings. Thus

ABOVE: the Opera House after the Great Fire, 1871.
RIGHT: Pullman, the ultimate company town, as it was 100 years ago.

it was that ambitious architects with powerful new designs were allowed free reign to build toward the clouds.

Three world masters led the charge: John Root, designer of the graceful Rookery and Monadnock buildings; Louis Sullivan, designer of the efficient Auditorium and Carson Pirie Scott buildings; and Sullivan's peerless protégé, Frank Lloyd Wright.

Brilliant innovators, they established Chicago's tradition of architectural leadership. Mies van der Rohe, the father of unadorned steel-and-glass modernism, nailed it down. Helmut Jahn, iconoclastic creator of the hotly disputed State of Illinois Center and Xerox building, helped to ensure its strength today.

Cultural birth

By 1890, Chicago was struggling out of an era of cut-throat Social Darwinism into an age of social reform. In the City Council, the avaricious "Gray Wolves," the bribery-wizened council men, still divvied up the boodle. But more civic-minded Chicagoans demanded social justice, a bit of high culture, and such public amenities as spacious parks and an uncluttered lakefront. The 1890s saw the establishment of the Art Institute, stocked with

OFFICIAL: THE COW IS INNOCENT

In the fall of 1997 the Chicago City Council rewrote history. It passed a resolution exonerating Mrs O'Leary's cow of blame for the 1871 Chicago Fire. Publication of research findings of Chicago amateur historian Richard Bales inspired the drastic action. Bales used real estate records to piece together a map of what Mrs O'Leary's neighborhood would have looked like, then used the map to argue against the account of the fire's origins given by witness Daniel "Peg Leg" Sullivan. At a hearing Peg Leg claimed he saw the fire from two houses away and hobbled 193 feet (59 meters) to Mrs O'Leary's barn to rescue her animals. Other buildings would have obstructed Peg Leg's view of the blaze and he could not possibly have hobbled the distance on a wooden leg in such short time, Bales argued. Conclusion: Peg Leg caused the fire and concocted the story to save face. The City Council agreed.

Lending weight to the "not guilty" verdict for Mrs O'Leary's cow is an account given over half a century ago by Chicago importer Louis M. Cohn. Mr Cohn, who died in 1942 at the age of 88, had claimed that, as an 18-year-old, he was among some boys amusing themselves shooting dice (they included Mrs O'Leary's son). And it was the boys, he said, who knocked over the fateful lamp.

Dutch Masters' paintings; the University of Chicago, founded with Rockefeller money on Marshall Field real estate; the Museum of Science and Industry, and the Columbian Exposition of 1893, a fabulously successful world's fair that introduced the Ferris wheel and the "shake" dancer Little Egypt. Her "exotic" bumps and grinds were undoubtedly modest by today's standards, but Little Egypt's act nonetheless drew condemnation from moralizing newspaper editors and clergymen who warned that she was instilling evil lust in the hearts and minds of her many male fans.

The Chicago Symphony Orchestra made its debut, although the conductor, Theodore Thomas, recruited from the New York Philharmonic, dared not offer many symphonies at first. Chicago's musical taste was too undeveloped; "light music" had to suffice as culture. Asked why he bothered to settle in Chicago at all, he explained: "I would go to hell if they would give me a permanent orchestra."

Thomas was one of those rare men of scope and vision who made Chicago what it is today. There were also others. There was A. Montgomery Ward, a stoical money man in the Jolliet mold who revealed the heart of a Marquette when he launched his 13-year court

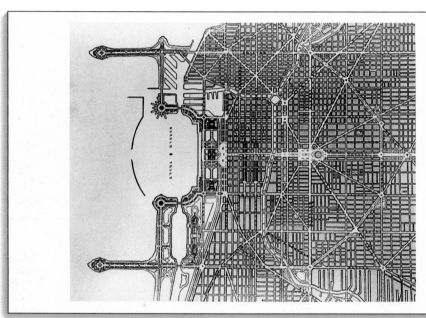

HULL HOUSE TODAY

The legacy of Jane Addams can be seen in contemporary Chicago in two institutions that carry her name – the Jane Addams Hull House Association, and the Jane Addams Hull House Museum. The association is the direct descendant of the organization created by Addams in 1889 when she was 29. The struggles that Addams fought personally (such as ending child labor and securing a minimum wage) have been replaced by more recent concerns of working-class life in Chicago. The non-profit organization offers programs in literacy; day care, family counseling; senior recreation and companionship; and independent living programs for "at-risk" young adults.

By the late 1990s there were as many as six community centers and 35 satellite locations in the Chicago area.

In contrast, the museum is a commemoration of the life and work of Addams, who involved herself in the international peace movement and has the distinction of being the first American woman to win the Nobel Peace Prize. The museum is located in the two original Hull House buildings, at 800 South Halsted Street on the campus of the University of Illinois at Chicago. The Charles J. Hull family built the mansion in 1856 and Jane Addams occupied it in 1889. The interior has been restored to look as it did when Addams used the building as her base for her work.

battle to save Grant Park from public buildings. City Hall, the press and the business community ganged up on the merchant, calling him an "obstructionist." But in the end Ward won, and legally established the principle that Chicago's entire lakefront should be preserved "forever open, clear and free."

There was the architect Daniel H. Burnham, who enshrined the principle of a pristine lakefront in his famous city plan of 1909. No other plan has so influenced Chicago's growth. The Burnham Plan of 1909 resulted in the creation of a string of lakefront parks and beaches, including Jackson Park and Washington Park;

humanitarianism; whatever the dynamics at work the city goes on benefiting.

Civic conscience

Social reform by 1890 was, in part, a survival tactic. Chicago seethed with labor unrest, and the city became an incubator for a national organized labor movement, then in its infancy. The class warfare, fueled by the loose alliance of young unions that were committed to better working and living conditions for all laborers, spooked Prairie Avenue's Millionaires' Row. In the 1880s and 1890s, a nationwide campaign for the eight-hour day and the minimum wage

the acquisition of a green belt of forest preserves on the city's periphery; the construction of Chicago's main post office; and the siting of the Eisenhower Expressway.

In many ways, it could be said that Chicago's renowned social consciousness was simply a natural reaction against the city's equally renowned and legendary greed. In this town of extremes, with its unofficial "Where's mine?" motto, it made a lot of sense for the backlash against rampant capitalism to be a particularly selfless, far-reaching brand of

triggered bloody confrontations. Thirteen men were killed in Chicago during one week. The National Guard was called out to quell a workers' riot outside Pullman's railcar plant. Seven policemen were killed in the Haymarket Riot of 1886. No one saw who threw the bomb, but four anarchists went to the gallows.

Pressures for social reform came from other quarters. From an emerging professional class stepped rebellious giants – social worker Jane Addams, attorney Clarence Darrow and muckraking journalist Upton Sinclair.

Addams, a proper young woman from Rockford, walked among the shabby sweatshops and immigrant tenements on the city's

---

LEFT: Burnham's 1909 Plan for Chicago.
ABOVE: back of the Union Stock Yard houses.

Near West Side and decided to devote her life to helping the people there. Chicago's population had reached 1 million by 1890, including hundreds of thousands of Irish, Italian and Eastern European immigrants living in conditions of squalor within a whiff of the stockyards.

Addams' Hull House, a settlement house tending to the needs of immigrants at Blue Island and Halsted, became a model for the nation, fighting for an end to child labor, for

THE MIGHTY PEN

The revelations by Upton Sinclair in *The Jungle* led to the passage of the Federal Food and Drug Act in 1906, the same year the book was published. Later, in *The Brass Check*, published in 1920, Sinclair criticized the American press for serving capitalist interests.

sense of self-esteem and hope in an exploited, downtrodden class of menial laborers.

Others have followed in Addams' footsteps. In the 1950s and 1960s, Saul Alinsky, the patriarch of militant community organizers, fought City Hall with his Back of the Yards Council and the Woodlawn Organization.

In later years Douglas Dobmeyer, president of the Chicago Coalition of the Homeless, led ragged demonstrations outside the yuppie

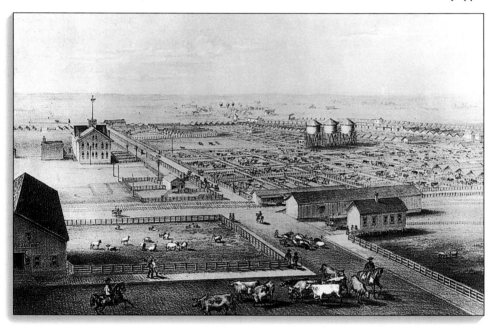

factory inspections and for a minimum wage. Jane Addams was some kind of crazy lady, according to the mavens of La Salle Street, Chicago's Wall Street – but, they had to admit, she was effective. Addams and her followers at Hull House and other settlement houses established throughout Chicago provided fresh clean milk for babies, taught immigrants English and set up day care centers. They provided a range of care and comfort that became a model for inner-city social welfare programs, from prescribing balanced diets for young families to describing how to open a bank account, enroll children in school or apply for a better job. These early social workers helped instill a

high-rises that displaced the Skid Row poor.

Upton Sinclair was crazier still. In *The Jungle*, his muckraking exposé of the stockyards, he wrote of "the secret rooms where the spoiled meats went to be doctored." He told of workmen whose feet were eaten away by acids in the fertilizer rooms. And he repeated dark tales of other workers who had fallen into steaming vats, and emerged as beef lard. Federal investigators checked out the allegations. All of these things were pretty true, they said.

But there was much more to the stockyards than the horrible sanitary and working conditions. There were the living conditions, often no less unsanitary. Families, many of them immigrants from Europe, were crowded into narrow wooden rowhouses in the neighborhood known as the Back of the Yards. Many of the workers were rural Europeans who spoke little or no English. Many were unfamiliar with living in America after hearing from friends and relatives, earlier immigrants, about how easy it was to get a high-paying job, and about how wealthy Chicago was.

What the immigrants didn't find out until they arrived was how hard they had to work, often in disgusting conditions; how much daily living cost, and how quickly those seemingly high wages disappeared; and how Chicago's

on more than one job. They often kept their children out of school in order to put them to work, too, so that the whole family might have enough money to move to a new neighborhood and find better jobs. These were the people, whose children worked long hours and didn't have the ways or means to keep their babies healthy, whom social reformers tried to help.

After World War I, an influx of blacks from the Southern states provided a new source of inexpensive labor to be exploited by the stockyards. Almost overnight, it seemed, much of Chicago's South Side became predominantly black neighborhoods. In its peak year of 1924,

vast wealth was accumulated and hoarded by a relative few who profited from the back-breaking labor of the new arrivals.

The Back of the Yards was a ghetto. Its "inmates" were never free of the stink of animal manure, slaughterhouses and rendering plants. In hopes of raising enough money to escape, or merely to meet the rents charged for their substandard housing, often owned by the companies using the stockyards, men and women worked long, grueling hours, sometimes taking

---

LEFT: Union Stock Yard, 1866.
ABOVE: traffic backup at Dearborn and Randolph Streets in the Loop, 1909.

the Union Stock Yard, a square mile of land down by Canaryville, employed over 30,000 workers and received more than 18.6 million head of cattle and calves, sheep and hogs. But in 1971 the big yard closed. Omaha and Iowa could cut a pork roast cheaper.

Sinclair was in the vanguard of the Chicago literary movement in the years before the Great Depression. Other notables included Carl Sandburg, the poet who wrote so eloquently of the city; Indiana native Theodore Dreiser, chronicler of big-city sins and small-town waifs, and Ben Hecht, the ex-newsman who told Broadway a secret: Chicago loves its rogues as much as its squares – sometimes it loves them even more. Writing a little later were James T. Farrell, Nelson Algren, Richard Wright and Saul Bellow, Chicago's Nobel Laureate in literature.

Machine guns, politics

After World War I, Chicago's focus of power shifted from industrialists to politicans. While heirs to Chicago's great retailing and meat-packing fortunes ensconced themselves on the North Shore, crooked politicians and bootleg-gers plundered the city. The handful of social reformers were too focused on good works to worry about the corruption of an entire political

operating his own beer breweries right in the middle of Chicago. To keep his operations going, he made the bribery of officials at every level, from City Hall to cops on the beat, an everyday fact of life that still plagues Chicago.

Capone, whose business card identified him as a "Second-hand Furniture Dealer," was short and pot-bellied and not particularly physically imposing. But Capone was nicknamed Scar-face for the parallel reminders of a knifing on his cheek, and he was a crudely brilliant and cunningly brutal organizer who ruled through a combination of fear and rewards, stick and car-rot. Those who did what he wanted could get

system, and they would probably have been no match for men with machine guns and brief-cases anyway. So the bootleggers dueled it out and more than 400 gangsters were killed over five years, including seven in the 1929 St Valentine's Day Massacre.

Bestriding the city during the Prohibition years – from 1920 to 1933 when a constitu-tional amendment outlawed alcoholic bever-ages of any sort throughout the United States – was that colossus of crime, Al Capone.

A one-time speakeasy bouncer who gradu-ated to running houses of prostitution, Capone built a vast bootlegging empire that included importing real whisky from Canada and

rich quickly. Those who refused his requests could get dead even more quickly.

He often made his points in a most dramatic way, sending out carloads of gunmen with non-musical violin cases or interrupting a black-tie banquet to kill a fellow diner, a disloyal lieu-tenant, with repeated blows to the back of the head with a baseball bat. Capone is listed in the *Guinness Book of Records* for the highest gross income ever accumulated by a private citizen in a single year: $105 million in 1927, when he was 28 years old.

Chicago in general boomed during the Roar-ing Twenties. Fortunes were made in the stock market. More big buildings went up. Flappers danced on speakeasy tables. Most people tolerated crime as a part of everyday life, as long as it wasn't one of their relatives or friends who was cut down in the latest careless crossfire among rival hoodlums.

Capone was finally brought down by a group of federal agents, led by Eliot Ness and known as "The Untouchables" for their determined refusal to take bribes.

Unable to pin murder or even bootlegging directly on the crafty Capone, Ness and his men instead cleverly went after the gangster for failing to pay taxes on his millions in illicit gain. In 1931 Capone was convicted and sentenced to

And when Prohibition-era Mayor William Thompson died, he left behind safe-deposit boxes containing $1,578,000 in cash, stocks, bonds and certificates. No one knows exactly how the mayor got so rich, or where that money came from. However, Al Capone always liked Thompson, to the point of keeping Big Bill's picture on his office wall.

Dream machine

Tony Cermak, the mayor who died stopping a bullet meant for President Franklin D. Roosevelt, dreamed up the political machine. Running as a Democrat against Thompson in the

11 years in prison (he actually served eight). He died in 1947, quietly, in bed, of syphilis.

But Capone didn't invent political corruption in Chicago. Back in 1837, on the very day Chicago voted to become a city, wagonloads of non-resident Irish canal diggers, technically ineligible to vote, were lugged to the convention hall to cast their ballots. Consider just two stealing mayors. When Fred A. Busse died, he left behind a safe-deposit box full of stock in a company that sold the city its manhole covers.

mayoral campaign of 1931, Cermak pieced together the first "balanced" party ticket – a Pole here, a German there, an Irishman here and there – and swept the white ethnic voting bloc. Only the blacks, still loyal to the party of Lincoln and Emancipation, backed Thompson. No surprise there: Chicago always has been a divided town – black here, white there, blood-red too often in between.

During the Civil War (1861–65), Irish canal diggers cheered Confederate victories. To celebrate, they poured out of Archer Avenue saloons and chased down blacks. In 1919, a black boy drifted into a white swimming area and was drowned when a white man on shore

---

LEFT: Al "Scarface" Capone, 1931 mugshot.
ABOVE: police officers survey the aftermath of gangland warfare.

hit him with a stone. The ensuing riots left 37 more dead. "The slums take their revenge," Carl Sandburg wrote. It would be fire the next time. In 1968, Dr Martin Luther King Jr was shot in Memphis and America's cities exploded. Chicago's West Side burned.

In the 1930s, the Great Depression hit hard. In Chicago, the jobless marched in protest down State Street. Businessmen cried. And yet, weak-kneed Chicago toddled along still. The city threw another world's fair in 1933, a Century of Progress, and gave the world Sally Rand, an exotic dancer who went on stage nude except for large stage props. Her titillating act,

as she enticingly maneuvered a large fan, feather boa or even a ball to provide provocative glimpses of bare flesh, drew mobs of men and made her notorious.

Their Daley bread

World War II jerked the nation out of its doldrums. Chicago worked, all out – grunted, groaned and sweated. What with all the bustle going on, nobody paid much notice when, in 1942, a team of physicists at the University of Chicago – an historically prestigious institution that claims more Nobel Prize winners than any other university in the world – built the first nuclear reactor.

The scientists, working under Italian-American physicist Enrico Fermi in a grim basement beneath the athletic stadium, toiled in secret through the early part of World War II. They rarely spoke of the practical applications of their work. In 1942, their "atomic pile" as they called it, created the first controlled nuclear chain reaction, and with it the technology for both nuclear power and the bomb.

By the 1950s, Chicago was more than 100 years old. It had moved through eras of settlement, furious growth, depression and war. One last period remained: the Era of Daley. Richard J. Daley, "Da Boss." He ruled Chicago for 21 years. Daley was a man far more complicated than any Jolliet or Marquette caricature. He was a getter, yes, but he sought power, not money. He was a giver, yes, but he sometimes gave you what you didn't want. Like the city's skyscrapers, Mayor Daley was a monument on the landscape, and, despite his excesses, his legacy has proven to be as durable as reinforced concrete.

THE NUCLEAR AGE IS BORN

"Properly carried through, it will become a place of pilgrimage for all the world; holy ground in the true modern sense." Those were the words of William H. McNeill, Chairman of the University of Chicago's History Department, speaking in the early 1960s of the then-planned monument to Enrico Fermi's successful nuclear chain reaction. The top-secret research that was conducted at the university yielded the advent of the nuclear age at 3:36pm, December 2, 1942. The monument *Nuclear Energy* was unveiled on the spot where the event happened at 3:36pm, 25 years later. It is a 12-foot (4-meter) high bronze sculpture designed by the British artist Henry Moore. At the

time Moore had been commissioned to create a 28-foot (9-meter) long bronze, *Reclining Figure,* for New York's Lincoln Center, a stone statue for Paris' UNESCO building, and a Portland stone screen for Time-Life.

Most certainly not all visitors to Chicago who take time to visit Moore's sculpture, which juxtaposes a mushroom cloud and a human skull, will consider it occupying "holy ground" because the nuclear age has the dual meaning of the benefits of nuclear power and the ravages of atomic weapons. But the spot at 57th Street and Ellis Avenue is perhaps the best place in the world to ponder the significance to the human race of Fermi's discovery.

He bulldozed whole communities, always against their wills, for expressways and plazas and universities. He plowed old ghettos and built segregating walls of high-rise public housing. Daley ran expressways toward the Loop. The business center thrived. But, by that time, the Loop's once-glittering nightlife was history.

Daley played kingmaker to a president, withholding the 1960 Chicago vote to see how the election was going and then delivering the winning margin to John F. Kennedy.

In 1968, at the height of the Vietnam conflict, Daley's cops beat up anti-war protesters outside the Conrad Hilton Hotel during the

Post-industrial Chicago is competing again in a service-oriented economy. In the late 1980s and early 1990s Chicago lost population and, in this respect at least, its "Second City" status. Los Angeles became the nation's second largest city after New York. But in 1997 the US Census Bureau reported that the Chicago metropolitan area's population had grown 4.9 percent since 1990. People had happily begun moving back into the city.

Today, Chicago theater, all but dormant since the heyday of the 1920s, struts again. The famed Chicago and Oriental theaters have been restored to their past glory. Midway, once an

Democratic National Convention. "The whole world is watching," demonstrators chanted.

Chicago redeemed its image in 1996 when it successfully hosted the Democratic Convention that nominated Bill Clinton for a second term.

Back to the future

So what of Chicago today? A city that stands as a monument to those who first passed through – Jolliet and Marquette, the getter and the giver. More Gold Coast. Less ghetto. More growth.

LEFT: Sally Rand has a ball.
ABOVE: the late Harold Washington, who was mayor of Chicago in the 1980s.

aviation ghost town, roars again. New immigrant groups flourish. School drop-out rates soar, but innovative schools churn out top-class scholars. The old political machine is losing people and power, and the long oppressed black minority is coming into its own.

A black man, the late Harold Washington, became mayor and built his own version of the Chicago machine in the 1980s, paving the way for the 1990s streamlined political framework of "Richie" Daley, the son of Da Boss.

Chicago is still a big town of genius and guts and verve. And it still ain't a sissy town. Jolliet just might love it. Marquette might now even like it, as well. ❏

THE GANG'S ALL HERE

If you can't beat 'em, make 'em work for you – Chicago gave up pretending that

Al Capone and his cronies didn't exist and turned them into a tourist attraction

Crime historian William J. Helmer said that those people concerned about Chicago's image never had a chance when they tried to purge the city of its history of gangs and gangsters, of firebombs and Tommy guns.

"I think that Americans have always had a rebellious streak that permits them to identify with certain kinds of lawbreakers," Helmer suggested. "Gangsters, like Capone, and outlaws, like Dillinger, seem enviably self-confident, unafraid of authority and unafraid of death, and to have an admirable ability to handle stress. If they also have style and élan, they discover that crime may not pay, but it can be a shortcut to immortality."

In the 1950s and 1960s, Mayor Richard J. Daley and other city fathers tried to make the world forget about "Scarface" Capone and the Thompson submachine guns that made the Twenties roar.

But times have changed and today the city is no longer demolishing any site associated with gangland lore, and the Chicago Historical Society no longer answers Capone queries with a blank, "Al who?"

Biograph ambush

In the last few years, Chicago has begun learning to live with, if not love, its gangland reputation through tours, exhibits and restaurants. Ironically, the structure with the strongest link to gangster lore has nothing to do with the infamous Capone.

The Biograph Theater at 2433 N. Lincoln Avenue became famous on July 22, 1934, when bank robber John Dillinger was gunned down by federal agents. Dillinger was not part of any crime syndicate; he was a freelancer who resembled Humphrey Bogart and came across as a regular guy.

His dramatic flair in relieving banks of their money, the gallantry he sometimes displayed and his success at playing cat-and-mouse with law enforcers contributed to his popularity. Dillinger's brooding good looks and reputation as a dashing playboy only enhanced his

standing among his many women admirers in every corner of the country.

When he was betrayed by "The Lady in Red" and ambushed by G-men, Dillinger died in an alley, just south of the Biograph. Women reportedly rushed to the scene to dip their handkerchiefs in the pool of his blood.

Gang society

Hardcore gangster enthusiasts can join the John Dillinger Died for You Society, a tongue-in-cheek fan club started in 1966 for followers of gangster lore. "Some called him Public Enemy Number One," noted Horace Naismith, the society president. "Actually, John Dillinger was a prominent economic reformer with unorthodox banking methods." Applicants to the society receive a membership card, a history of the group, a catalog of gangster accoutrements and notices of meetings where an empty chair is always left for the club's namesake.

Chicago's oldest crime structure stands at Dearborn and Hubbard streets. It is the old

Criminal Courts Building, a gray stone fortress that has been renovated for private offices. Behind it, where a firehouse now stands, was the old jail where executions were carried out.

It was here, on November 12, 1887, that the four celebrated Haymarket anarchists went to the gallows. (Eight activists were originally charged with incitement to murder after a political riot which ended in several deaths. But sympathy for the accused led to the pardoning of the four survivors.)

In all, 92 prisoners were hanged in the old jail between 1882 and 1929. It would have been 93, but in 1921 "Terrible" Tommy O'Connor,

condemned to hang for murdering a police detective, escaped four days before his date with the hangman's knot.

The perpetrators of gangland murders were rarely arrested by the police, however, let alone sentenced to death. Instead, their courtrooms were the smoke-filled headquarters of gangster bosses, and their executions were carried out in public or private by gunmen whose own days were numbered.

PRECEDING PAGES: the often-printed *Chicago Sun-Times* photograph of Capone at his Florida winter retreat.
LEFT: actor Robert Stack as federal agent Eliot Ness.
ABOVE: federal agent Eliot Ness as he really was.

Flavored death

During the 1920s, most of the death sentences delivered by gangsters were the result of territorial wars that began over bootlegging and quickly expanded to extortion, gambling, prostitution, labor racketeering and corruption of public officials. The methods of punishment were swift and often ingenious, such as rubbing the bullet tips with garlic so that if they happened to miss a vital organ the victim could still die of gangrene.

At first, the gangs were content to keep to their own sides of town, but eventually greed got the best of them and entrepreneurs sparked open warfare.

In July of 1921, independent businessman Steve Wisniewski hijacked a beer truck belonging to Dion O'Banion. Deanie, as close friends knew him, had been an altar boy and a singing waiter. But by 1921, O'Banion was the undisputed crime boss of the city's North Side. His top lieutenant, Earl "Hymie" Weiss, forced Wisniewski into a car at gunpoint at the corner of Halsted and 14th streets, now the edge of the Maxwell Street flea market district. Wisniewski got his brains blown out and made history by being the first victim to be "taken for a ride."

O'Banion ran his operation from a flower shop at 738 N. State Street, now a parking lot. He himself had become a thorn for South Side crime boss Johnny Torrio. On November 10, 1924, Capone – who at the time was Torrio's top lieutenant – sent a trio of killers into O'Banion's flower shop to silence the Irish tenor forever.

Weiss took over O'Banion's gang, but not for long. On October 11, 1926, Weiss and his driver, Sam Peller, died in a storm of machine gun bullets on the steps of Holy Name Cathedral at 735 N. State Street. Both Weiss and O'Banion were taken to a mortuary at 703 N. Wells Street, now an art gallery. Back then, it was the site of some of Chicago's most lavish gangster funerals. O'Banion's funeral procession included 122 cars and 26 trucks loaded with flowers.

Scarface surfaces

By now, Al Capone had taken over from Torrio, who survived an assassination attempt and decided to retire amid the city's longest running gang war. Its violence was so blatant that Tony Lombardo, Capone's *consigliere*, was gunned down on a Friday afternoon, September 7, 1928, walking east on the south side of Madison, between State and Dearborn. At the time, State and Madison was known as "the world's busiest corner."

But the most notorious of all gangland attacks, the one that would forever burn Capone into Chicago's history, came on St Valentine's Day in 1929.

At 2122 N. Clark Street, now a grassy lot in front of a senior citizens' home, stood the SMC Cartage Co. It was at this garage that Capone's boys, masquerading as cops, lined seven members and associates of the rival Bugs Moran

gang against a brick wall and riddled them with machine gun bullets. Moran, who had inherited the O'Banion-Weiss organization, was not present at the massacre, and so lived to learn what others already knew: Chicago had become Capone's city.

Capone, whose estimated income surpassed an astonishing $105 million in 1927 – still a Guinness world record six decades later – was at last convicted in 1931 of income tax evasion and served eight years in prison.

His final headquarters were at the corner of Michigan Avenue and 22nd Street, now a vacant, 10-story eyesore building with a sign

THE UNTOUCHABLES

Al Capone and his mob were pursued relentlessly by federal Prohibition agent Eliot Ness and his handpicked team of nine elite agents, who sought to destroy Capone's thriving beer-and-liquor empire. After banding together, Ness quickly grabbed Capone's attention by raiding 18 of the mobster's Chicago Heights stills in one night.

Initially reluctant to have the members of this federal team killed, Capone had his men offer the agents bribes, which were refused. One mobster threw an envelope stuffed with cash into an agent's car he passed on the road. The agent caught up with the car and threw back the envelope. When the press learned of the failed bribe attempts,

Ness and his men were dubbed "The Untouchables". The Untouchables continued to damage Capone's illegal business, and an enraged Capone made unsuccessful attempts to kill members of the team, including Ness. The federal government eventually prosecuted Capone, who was found guilty of tax evasion and sentenced to 11 years in prison (although he served only eight). Although Capone was never prosecuted on the Prohibition violations the Untouchables had uncovered, Ness had the satisfaction of personally escorting his elusive quarry to the train that took him to prison in 1932. The story was marketed to a new generation in Brian De Palma's 1987 film, *The Untouchables*.

over the boarded entrance that reads the New Michigan Hotel. It used to be the Lexington Hotel, where Capone's office was on the fourth floor, behind the rounded turret windows at the front corner.

Capone died in 1947 in Florida, his body ravaged by syphilis because, for all his ruthlessness and savagery in dealing with those who got in his way, he himself had a fear of needles, even those backed by penicillin. His body was transported back to Chicago and buried in the family plot at Mount Carmel

hitmen left a seasonal calling card in inimitable gangster style – a blood-red valentine pressed into McGurn's lifeless left hand.

CHICAGO MELODRAMA

Just before his death outside the Biograph Theater, John Dillinger, his girlfriend Polly, and "The Lady in Red" watched *Manhattan Melodrama*, starring Clark Gable.

Guided tours

Untouchable Tours (773-881-1195), a theater on wheels with a couple of real actors doing a fine job of combining the dual role of character and guide, offers a nostalgic, lively and entertaining two and a half hour trip to many gang-era landmarks. The tours are available most days of the week, depending on the

Cemetery in the western suburb of Hillside, about a 40-minute car drive from downtown.

As for "Machine Gun Jack" McGurn, who masterminded the St Valentine's Day Massacre, his life came to a close on the seventh anniversary of the event. The building at 805 N. Milwaukee Avenue now houses an office furniture store. In 1936, it was a bowling alley, where two remnants of the Moran gang wreaked revenge and mowed McGurn down with Tommy guns. As a parting gesture the

demand, and depart from 610 N Clark Street.

The tour's dinner package winds up at Tommy Gun's Garage, 1239 S. State Street. Tommy Gun's, a block from Chicago Police Headquarters, offers dinner and an entertaining floor show set in the 1920s. There's a machine gun-toting bouncer and plenty of flappers. The place is usually packed with both locals and visitors from around the globe who buy up the "I Got Massacred" T-shirts.

"Any place in the world, people will associate Chicago with Al Capone. That's what Chicago's known for, like it or not," says the proprietor Sandy Mangen. "Right now, it's a negative image. Let's make it a fun one." ❑

LEFT: a police re-creation of the St Valentine's Day Massacre, 1929.
ABOVE: the aftermath of the real thing.

THE WINDS OF POLITICS

Probably more than any other US city, Chicago is renowned for its politicking and,

as every savvy political player in town knows, it is ruled by the Boss, the mayor

The prevailing political breezes in Chicago, the Windy City, come from the fifth-floor City Hall office of the mayor. Blowing through the glass and limestone office canyons of LaSalle Street and the Loop, up along the lakefront and into the neighborhoods, they shape and define Chicago's political character in the mayor's likeness – whoever happens to be the mayor at that particular moment.

Chicago's political winds can, depending on the given mayor, flatten the 50-member City Council like a field of wheat in a Midwestern summer storm, or puff up the ambitions of a would-be foe like the spinnaker of a yacht plying Lake Michigan before a zephyr.

Presidents, governors, congressmen and every sort of political wanna-be have been well advised not to sally far into precincts from Rogers Park to Beverly without first lifting a finger toward City Hall to gauge wind velocity and direction, lest they end up turned as inside-out as an umbrella on State Street in April.

This city of 1.5 million registered voters – three-fourths of them inclined to vote Democratic in major elections – has perhaps the most famous (or infamous depending on one's point of view) reputation for politics of any major US city. And mayors are alway sat the center.

Daley duties

Richard J. Daley was the mayor most closely identified with the city. Elected to a record six terms, he died in office after serving 21 consecutive years and pulling the levers of the nation's last partisan political machine.

He also served as Cook County Democratic Party chairman – the only mayor ever to hold both posts at the same time – and handpicked candidates for office. Thus he saw to it that the Machine, fueled by some 40,000 city jobs he controlled and 20,000 more he influenced, churned out sure-bet Democratic pluralities

every time. With an accountant's precision, Daley kept tabs on party loyalty and used jobs as a means of rewarding friends and punishing enemies. During Daley's regime, the local political lexicon became salted with terms such as "clout" and "Boss." Cynical slogans, such as "Vote early and vote often," became popular

clichés for how the Machine succeeded, but the mayor's favorite maxim was "Good politics makes good government." Pithy advice along the lines of "Don't make no waves, don't back no losers," stated the Machine philosophy.

Daley's accomplishments, however, were not simply raw political power. In the tradition of Chicago's most successful mayors, he was a master builder and the business community loved him. "The City that Works" was coined under Daley as the local motto that Chicago mayors have clung to ever since.

After Daley died in 1976, there were five mayors in 12 years. But the Daley name remained linked with the office in voters' minds,

LEFT: "Hizzoner Da Mare."
RIGHT: William B. Ogden, the New York state legislator who became the first mayor of Chicago.

so much so that his son, Richard M. Daley – also known as Richard II, or simply Richie – was elected mayor in 1989.

Punchy quotes

Until landmark federal court rulings curtailed the use of partisan patronage hiring, politics was as avidly participatory in Chicago as 16-inch softball, and it continues to rank with Chicago's professional sports franchises as a top spectator activity.

People identify Chicago more with gangsterism than with deep-dish pizza, and so too are they more apt to remember its punch-in-

the-nose style of politics than its renowned symphony. It is difficult to know exactly which piece of the legacy is most responsible for Chicago's hurly-burly political reputation.

As for punches in the nose, Chicago politics was typified earlier this century when William Hale Thompson, a three-term mayor, boasted that he would like to sock the King of England in the snoot. While Thompson's comment was reviled by most of the civilized world, Chicagoans laughed it off as a stunt to attract Irish voters and reaffirm the city's "leave us alone" world view. Thompson, who consorted with Al Capone and died with $1.4 million stuffed into safety-deposit boxes, was one in a long line of the larger-than-life characters that Chicagoans are used to having for their mayors.

Another memorable comment came from alderman and saloon keeper Mathias "Paddy" Bauler when Daley was first elected in 1955: "Chicago ain't ready for reform." In 1968, when his police and the military clashed with hippies and other Vietnam War protesters outside the Democratic National Convention, Daley came up with one of his classic malapropisms, declaring that the National Guard had been called out "to preserve disorder."

The graveyard vote

It is said that Democratic nominee Hubert H. Humphrey lost the election to Republican Richard Nixon that autumn largely because of the convention, as emblematic a Chicago political event as Daley's having "stolen" the presidency for Democrat John F. Kennedy. Illinois was a key state in the 1960 Nixon-Kennedy race, and Daley reputedly withheld Chicago's returns – possibly padding them out with ballots cast in the names of deceased supporters – until the last moment, when the city miraculously supplied just enough of a margin for JFK to carry the state and eventually the nation.

Chicago's tough reputation got tougher during the 1969 "Chicago Seven" conspiracy trial, a legal circus that led to overturned convictions for abuse of the judicial system, and as a result of the "Days of Rage" rampage by a militant faction of Students for a Democratic Society. The students took their Weathermen name from the Bob Dylan lyrics – appropriate

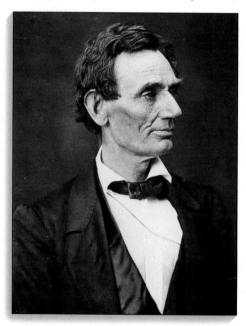

How the Daleys Won the Day

● Richard J. Daley's career of public service began in 1936 as a Republican by chance: an unopposed Republican State Senator died right before elections so the Democrats just wrote Daley in the Republican side.
● Harold Washington's immediate successor after his death in 1987 was Eugene Sawyer who had risen through the Machine ranks. He was defeated by Richard the Second in the Democratic primary. Timothy Evans, Washington's floor leader in the City Council, challenged Daley in the general election with a third party candidacy. With a $7 million campaign and the swing vote in his column, Richard M. Daley won.

Left: Abraham Lincoln, 1860.
Right: National Guard, 1968 Democratic Convention.

for a city like Chicago – about not needing a weatherman to tell which way the wind blows.

Nicknames

But Chicago's link with seamy politics was nothing new in the 1960s. For the whole of the previous 100 years, the city reigned as the nation's smoke-filled-backroom capital, hosting 24 Democratic and Republican national conventions. The first was a raucous 1860 Republican Party affair when dark horse presidential candidate and Illinois native son Abraham Lincoln was nominated.

In a city with several nicknames, it's fitting that Chicago's colorful political characters had colorful nicknames of their own. Daley, of course, was "Da Mare," a linguistic bow to his own syntax, fractured as a result of growing up a sheet metal worker's son in a Back of the Yards neighborhood. The strapping Mayor Thompson was "Big Bill." Six-foot, six-inch, 300-pound Mayor "Long John" Wentworth was one of two newspaper publisher-mayors who served before the turn of the century, the other being Joseph Medill of the *Tribune*. The imperious, mercurial Jane Byrne, swept into office as Chicago's first woman mayor by voters fed up with Michael Bilandic's inept handling of

RIOTING IN THE STREETS

What started as a peaceful march, protesting the Vietnam War up Michigan Avenue, turned treacherous in 1968 when the Democratic National Convention was held in Chicago.

Emotions ran high during this year. The war in Vietnam was going on, Martin Luther King Jr had been killed, Senator Robert F. Kennedy had been assassinated and the Soviets had invaded Czechoslovakia. Adding to the unrest, media reports appeared that cited protesters' threats to, among other things, spike Chicago's drinking water with LSD during the convention.

Although this threat was most likely a lie spread by the city's politicians to further their own ends, it fanned the flames of unrest. Panicked, Daley sent hundreds of police into the streets to contain the demonstration. Violence quickly broke out. Thanks to the battery of television cameras trained on the action, the world watched in horror as police clubbed viciously at the demonstrators. Other law enforcement personnel were armed with tear gas and machine guns. Hoffman and other anti-war leaders were subsequently prosecuted in the Chicago Seven trial for conspiracy to riot, but later acquitted. Almost 30 years passed before the Democratic National Convention was held again in Chicago. In contrast to its predecessor, the 1996 convention went ahead without a hitch.

the 1979 blizzard, was known as "Lady Jane."

Alderman "Bathhouse John" Coughlin and Michael "Hinky Dink" Kenna were flamboyant lords of the Levee, the downtown vice district, who controlled City Council politics and "boodle," or graft, from the 1890s until Prohibition. "Fast Eddie" Vrdolyak was a latter-day political sharpster who became the City Council kingpin after Daley's death but surrendered his Democratic Party chairmanship for disastrous

THE POWERS THAT BE

Chicago has 50 wards, each represented by an alderman. Neighborhoods within the wards have precinct captains who report to a committeeman, who reports to the Cook County Democratic Party. And the voters wonder why it takes so long to get things done.

Lifetime jobs

A handful of governors and US senators from Chicago gained fame – and sometimes infamy – in the shadow of the mayor's office. Otto Kerner was a popular governor later convicted of corruption by Thompson. Adlai Stevenson II was an ex-governor who lost two successive presidential elections as the Democratic nominee, despite Daley's support.

When Daley saw Stevenson's son and namesake as a potential

mayoral candidacies, one as a third-party candidate and the other as the Republican nominee, when Chicago politics began to hinge on black-white racial issues in the mid-1980s.

Populist "Walkin' Dan" Walker as a Chicago attorney authored the national report that depicted the 1968 convention fiasco as a police riot. Daley's lasting enmity helped Walker win the governor's office in 1972 after defeating the mayor's handpicked candidate in the Democratic primary. "Big Jim" Thompson, another six-and-a-half-footer, was the federal prosecutor who put some of Daley's closest protégés in jail in the early 1970s, and went on to become Illinois' longest-serving governor.

rival, he helped get Adlai III elected to the US Senate and safely out of town, 700 miles (1,120 km) away in Washington, DC.

The mayoralty is viewed by most Chicago politicos as second only to the presidency. But just one Chicagoan – Edward Dunne, elected governor in 1912 – has actually risen to higher office. While many, particularly the city's early mayors, might have seen City Hall as a beginner's step to the White House, the fifth-floor office has now come to be viewed as a "career cul-de-sac."

Besides, the job carries a relatively low life expectancy: four of Chicago's 41 mayors have died in office, two by assassination. Carter

Harrison I, widely viewed as the city's first modern professional politician-mayor, was slain at his home by a disgruntled patronage job seeker. Cermak was in his first term in 1933 when he was felled by a bullet intended for President-elect Franklin Roosevelt. Daley died in 1976 after he was stricken by a heart attack, the same fate that befell Harold Washington, Chicago's first black mayor, in 1987.

Jesse's push

Without question the city's most famous non-elected politician has been Jesse Louis Jackson, unsuccessful but highly visible in his South Side operation PUSH (People United to Save Humanity) as a revival meeting-cum-political rally venue to mobilize black voters outside the Democratic Machine. He directed voter registration drives and boycotts that helped build a monolithic black electoral movement, supporting Washington and other black candidates – including Jesse Jackson.

Anathema to the white Democratic Party establishment in Illinois and distrusted by black Machine regulars, not to mention some of his own allies in the independent movement, for his "me-first style," Jackson packed up his aspirations for national office and Rainbow

campaigns for the Democratic presidential nomination. The peripatetic civil rights activist played an integral role in the establishment of the political dynamics now at work in Chicago.

Jackson marched with Martin Luther King Jr through Chicago's segregated white neighborhoods in the mid-1960s, and was a prominent minority voice in denouncing Daley's infamous "Shoot to kill" order in the wake of rioting touched off by King's 1968 assassination. In the 1970s and 1980s, Jackson used his Coalition operations in 1989, after 25 years in Chicago, and moved to Washington, DC.

A split city

What Jackson left behind is an overwhelmingly Democratic city; in 1989, for example, the Republican mayoral candidate, "Fast Eddie" Vrdolyak, was slowed to a crawl with barely 3 percent of the vote. But Chicago also remains a city in which the Democratic Party continues to be fractured by race.

White ethnic and black Democrats typically offset each other. Sometimes, close elections are swung by "lakefront liberals," and Hispanics, the fastest-growing minority in the

LEFT: thumbs up from Jesse Jackson.
ABOVE: the political group known as the Chicago Seven, plus Jerry Rubin's girlfriend.

city. Since 1837, when William Butler Ogden became the city's first mayor, the key to winning elections has been knitting together a majority coalition from an ethnically diverse populace. The Republican Party lost its domination of the City Council in 1931 when Anton Cermak defeated the last mayor it produced, "Big Bill" Thompson. Cermak melded, for the first time, white ethnic immigrants and black voters who had been Republicans and put an end to Irish domination of the Democratic Party.

> ### CRIME AND REASON
> Embarrassingly, Chicago maintains an average of more than one alderman indicted per year. Charges range from tax evasion to sex with minors.

sufficient showing among Hispanics and "limousine liberals" to capture 52 percent of the vote. Given his huge popularity in the community, no black politician dared oppose him. His returns were much the same in 1987 in a primary rematch with Byrne.

Daley redux

Seven months after his re-election, however, the mayor's office claimed another victim, and Washington was dead. The city reverberated with shock, and the prospect of a bitter succession battle.

Bridgeport bossism

With his untimely death, however, Cermak's new version of the Machine fell into the hands of Irish politicians yet again, specifically those from influential Bridgeport. Born and reared in this Back of the Yards enclave of packing houses, saloons, shops and bungalows were the next four mayors: Edward Kelly, Martin Kennelly, Richard Daley and Michael A. Bilandic.

Theend of the old Machine came four years later when Jane Byrne and young Richard M. Daley split the white vote, allowing Harold Washington to capture the Democratic nomination. Washington's winning coalition was built on a strong black turnout and a

Washington's base was split and it was the black political community's turn for a double-barreled shot at the mayoralty in a special 1989 election. Richard M. Daley prevailed. Beginning his tenure by shunning the trappings of bossism that his father took on so eagerly, he won high marks for fairness, and quickly consolidated Hispanic and liberal support beyond that which Washington enjoyed. As a result, Daley, by then known to Chicagoans simply as "Richie," was re-elected in early 1991. He has been in office ever since. ❏

ABOVE: taking a stand – heir and mayor apparent, Richard M. Daley in 1990.

Schooled in Scandal

The author Nelson Algren once wrote: "I too wish to defend my city from people who keep saying it is crooked. In what other city can you be so sure a judge will keep his word for $500?"

Scandal is a fact of life in Chicago. Politics, Chicago's favorite pastime, has bred a local strain of unscrupulousness, born of audacity and disrespect for both the public and public office. At the same time, Chicago has a bumptious journalistic community with a long tradition of irreverence toward authority in general and politicians in particular. The result is both more wrongdoing, and more reporting of that wrongdoing, than perhaps anywhere else.

Any "greatest hits" of Chicago scandals and "stings" must include Operation Greylord, the Federal Bureau of Investigation probe into court corruption. Between 1979 and 1983, FBI agents masquerading as defendants, attorneys, prosecutors and even a judge uncovered widespread bribery, extortion and fraud in the courts. Fourteen judges and 75 attorneys and court staffers were convicted.

Corruption is hardly new in Chicago, of course. In the 1880s, aldermen "Bathhouse" John Coughlin and Michael "Hinky Dink" Kenna offered protection from police interference to vice dealers in exchange for votes. One historian claims that during the 1890s, at least 56 of the 68 aldermen took bribes.

In the 1977 Mirage Tavern sting, the *Chicago Sun-Times* set up a bar manned by undercover reporters. They found that for modest sums building, plumbing, electrical, food, liquor and fire inspectors would overlook violations. The reporters were able to bribe all but one of them. Two weeks after the story broke, the same inspectors were again seeking bribes – except that they had upped the ante. Eventually a third of the city's electrical inspectors were convicted.

In 1985, Operation Incubator stung the administration of the late mayor Harold Washington. An undercover FBI "mole" posed as a representative of a company seeking city contracts. The mole reportedly bribed city

officials. Several officials and aldermen were convicted, and the public was entertained by videotapes of one former mayoral aide dickering over the exact amount of his bribe.

A commercial scandal hit the hallowed halls of the Chicago Board of Trade and the Chicago Mercantile Exchange in 1988. Federal undercover agents went into the trading pits and returned with evidence of fraud: floor traders were trading for themselves at more favorable prices than they traded for their customers.

More recently, sex scandals and the misuse of funds by officials have been making headlines. In 1995, US Representative from

Illinois Mel Reynolds was sentenced to five years in prison for having an affair with a 16-year-old campaign volunteer. Then there was Operation Silver Shovel which began as an investigation of illegal dumping of construction debris in the city and turned into a ratting session as aldermen raced to save themselves. The most shocking conviction, however, was that of Dan Rostenkowski. The former Chairman of House Ways and Means committee went to jail in 1996 for 17 months, indicted on 17 counts of embezzling and misusing hundreds of thousands of dollars of government money in the operation of his congressional office. ❑

RIGHT: Mirage Tavern, site of the 1977 *Chicago Sun-Times* sting.

A HUSTLIN' TOWN

The entrepreneurial style of "the city that works" continues to flourish, in keeping with the Chicagoan approach to life summed up in two words: "Where's mine?"

Chicago is considered by many native Chicagoans to be the greatest city in America, and hence in the world. It was built by thriving commerce and philanthropy in the days before tax write-offs when millionaires unbuttoned their pocketbooks for civic halls, museums and monuments of great splendor. Skyscrapers, the first the world had known, pierced the low-lying prairie clouds. Visionary architects such as Louis Sullivan and Frank Lloyd Wright constructed elaborate buildings. H.L. Mencken said that everything interesting in American writing seemed to be coming out of Chicago. With its central location, in the heart of the Heartland, Chicago seemed sure to grow and flourish.

Chicago, currently on an upswing, has had a tumultuous economic history. Different people, historians among them, give different reasons: that Chicago lost its hopes of pre-eminence when its businessmen refused to bestir themselves to wrest the automobile industry from Detroit; that air travel deflated the city's aspirations, because with the advent of commercial flights people no longer needed to stop in Chicago en route coast to coast; that the opening of the St Lawrence Seaway, which was supposed to make Chicago a great international port, turned out a failure; that Chicago never really recovered from the Depression, or made up for the loss of the stockyards, or was able to live down its reputation as a crime-syndicate town – and so on and so forth.

Faded rivalry

Other people, other opinions, other historians, other causes. Whatever the opinions, whichever the causes, it can't be disputed that Chicago today is in the best shape it has ever been in. After bottoming out in the 1990 census, Chicago's population is on the increase again.

PRECEDING PAGES: Shriners on the march; voter registration.
LEFT: Belmont St Market in full swing.
RIGHT: Keeping a watchful eye.

Yet the epithet "second city" no longer seems quite accurate and not just because Los Angeles has overtaken Chicago in population number. In the nine years Richard Daley has been mayor, Chicago has undergone a dramatic transformation. Public schools have improved, failed housing projects have been torn down

and new construction is everywhere. Critics have even gone as far as to accuse Daley of gentrifying the city and turning it into one big suburb. The old inter-city, one-on-one rivalry between Chicago and New York, seems to have all but disappeared.

Ah, New York, New York – if you can make it there, the song goes, you can make it anywhere. Of Chicago, the exact reverse used to be said: If you can't make it here, you can't make it anywhere. The sentiment was meant to stand as a tribute to the wide vocational opportunities Chicago then provided. It was probably never very true – to those who work without family money or other nets to catch them, every big city presents the possibility of a dangerous fall – and it may be even less true now. For many who choose to live in Chicago, one of the city's special delights is precisely that it is not New York.

Judged by its vibrancy, tumult, concentration of talent and sheer excitement, New York is far and away America's greatest city – in fact, the country's only world city. Yet Chicago, for reasons that visitors often find difficult to grasp, nonetheless remains, for many of those who have lived in it, America's best city.

The city is at its best, when it creates its own style. From "haute cuisine" restaurants to high

society social events, pretensions somehow do not work in this town, though that doesn't stop people from trying

A hustlin' town

Among modern writers, Nelson Algren probably has impressed on the national consciousness the strongest notion of what Chicago is. For Algren, Chicago was above all a hustler's town. "Right from go it was a broker's town and the brokers run it yet," he wrote in a lengthy 1951 prose-poem entitled *Chicago: City on The Make*. Much of the poetry in his prose-poem is of a hopeless sort, yet every once in a while Algren hits a note that resounds with true feeling, as when he remarks that loving Chicago is "like loving a woman with a broken nose, you may well find lovelier lovelies. But never a lovely so real."

To end the litany of clichés about Chicago, one can scarcely do better than consult a volume entitled *Chicago* by Studs Terkel. A self-advertised man of the people, Terkel, with his Uher tape recorder, became over the years Chicago's recording angel, and hence himself something of a cliché. Slim though Terkel's *Chicago* is, thick and fast fly the clichés that make up its substance.

Room for all

From the Pottawattomies to the Haymarket Riot to the bag lady in Uptown, the history of Chicago, in Terkel's view, is that of big guys screwing little guys, with occasional heroes such as Saul Alinsky popping in for cameo appearances; with plenty of villains such as the general run of businessmen, politicians and, currently, the prosperous young; and with just enough room left over for a feisty little guy with a cigar and a tape recorder to squeeze in and make a nice living. But then Chicago has always been a hustler's town. Everyone understands that everyone else has to make a buck. And "no" simply means "not now."

In the age of the computer, America's major-league hustlers could be anywhere. Yet the odds are they are taking important meetings in Los Angeles, doing power lunches in New York, cutting serious deals in Washington, or phoning

LEFT: Maxwell St Market.
RIGHT: a cheerful sidewalk philosopher who leans towards the left.

in their instructions from Tokyo or London. The notion of Chicago as a powerful organized-crime town no longer seems quite convincing. Even in the post-Capone 1940s, the so-called Syndicate was still the behind-the-scenes explanation for everything that went on in the city; it was said to have taken its tribute for every jukebox, case of soda pop, carton of cigarettes and, if rumor were to be believed, nearly every other thing bought and sold in the city.

The Boys themselves were fierce characters, with nicknames (always printed in the press within quotation marks) like "Teets," or "The Camel" or "Big Tuna." Now they mostly seem to be either dead or old bulls gone weak in the knees. Their successors, though doubtless quite as vicious, are younger men with pot bellies and ambitious hairdos who live with their families in gaudily decorated ranch houses in the western suburbs. Chicago no longer seems the mainline crime-boss town it once was.

Perverse pride

Chicagoans generally have taken an old pride in their city's corruption. Not so long ago, when one needed special consideration of one kind or another, somebody always knew somebody who knew somebody else who could fix it. "I

JUST FOR THE RECORD

Theodore Dreiser, an Indiana native, grew up in squalor but had dreams of living in the big city, which he achieved through journalism and later, novels. In Dreiser's view American cities had stories to tell, and his early career as a Chicago journalist taught him how to capture a reader's imagination. Ultimately he was seen as a literary pioneer.

His first feature story, a piece on Chicago slum life, exhibited as much his literary skills as it did the city around him: "Saloon lights and smells and lamps gleaming smokily from behind broken lattices and from below wooden sidewalk levels gave it a shameless and dangerous color." His first novel was *Sister Carrie*, which was withdrawn following public uproar. The American public wasn't ready for Dreiser's presentation of baddies who get away with it, or for his airing of sexual issues. Dreiser analyzed the cultural role of the intellectual, the role of mass consumption, and the intersection of class, gender and power long before it became fashionable. The references to elements of life in the late 19th century which would have otherwise gone unrecorded are the components on which a Dreiser story is built. His characters are survivors; he takes his readers through their compromising positions, difficult decisions, horrible grief and ultimate successes, but in the end, he is telling the story of life in the city.

got a guy," went the phrase. From a broken curb to a black-market baby adoption, everybody had a "guy" to get the job done. In those days, the phrase "everything's on the up and up" was pressed into frequent service, probably because it was difficult to believe many things actually were on the up and up.

The big-city view

The suspicion that things aren't what they seem, aren't quite "on the up and up", has long seemed one of the qualities that mark people raised in Chicago. In its gentler, and hence more pleasing aspect, it comes across as a humorous dubiety. It also qualifies as part of what is known as the big-city view. In Chicago it doesn't have the hard edge of nastiness that it can take on so readily in the Big Apple. This is the Chicago skepticism that takes little or nothing at face value, that gets a little nervous when a "yes" answer comes back a bit too quickly, and that checks to see if the wallet is still where it's supposed to be after all large public functions at which a clergyman has been asked to give a benediction.

Chicagoans seem notable among Americans for being deeply suspicious of the next fellow's motives and then being delighted at having

THE GANG CULTURE

Today's hustlers can't be romanticized like the mafia and the dirty politicians of the recent past because they are too much a reality. Today's hustlers are the Chicago gangs. There are at least 40 organized street gangs in Chicago with an estimated 38,000 members representing all races and ethnic groups. Most often gang crime is related to turf, narcotics activity or both. Gangs display their unity in obvious ways such as colored clothing, jewelry and signals. Members stay together in quiet times and in times of conflict. The reward of this twisted loyalty is acceptance and recognition as gang members. Virtually all gangs have oaths, pledges, initiation rites, mission statements and a set of rules known as "laws" which each member must loyally memorize and adhere to. Gang violence hit its peak in the early 1990s when a series of vicious turf wars erupted between the Black Disciples and Larry Hoover's Black Gangster Disciples.

Violence in the Latino community, led by the Latin Kings who have satellite branches on the East Coast, also peaked at this time and shoot-outs between rival gangs were common. Police presence in schools, prevention programs and strong neighborhood involvement has helped curb the gang influence but it nonetheless remains a huge problem, particularly for the poorer neighborhoods.

these suspicions confirmed. This characteristic applies particularly to public life. A large public scandal in Chicago seems to get the salivary glands working like nothing else. The minicams come roaring out on to the streets like fire engines. The editorialists work themselves up into high moral dudgeon. And, in truth, almost none of it really matters very much in the end. Black or white, a Chicago politician remains a Chicago politician; and Chicago remains resolutely a

BOOM TOWN

A parcel of land bought in Chicago for a modest $450 in 1833, the year the town was incorporated as a village, sold for a staggering $200,000 just over 50 years later.

differences between the two neighborhoods, their common interest in art, liberal politics and what their denizens take to be good taste. A lake culture persists, although now somewhat shriveled in Hyde Park and somewhat expanded beyond Lincoln Park. Life in Chicago, to adapt the local weatherman's phrase, is somewhat cooler near the lake. Yet the lake culture, though Chicago would be a barbarous place without it, is far from characteristic of the entire city.

city that stands in refutation of Lord Acton's celebrated maxim by demonstrating, again and again, that only a small amount of power can corrupt absolutely.

Lake tastes

Lake Michigan is about the only interesting natural feature in the city. The Chicago writer Isaac Rosenfeld used to refer to "the lake culture," by which he meant chiefly Hyde Park and the Near North Side with, despite the many

LEFT: there's always room for more pizza.
ABOVE: like markets all around the world, Maxwell Street Market has artists eager to paint your portrait.

Of course it is always the lake that people from out of town see and remember and remark upon. And why not? If they come to Chicago "holding," to use the old race track term to describe horse players who had money in their pockets, they might stay at the Drake Hotel or the Four Seasons, shop amid the glitz of Water Tower Place, dine at some upscale slow-food joint such as the Everest, buy some art in River North and listen to a sumptuous opera at the Lyric. All of which is fine, splendid even. "Enjoy," as the waitresses love to say to the diners who turn up at the numerous Italian eateries that cluster around 26th and Oakley. Between the Campbell Soup factory and the

Fine Arts Building, the Black P-Stone Nation gang and the plummy announcers for WFMT, Chicago provides plenty in the way of extremes. Yet representative Chicago is not really found in the extremes between the proud and the profane. It is less likely to be found in a four-bedroom, five-bath condominium in the John Hancock Center than in Jefferson Park (with bachelor Uncle Sven installed in the basement apartment), not in the lockup at 26th and California but on bingo night at Saint Dominic's Parish.

Chicago's solidity may derive from its flatness, an unrelieved stretch of prairie now covered principally by apartments and bungalows, squat factory buildings and shops, and punctuated only by the occasional grandeur of a Catholic church built decades ago. True, there is a magnificent skyline with, to quote Louis Sullivan, its "proud and soaring" qualities, but one generally doesn't live in a skyline.

A city divided

The neighborhood has always been and remains Chicago's chief unit of social organization. Not many people really grew up in Chicago at all; instead they grew up in Austin, or South Shore, or Englewood or

POLITICIANS, CHICAGO STYLE

In the 1880s, first Ward Aldermen John "Bathhouse" Coughlin and Michael "Hinky Dink" Kenna presided over Chicago's district of vice known as "The Levee" whose working population consisted of thousands of bums, thugs, pimps, madams and thieves.

From Lake Michigan to the river and between 12th to 24th streets, the Levee boasted dice joints, peep shows, dance halls, burlesque houses and brothels. In 1910, a commission of concerned Chicagoans investigated the Levee and the situation it created and found there were 27,300,000 paid-for couplings annually (the population was 2,185,283). Gross income from prostitution was estimated at $30 million, with half this amount going to politicians and police. Kenna and Coughlin, acknowledged Lords of the Levee, exacted tribute regularly. The Bath and Hinky Dink were able to provide protection because, through their control of the First Ward vote, they had men beholden to them in every city, county and federal office.

The Democrats' slogan for the First Ward was "Vote early and often." Kenna and Coughlin ensured their re-election by finding jobs for the down-and-out and then, on voting day, marshaling them to party headquarters to vote.

Coughlin and Kenna. Two examples of Chicago style politicians who used their office to fill their own pockets.

Albany Park or Ravenswood or Pullman or Gage Park. To this day there are North Siders who have never been south of the Museum of Science and Industry, and South Siders who have never been north of the Lincoln Park Zoo, and who are perfectly content to be so circumscribed in their local peregrinations.

Growing up in a Chicago neighborhood, the chances are great that one grew up among one's own, among one's fellow Swedes or Poles or Irish or Germans or Jews or blacks or Chinese or Ukrainians or Greeks or (more recently) Koreans or East Indians.

As social units go, the neighborhood is long on familiarity and, in most instances, security. It is not strong on imagination; that is to say, growing up in a Chicago neighborhood, it is a bit difficult to imagine life outside the neighborhood. The reigning spirit of the neighborhood is generally very conservative and traditional.

Yet it is Chicago's organization around its many neighborhoods that largely gave (and for the most part still gives these days) the city its strong feeling of solidity, solidity of a kind not necessarily so readily available elsewhere in the country.

Peasant origins

As for physical solidity, Chicagoans, as a general type, tend to be somewhat beefier than people in New York (where anxiety probably peels away pounds) or San Francisco (where elegance is obligatory). Perhaps this is due to the peasant origins of so many of Chicago's early immigrants from Europe. Perhaps it is due to the Chicago diet, which tends to feature such fine and life-threatening items as pizza, ribs and every permutation played on beef. (Much fuss is made over hot dogs in Chicago, but the great, the archetypal Chicago sandwich is the Italian beef and sausage combo. There is no way to eat it without being reminded of one's prehistoric origins; upon finishing it one can almost hear the arteries leading to one's heart creaking to a close; and, unless one's taste buds have been ruined by the food served in spurious French restaurants, it happens to be delicious.)

LEFT: feathered friends get together.
RIGHT: unlike other US cities, Chicago has room for diversity.

Squinty-eyed realism

In Chicago it's all right to be the way you are. In New York, if you are homely you had better be smart; in Los Angeles, the capital of cosmetic surgery, homeliness means unhappiness. In Chicago, however, a city of diversity, there is room for individuality. A city that conveys so emphatic a feeling of solidity tends to induce in its citizens an habitual squinty-eyed realism.

Gabble about the rich ethnic diversity of Chicago, for example, is all right coming from politicians, whom no one takes seriously anyhow, but anyone who has grown up in Chicago knows that the Italians don't trust the Jews, who

don't think much of the Germans, who tend to be contemptuous of the Irish, who don't care much for the Poles, who could live nicely without the Greeks, who feel the East Indians are a pain, and who themselves wish the city's Spanish-speaking population would get their damn kids under some kind of control. Ethnic diversity doesn't get much richer than that.

Still toddlin'

The wonder of Chicago is that, despite its endemic corruption, its historic group animosities, the city keeps chugging along. Major hospitals and numerous schools and universities dot the cityscape. The Chicago Symphony, the

Art Institute and the University of Chicago remain internationally renowned; the Lyric Opera is rapidly entering world-class, if it is not there already. The city has great department stores and malls. Northwestern University not only has lived up to its potential to be one of America's elite academic institutions but is also developing an excellent athletic department. The Chicago Public Library has opened a monumental new main library. So much of the recent development and growth in Chicago is

> ### DESIGNED TO BE SLUMS
>
> The tenements of Greek Town and Little Italy were built to be slums. They were meant to keep the poor living at subsistence level and thus a captive working force.

reflective of the city's interest in culture. The variety of activity in the city remains impressive. It is comforting to think that while the ensemble called The Music of the Baroque gathers in one Chicago-area church for a concert, the members of the group known as Gamblers Anonymous get together in another for one of their meetings.

It is reassuring to know that one can eat reasonably and well at Stefani's on Fullerton, walk a few blocks east to an enormous used bookstore on Lincoln Avenue, then go off from there to a basketball game, or a blues bar or a production of a Greek play at the Court Theatre in Hyde Park. Another wonder is Chicago talent,

which keeps cropping up in odd and expected places. The Gilbert and Sullivan Society, for instance, performs elegant operettas in the battered auditorium of Saint Ignatius Church. Amid the ramshackle buildings of East Howard Street just off an alley, one comes upon a shop called Fritz Reuter and Sons, Master Violin Maker, Restorations and Appraisals. Or on 25th Avenue in Melrose Park, on a street doubtless zoned light industrial, a Chinese chef of unsurpassed quality named Ben Moy runs a restaurant frequented by many of the city's best-known artists and intellectuals.

Such is Chicago – the figurative width of the place – that its wealth of cultural resources cannot be adequately covered by a single analysis or a single visit.

No surprises

There is a way that Chicagoans speak, and it has nothing to do with giving the letter "a" a harsh sound or reverting from time to time to "dems" and "doses" in the manner of the late Mayor Daley. This way of speaking, this characteristic Chicago voice, combines cynicism with love of life, knowingness with occasional sentimentality. To those that speak it, nothing in the way of corruption comes as shocking news: the language itself has already been "corrupted."

The Chicago voice is a big city voice, and the people who speak with it tend to be old shoe, which is to say familiar and comfortable, for they know that pretensions will take you just so far and that life is a struggle that everyone loses in the end, so you may as well relax and make the best of things.

To a serious Chicagoan, life is inexhaustibly interesting, full of secret splendors and, when you come to consider the alternative, a damn fine thing. And Chicago is a good place to view life, a city where the sensible and accepted working assumption is that everyone and everything is a fake, except those people and things that one discovers are not, of which Chicago, being the kind of city that it is, has a great deal more than its share. ❏

LEFT: a sweet Chicago smile.
RIGHT: fair and freckled.

VOICES OF CHICAGO

The voices eventually and inevitably change, but in this city the message
tends to remain the same: abandon all pretensions, ye who enter here

Chicago enters the new millennium with a changing of the literary guard. In one year, 1997, two of its literary giants, the columnist Mike Royko and the novelist Leon Forrest, died. That same year another literary institution, Studs Terkel, retired from his radio interview show at the age of 85.

The mantle has been passed on to a new generation. John Kass was hired by the *Chicago Tribune* to fill Royko's shoes. Illinois' Poet Laureate, Gwendolyn Brooks, identified Marvin Gladney (author of *Sankofetic*) as a poet of "great promise." Among novelists, the attorney Scott Turow, author of best-seller *Presumed Innocent*, is the most prominent.

The working-class sentimentality and acerbic wit of Royko was characteristic of a Chicago literary voice that has been evolving for some 100 years. It can be traced directly to earlier notable Chicago newsmen and writers and the penny newspapers of the 1890s.

Touch of gold

Before Royko there was the writer Nelson Algren, best known for his novel *The Man With the Golden Arm*, for which he won the first National Book Award for fiction in 1950; the prose-poem *Chicago: City on The Make*; and an excellent collection of short stories, *The Neo Wilderness*. Algren's most famous words of advice easily could have been written by Royko: "Never play cards with a guy named Doc. Never eat at a place called Mom's. And never sleep with someone whose problems are greater than your own."

Before Algren there was that master of the short story, Ring Lardner, who developed his style as a Chicago sportswriter. Lardner, the model for Abe North in F. Scott Fitzgerald's *Tender is the Night*, is best remembered for his two collections of baseball stories, *You Know*

Me Al and *Alibi Ike*. And before Lardner there was the syndicated Chicago newspaper columnist Finley Peter Dunne, whose literary alter ego, Martin J. Dooley, an Irish immigrant saloonkeeper of droll wit, entertained readers across the nation. Dooley had a knack for slicing through pretense, much in the manner

LEFT: the Tribune Tower entrance lights up Michigan Avenue.
RIGHT: 1976 Nobel Prize winner Saul Bellow is an important voice in the city.

of Royko's own alter ego, Slats Grobnik. It was Dooley who first said, "Trust iv'rybody, but cut the cards."

Like Royko, these earlier Chicago writers wrote for regular Joes, with bluntness and humor, in the language of the common man. Lardner, in particular, is credited by H. L. Mencken with "reducing the American language to print." While East Coast writers in the years before World War I still adhered dutifully to every rule of proper syntax and grammar, Lardner was

banging out dialogue such as: "I didn't used to eat no lunch in the playing season except when I knowed I was not going to work."

Literary capital

From about 1890 to 1925, Chicago was a national hub of literary bustle. Mencken, writing in 1917, declared Chicago "the literary capital of the United States" and insisted that all the great American writers of his day had lived at least for a time in Chicago.

"Chicago has drawn them in from their remote wheat towns and far-flung railroad junctions, and it has given them an impulse that New York simply cannot match – an impulse toward independence, toward honesty, toward a peculiar vividness and naivete," he wrote. "New York, when it lures such a recruit eastward, makes a compliant conformist of him, and so ruins him out of hand. But Chicago, however short the time it has him, leaves him irrevocably his own man, with pride sufficient to carry through a decisive trail of his talents. Witness (Sherwood) Anderson, (Theodore) Dreiser, (Edgar Lee) Masters, (Carl) Sandburg and (George) Ade."

Some historians say Chicago's reputation as a writer's town is rooted in the newspaper circulation wars of a century ago, when the morning papers dropped their prices from two cents to a penny. With the price cut, newspapers found their way into the hands of more average Chicagoans than ever before.

Blooming times

Many of the major papers, such as the *Daily News* and the *Inter-Ocean*, attempted to cater to their expanded readership by adopting a more democratic editorial tone. Even the staid *Tribune* made adjustments, such as giving news coverage for the first time to the plebeian sport of boxing and coming out in favor of the shocking new fad of bloomers.

The papers courted journalists who could write in an entertaining and personal style, almost always employing elements of spoken American English. One such pioneer, Eugene Field, wrote both journalism and poetry in his "Sharps and Flats" column for the *Daily News*. He used contractions, slang and offensive words such as "ain't" in his poetry. His most enduring works are his children's poems *Little Boy Blue* and *Wynken, Blinken and Nod*. George Ade was another Chicago pioneer. He came to Chicago in 1890, got a job alongside Field at the *Daily News*, and within three years was a star columnist. In his own words, he showed a "criminal preference for the Midwest vernacular."

But Chicago newspapers did more for literature than allow plain speech to get down on paper. In an age before writers' conferences and creative writing fellowships, the papers offered aspiring writers a sort of hardball literary apprenticeship. Dreiser, Sandburg, Field, Edna

---

BLACK CHICAGO

Richard Wright might be the most famous black Chicago writer, but Dempsey Travis is the most prolific. Travis has written over 11 books on the black experience.

Ferber and Ben Hecht were among those who put in time on Chicago newspapers, happy for the paycheck and camaraderie.

Until the day it folded in 1978, the *Daily News* remained Chicago's most literate newspaper, conscientiously nurturing such talents as Field, Ade, Sandburg, Hecht and Royko, even when it meant allowing them to freelance a bit on company time. Editor Henry Justin Smith referred to his stable of writers as "budding Balzacs" and cut them a good deal of slack.

Sandburg covered the 1919 Chicago race riots for the *Daily News* and wrote a book about the tragedy. He later won Pulitzer Prizes – two for poetry and one for his biography of Abraham Lincoln – and wrote the poem that would become a Chicago cliché: "*Hog Butcher for the World, Tool Maker, Stacker of Wheat, Player with Railroads and the Nation's Freight Handler, Stormy, Husky, Brawling, City of the Big Shoulders.*" The stockyards are gone and the big shoulders wear Brooks Brothers, but the poem is still quoted and the image sticks.

Creative nonfiction

Smith hired Sandburg as much for his poetry as his journalism, so he assigned him the easy task of reviewing "picture plays" for the *News* and left him free to write poetry the rest of the day. Smith prized good writing above all else, possibly even facts. He once hired a reporter who had faked a story about a local resident living to a prodigious age, explaining that "accuracy can be taught, imagination cannot."

Hecht worked at the *Daily News* alongside Sandburg. It was Hecht, in fact, who got Sandburg the job. Hecht was an outstanding reporter and columnist, but notoriously lazy about doing his legwork. When a deadline loomed, he sometimes made up material. On one occasion he and a *News* photographer cajoled a police captain into posing for a picture aboard a police boat, gun in hand, with Hecht concocting the totally unsubstantiated headline: "Police Pursue River Bandits."

It made for bad journalism, but good times. Hecht immortalized the Chicago school of high-jinks journalism in his smash play *The Front Page*, which later became a movie that has been remade again and again.

Outside the city's newsrooms, Chicago's literary scene during the 1910s and 1920s was anchored by the poet and editor Harriet Monroe. The magazine she founded, *Poetry*, was the official organ of the American Modernist movement and the first to publish T.S. Eliot, Marianne Moore, William Carlos Williams and Ezra Pound.

Literary obsessions

During the next three decades, while the nation struggled through the Great Depression and another world war, Chicago produced four more nationally important writers, all of a pro-

letarian bent: Algren, Richard Wright, Jack Conroy and James T. Farrell. They all shared a fascination with Marxism politics and an obsessive interest in the underdog.

Wright, who moved up to Chicago from Mississippi in the 1920s, worked as a postal clerk by day and wrote by night. His best works, including the novel *Native Son*, which was set in Chicago, were strongly influenced by Dreiser's naturalistic fiction. Conroy, a writer and editor in Chicago for some 40 years, is best remembered today for his 1933 proletarian novel *The Disinherited*. As editor of several leftist literary journals in the 1930s and 1940s, he also published the early work of

Wright and Algren. Of Algren, Conroy once said: "The gates of his soul opened on the hell side." Farrell, a second-generation South Side Irishman, wrote more than 50 books. His brutally realistic trilogy of books about Studs Lonigan, an aimless youth growing up in Chicago from the early 1900s to the Depression, holds up well a century later.

Homeless Papa

Conspicuously absent from this rundown of Chicago writers is the big daddy of them all,

Ernest Hemingway, who grew up in Oak Park. Hemingway skipped town after high school and never looked back. He belonged to Paris, Cuba and the world, but never to Chicago.

It is equally axiomatic that almost all Chicago writers eventually leave town, though seldom with Hemingway's haste. Dunne, Lardner, Dreiser, Sandburg, Hecht, Wright, Farrell and Algren are among those lured away by the energy of New York or the wealth of Hollywood and the West Coast.

In Algren's case, it was also a matter of hurt feelings. In his introduction to *The Neo Wilderness*, Algren groused that his books could be found in translation "in the libraries of all the

---

> ### PROSE PRIZE
>
> New York has the Pulitzer. Oslo has the Nobel. Chicago has the *Chicago Tribune*'s Heartland Prize for fiction. Jane Smiley's novel *A Thousand Acres* won it in 1992.

---

large cities of Europe," but not "in the library of the city about which they were written."

Streets seen

Shortly after Algren's death, an alderman proposed to honor him by changing the name of West Evergreen Street to West Algren Street. But folks on the street objected, so the alderman abandoned the plan. The living sometimes vote in Chicago, while the dead usually don't. On the other hand, stretches of two (non-residential) downtown streets are named after two well-known columnists and broadcasters, Irv Kupcinet and Paul Harvey.

Chicago remains a writer's town, if no longer a literary titan. Among the critically acclaimed writers making their homes in Chicago in the 1990s are Pulitzer Prize winner Gwendolyn Brooks, National Book Award recipient Larry Heinemann, Cyrus Colter, Harry Mark Petrakis, Charles Dickinson, Bill Granger, Sara Paretsky, Richard Stern, Stuart Kaminsky and Stuart Dybek. And David Mamet developed his craft as a great playwright in Chicago; it's doubtful that anyone has ever really captured the profane, hustling attitude of Chicago in crisper dialogue than his real estate salesmen in *Glengarry Glen Ross*.

Over the past quarter-century, however, Chicago has been able to boast of only one bona fide literary superstar: Saul Bellow, who in 1976 won the Nobel Prize for literature.

Like Algren and the many others before, Bellow eventually left the city. But by the late 1990s the *Chicago Sun-Times* was suggesting that physical location might be of declining importance to the Chicago writer's craft.

"Today Chicago, as have other cities, has become a way station where writers hang their hats, briefly teaching at local colleges and universities before moving on to the next academic appointment," the paper lamented. "In this postmodern world, marked by an ease of mobility as well as instant communications, ideas tend toward the global. Regional literature has been flattened." It will be up to the likes of Gladney, Turow and Kass to prove if such a prognostication is correct. ❏

LEFT: the 1974 movie remake of *The Front Page*.
RIGHT: Harold Washington.

He is a great LEGISLATOR
He is a great CONGRESSMAN
He will be a GREAT MAYOR
Harold WASHINGTON ⑧

GAY CHICAGO

Chicago's gay community is out of the closet, confidently claims its own
neighborhood, and has developed a powerful voice, politically and culturally

Just as Chicago's neighborhoods are often defined by ethnicity, there is a Chicago neighborhood, known as "Boys' Town," defined by … sexuality.

Boys' Town, which begins at Roscoe Street and Halsted and extends north to Addison Street and Halsted, is known more than any other area of Chicago for its gay bars, businesses and general population of gays, lesbians and bisexuals. While the gay community extends further afield to neighborhoods such as Andersonville and Bucktown, Boys' Town is the area of the city where it took root in the 1970s.

Chicago's gay community is without a doubt out of the closet. In 1996, 6 percent of voters under the age of 40 identified themselves as gay, lesbian or bisexual. These numbers put the gay voting block ahead of Jews, Latinos and Asian-Americans in terms of size. The 1998 AIDS Walk, which is a six-mile (10-km) hike up the lakefront to raise money for Aids research, drew over 30,000 people.

Today the gay and lesbian community has grown and flourished to become a highly visible and influential part of Chicago's political, social and cultural structure. Over the years Boys' Town has been particularly known for its wild bars, racy bookshops and exotic clothing stores. Although these places remain, today the North Halsted strip also has good restaurants, smart homes and enticing stores for any shopper.

Pillars of society

At its north and south ends Boys' Town is marked by distinctive curved pillars. The pillars, decorated with the colors of the rainbow, not only signify the North Halsted "Boys' Town" district but also represent the fight against racism. The rainbow, which is displayed throughout the community, evolved from the Color Triangle Project whose goal is to fight racism in Chicago's gay, lesbian and bisexual community. Most of the stores, bars and restaurants on the North Halsted strip display the color triangle; the colors of the rainbow, often displayed as a sticker in a store window or a flag hanging from the front of a business, represent a store's willingness to serve and accept the gay community.

Preserving its flair, Boys' Town" is in part characterized by the tongue-in-cheek names it

FINDING ITS CENTER

The Gerber/Hart Library, which opened its doors in 1981, is the Midwest's largest gay circulating library, archives and resource center. It's named for Henry Gerber, a US Post Office employee who in the 1920s founded the country's first gay rights organization, the Society for Human Rights, and civil liberties attorney Pearl Hart. In 1999, the library moved to larger premises to make room for its growing collection and also to expand its role as a resource center to include a cultural center for the gay community. The center promotes the work of gay artists, and events include music and theater festivals and theater readings.

gives to many of its businesses. The Ram Bookstore, the Gay Mart, Banana Video and the OutSpoke'n bike store are all to be found in the neighborhood. There is no shortage, however, of organizations that exist to take the problems of the gay community a lot more seriously. Just a few are Horizons, whose services include social service and legal referrals, the Aids Foundation of Chicago, Lesbian Parents Group, Gay and Lesbian Physicians of Chicago, Lesbian and Gay Bar Association and the Chicago Area Gay and Lesbian Chamber of Commerce (*for detailed information, see the Travel Tips section at the end of this book*).

community since 1980, the New Town Writers have fostered gay literary expression through novels, prose and poetry.

March in June

There are year-round pride events, the biggest being the colorful, traffic-stopping Annual Gay and Lesbian Parade. Held on the last Sunday in June, the parade takes over Chicago for the day and is symbolic of the progress of the gay movement since the time in 1974 when a group of drag queens had a run-in with the police at the Stonewall Inn in New York.

Unlike many other cities, the Chicago gay

Publications aimed at the gay community include *The Windy City Times*, *Gay Chicago* and *Outlines*, all free of charge. The publisher of *Outlines* also produces *Out!*, a comprehensive – and again free – Chicago resource guide. All the above can easily be found in bundles in the doorways or near the fronts of numerous gay-friendly establishments

There are also artists' groups, such as the New Town Writers, that were founded by and address gay and lesbian issues. Active in the

LEFT AND ABOVE: the Annual Gay and Lesbian Parade, held on a Sunday in June, is part politics and part party and entertainment.

community enjoys the support of the mayor, Richard M. Daley. During his period in office Daley has passed a domestic partnership ordinance, set up a police department gay and lesbian advisory committee for the first time, and poured $3 million of city money into a street enhancement scheme as a thank-you gesture for the gay sector's contribution to Chicago. He has also committed himself to pushing the federal government to introduce a hate crimes law that would include gays.

Some people believe, not altogether improbably, that in the future Boys' Town will be like a "museum" that people visit, to remember the early days of the gay movement. ❑

THE CHICAGO BLUES

The early blues originally came from the Mississippi delta but Chicago
has long since developed its own particular, influential style

The long blond-wood bar of the neighborhood tavern was propping up only a few people. Three older black guys in short-sleeved shirts and snappy straw hats trash-talked and cackled back and forth as they sipped their beer, while a younger, thinner black guy in an identical hat looked around coolly as he nursed a fruit juice. A fat white man wearing a plaid shirt and a loud and lurid paisley tie grinned at the three old black guys as he worked on a whiskey.

A newcomer, a Hispanic wearing baggy trousers and several earrings, made straight for the older black guys. After a few minutes of chatting and laughing, the whole group gradually migrated to the far end of the room. Two of the men nonchalantly slung guitars over their shoulders, while another settled behind a drum kit. Another adjusted a mike and yet another blew a few tentative notes on his harmonica.

Their music hit the ground running: the heavy beat, the surging bass, the overlay of harp and, leading it all, the whine and squeal of the lead guitar. They grinned at each other. It didn't matter that there were only half a dozen people in the bar. Within minutes, however, the place was jammed with people: more old black guys, nodding their heads in time, and a bunch of young whites who were shouting along, clapping and boogying on their stools. Some started dancing in front of the band, pausing between songs to shake hands with the musicians or offer some words of approval.

It was 3.30 on a Wednesday afternoon in a residential neighborhood. Welcome to the blues, Chicago style.

Blue notes

The Chicago blues hold a secure niche in both the annals of American music and today's popular entertainment, as much a part of the town

as Dixieland jazz is to New Orleans. It is a loud, showy, rocking type of music that takes traditional blues themes, chords and bent notes, and then juices them up with amplification. Musicologists could go on and on about the characteristic 12-bar, three-chord schematics and "the dominant seventh," with split quarter tones.

To music scholars, blues music does not refer to "blue" themes in lyrics, but to the "blue" notes that have been played natural or flatted, often deliberately out of tune. It's a style that has been described as getting music out of the cracks between the piano keys. To non-experts, the overriding musical feature of the Chicago blues is that the music is guitar-driven.

It would be difficult to overstate the influence of the Chicago blues and Chicago bluesmen on today's popular music, particularly mainstream rock 'n' roll. Anyone who listens to a set of live blues anywhere in Chicago is sure to mark it as the roots of rock. "Musicians treat the blues like gospel; it's a kind of honesty meter, a

PRECEDING PAGES: rockin' all night long at the Chicago Blues Fest.
LEFT: Koko Taylor, Chicago's Queen of the Blues.
RIGHT: backyard barbecue blues.

measure of belief," according to Paris-based music critic Mike Zwerin. "'He can't even play the blues', is to say he's hopeless. Chicago remains the point of reference – a mecca."

African roots

Everyone has a personal interpretation and feel for the blues, as with any other art form. But to appreciate the development of Chicago blues, it is important to understand the people who created it. The genesis of the blues can be traced back to Africa, where tribes developed strong oral traditions of passing down their lessons and legends. In some African cultures, one sign of masculinity was the falsetto singing that has become such a part of modern blues, rhythm and blues, soul and rock music.

The Africans who became slaves in America brought their traditions with them, and hung on to vestiges of those traditions despite the cultural influences that led them to speak the language, wear the clothes and use the manners forced on them by white owners.

The blues grew out of the "field hollers" of slave times, when the workers bending over cotton or other crops would communicate with each other in long slow chants and songs. Many owners refused to let their slaves talk to each

other, but didn't mind them singing while they worked. For many, the holler messages passed from field to field, from plantation to plantation, were the only way of keeping in touch with their African traditions, and sometimes the only way of tracking down family members.

Negro spirituals

As African rhythms melded with European styles of harmony, the field hollers led to the Negro spirituals and hymns that looked toward happiness some day, but not in this lifetime. The early blues, often referred to as the "downhome" or "country" blues, were rooted in the Mississippi delta, and featured songs that were typically more personal than spiritual. They were songs about loving and leaving, about loyalty and betrayal, about desire and temptation. They were sung for friends at home, for cellmates in prison or for tips on the street.

Accompanied at first by finger-snapping, stomping, "hambone" thigh-slapping and other crude forms of percussion, the downhome blues ultimately became associated with the acoustic guitar, particularly the homemade "bottleneck" style. Some black freemen became wandering minstrels, taking the field hollers and early blues on the road to perform for and entertain slave and master alike.

servicemen, many came to Chicago to get an education and become professionals. Thousands took up the jobs – generally menial, but relatively high paying – offered by the ever-growing stockyards.

Chicago's two large black-dominated neighborhoods developed because the migrants from the South typically got off the trains at one of two stops. If they got off at the 63rd Street station, they usually settled right there on the South Side; if they got off at the 12th Street station, they generally ended up on the West Side. The Southern musicians, naturally, followed their audience.

Moving north

In the post-slavery industrial era, the expanding mills and factories of the North brought many blacks up the Mississippi Valley to Chicago. The migration varied between a trickle and a steady stream for much of the first half of this century, but after World War II it became a positive flood as young blacks, often with their families, sought out the bright lights and higher-paying jobs.

Using the government aid for returning

One of the men who acted as a bridge between the delta and the city, from Mississippi to Chicago, from downhome to urban blues, was Big Bill Broonzy. He was also one of the first American artists to take the blues to Europe, where it was embraced by sophisticated audiences.

Chicago performers often bracket dates in small clubs in their home neighborhoods with tours of big halls in Europe, and a handful of Chicago blues expatriate shave resettled in Europe to take advantage of the enthusiastic audiences.

The famous guitarist Luther Allison was based in Paris before he died. In Chicago,

LEFT: Junior Wells, who shared with Buddy Guy the unofficial title of "greatest ever Chicago bluesmen."
ABOVE: Ruth Brown, wide and wailin'.

visiting Europeans often seek out the blues bars and clubs, and the annual weekend Chicago Blues Fest held in Grant Park has become a focus for many foreign tourists.

Birth of the blues

Though still popular after World War II, the rural, relatively simple downhome blues – typically one man with one guitar, mourning the love he done lost – eventually gave way to a faster, more raucous, and often more joyful music.

When the electric guitar came along in the 1950s, it was embraced wholeheartedly in the black clubs and the living rooms and the back yards, and thus was the Chicago blues born.

The man with the guitar not only had an amplifier, but he also had an electric bass player, a drummer, a harmonica player, a saxophone player and perhaps even a lady – sometimes slim and sultry, sometimes wide and wailin' – to sing the blues.

The resulting Chicago blues, however, retained and intensified many of the features experts use to characterize downhome blues: vocal moans and drones, for example, along with "constant repetition of melodic figures, harmonica tremeloes, a heavy sound and rough

BLUES HEAVEN

One of the most famous addresses in Chicago is 2120 South Michigan Avenue. For a decade it was the headquarters of Chess, one of the most influential record labels in the history of the blues.

The independent label recorded such legends as Muddy Waters, John Lee Hooker, Bo Diddley, Koko Taylor, Little Walter, Howlin' Wolf, Sonny Boy Williamson, and Willie Dixon. Non-blues artists – such as Aretha Franklin, Chuck Berry, Ramsey Lewis, and Ahmad Jamal – also recorded there. After the Rolling Stones visited the studios in 1964 and met some of the bluesmen who were so influential on their music, the band paid tribute to the experience by recording the instrumental *2120 South Michigan Avenue*.

In 1996, when the building was idle for some time, Willie Dixon's family, true to his wishes before Dixon died in 1992, announced that they would establish the Blues Heaven Foundation in the building. Two years and half a million dollars later, they opened the foundation's doors. The Foundation preserves the history of the blues, counsels the oft-exploited blues artists on their rights, and promotes the music in schools. It is an impressive legacy to one of the blues' most talented composers, the man who wrote such classics as Muddy Waters' *Hoochie Coochie Man* and *I Just Want to Make Love to You.*

intensity," according to the noted blues author Charles Keil.

The delta bluesmen who defined and refined the new style in the 1950s included J.B. Lenoir, Jimmy Reed, Little Walter, Howlin' Wolf, Sonny Boy Williamson, John Lee Hooker and Muddy Waters, who became the single performer most identified with the earthy, vibrant, driving style of Chicago blues.

Theme of sorrow

Waters' songs, such as *Hoochie Coochie Man*, *Got My Mojo Workin'* and *I'm Ready*, epitomize the rollicking sexual boastfulness

more sophisticated, of course, and humor is one of the strongest undercurrents in the Chicago blues, as when the singer complains about a straying spouse or a meddling mother-in-law. A modern bluesman – or woman – may complain about a lover who cheats, but may also threaten to kick that lover's ass. Willie Dixon sang many of his own songs, but his true legacy will be the hundreds he wrote for other artists, often tailoring the themes, lyrics and rhythms to a performer's individual style. To Dixon, who said, "The wisdom of the blues is the true facts of life," everything that did and could happen was fair game for a blues song.

that often replaced the theme of sorrow and helplessness so common in the downhome blues. In *Tiger in Your Tank*, Waters sang:

> I can raise your hood.
> I can clean your coils.
> Check the transmissions,
> And give you the oils.
> I don't care what the people think,
> I want to put a tiger,
> You know, in your tank.

Many of the themes and lyrics have become

Chess game

One of the cornerstones of the development of the Chicago blues in the 1950s and 1960s was Chess Records, the recording company operated by Leonard Chess, his brother Phil and Leonard's son Marshall. Many of the leading talents in blues cut records with the Chess family. Muddy Waters was with them for years with no contract beyond a handshake. Willie Dixon, who was an accomplished upright bass player as well as songwriter, was a Chess stalwart who often used his basement to audition new talent for the Chess family.

Today, more than 20 years after guiding light Leonard Chess died and the studio was closed,

LEFT: the bassist and songwriter Willie Dixon with Muddy Waters.
ABOVE: Marshall Chess in his vinyl days.

Blues joints

Checking out blues clubs is one of the best treats in a visit to Chicago. Three names most associated with contemporary Chicago blues are the guitarists Buddy Guy and Son Seals, and the vocalist Koko Taylor. The smart visitor to the city should find the "joints" where they are performing.

There are a number of popular blues clubs on the North Side of Chicago. The best North Side and downtown clubs include Blue Chicago, BLUES, Kingston Mines and Buddy

Guy's Legends. It's always advisable to check in advance with these to see if booking is necessary; on weekends or when well-known performers are playing, tickets can be tight. Cover charges vary, depending on the night of the week and who's performing.

For a real plunge into urban blues, nothing compares with the South Side, particularly the Checker Board, also known recently as the New Checkerboard Lounge. For years, the Checker Board has been the unofficial headquarters of the Chicago blues for the South Side bluesmen, but it's in a tough neighborhood where visitors should take care. The cover charge at the Checker Board is usually

only a few dollars. Once inside, the club is remarkably small for having such a big reputation. It has seats for perhaps 100 and standing room (which is more usual) for about 300, but in fact it only takes about 30 people to make the place look crowded.

Though the neighborhood outside may be threatening to some, once inside it's easy to make friends among the locals and the bluesmen themselves, who especially appreciate out-of-towners and love the idea of someone crossing an ocean to hear them play. You cannot book or make advance reservations on the South Side, by the way.

For the hard-core late-night prowlers, Kingston Mines, with its two alternating stages, can be a gold mine for the blues. One of Chicago's northernmost blues clubs (on North Halsted), it's not exactly a fancy club, but it's one of those places that looks better as the night goes on. And the night does go on at Kingston Mines, usually until 4am. On Saturday nights and Sunday mornings, the music rolls until 5am. Other blues performers around the city finish their regular gigs at two or three in the morning and then head for Kingston Mines, where they jam and "talk country" at each other, much to the delight of aficionados.

In November 1996 the House of Blues chain opened a location in Chicago at Marina City, 300 N. State Street. But *caveat emptor*: the blues aficionado should note that most of the acts featured at the House of Blues are not blues at all (*see opposite*). A call ahead before going is the best strategy to avoid disappointment.

In 1990, the city granted landmark status to the building at 2120 South Michigan Avenue that once housed Chess Recording Co. and its legendary music studios. In 1997, the doors of the building were reopened as the home of the Blues Heaven Foundation, the closest thing in Chicago to a blues museum. It is open for tours (*see Travel Tips*).

And, of course, the Chicago Blues Fest has become an avidly awaited annual summer tradition. It's free, held in downtown's grassy Grant Park, and typically features dozens of artists from Chicago and elsewhere. ❑

LEFT: John Lee Hooker.
RIGHT: the Blues Brothers back up Aretha Franklin.

the debate continues in Chicago over the role of the Chess family. Were they whites who exploited black talent? Would the Chicago blues have become as popular as they did if they hadn't given so many unheard artists a chance to record?

English invasion

One thing not in doubt is that many of the architects of modern rock 'n' roll made formative pilgrimages to the tiny Chess studio on South Michigan Avenue. Prominent rock singers and guitarists, particularly the leaders of the 1960s "English invasion" such as the Rolling Stones, paid personal homage to Chess's blues artists. For a time, Marshall Chess managed the Rolling Stones, who took their name from a Muddy Waters song. They and other modern rock stars not only re-recorded many Chicago blues songs to create international hits, but often borrowed or stole outright individual guitarists' distinctive riffs.

When Howlin' Wolf recorded Willie Dixon's *Little Red Rooster*, for example, it sold 20,000 copies, a big hit for a local blues record. When the Rolling Stones re-recorded the song in a nearly identical manner, it sold more than 500,000 copies. Tom Marker, a longtime

HOUSE OF BLUES

Koko Taylor has performed there. So has Bobby "Blue" Bland, another Chicago blues legend. *The Blues Brothers* star Dan Aykroyd is an investor. But do not expect to see a line-up of Chicago's top blues acts there. The reason is that the House of Blues was opened to promote blues music but not promote it exclusively. In fact, according to House of Blues founder Isaac Tigrett, the business might not succeed if the House of Blues offered only blues.

"You have a dwindling media appeal, you just don't find it on radio, you never read about it in the mainstream press," Tigrett said during an interview with Associated Press when the club opened. "Because commercially it has not been successful for a lot of people, no one's investing in the culture."

Because it was known Chicago's House of Blues would not be a blues joint and the owners were not even black and from the blues community, its debut in November 1996 got a skeptical reception from some quarters. However, since then it has succeeded in winning over many by establishing itself as the place in town to hear acts that some blues aficionados believed might have retired or died. War, the Staple Singers, and The Wailers (without Bob Marley, of course) are among the groups whose careers the House of Blues has helped to keep alive.

Chicago blues disc jockey, recalled that the English rockers, especially the Stones, were "just crazy" about the blues. "Those guys were big fans of the Chicago sound when they were getting their blues thing together themselves," he said. "They were just trying to copy the stuff. Sometimes they would copy the song lick for lick." The black bluesmen made the music, and the white rockers made it famous.

Shoestring existence

Many blues performers literally sang for their supper and not much more. Even name performers often lived on a shoestring – and still

do. For example, Koko Taylor, known in Chicago as the Queen of the Blues, needed the receipts of a benefit thrown by friends and fellow performers to pay the bills after she and several band members were injured in a 1988 auto accident.

"Musicians all over Chicago are working hard, but they're working for almost nothing," Taylor told the *Chicago Tribune*. "You sing the blues, die and they have a benefit to bury you. That's the pattern," added Valerie Wellingtons, who, until she died on January 2, 1993, at the

LEFT AND ABOVE: "Musicians all over Chicago are working hard," according to singer Koko Taylor.

tender age of 33, was one of the brightest young blues singers. Wellington and a number of other performers had formed the Chicago Blues Artists Coalition, a sort of blues-rights organization that aimed to help performers learn how to handle their own business and financial affairs. Blues Heaven – the de facto blues museum that Willie Dixon's family opened in 1997 in the old Chess Records building – was started with the goal of also helping blues artists handle their affairs.

Not all blues artists end up down and out, of course. The Chicago blues have made a lot of money for some artists who have reclaimed the traditions from the white-dominated world of rock. Though not from Chicago, the influence of the Chicago style is heard in many of the tunes of artists B.B. King and Robert Cray. The Chess recording studio is gone, and so are some of the classic South Side blues clubs such as Theresa's, but the Chicago blues scene remains as lively in the 1990s as ever.

Following the death of Muddy Waters, guitarist Buddy Guy and singer-harpist Junior Wells shared the unofficial title of greatest living Chicago bluesmen. Junior Wells died in 1998, leaving Buddy Guy to carry the torch alone. Eric Clapton says Buddy Guy is the world's greatest guitarist.

New guard

Sadly, many of Chicago's finest blues musicians and singers passed away in the 1990s, including Johnny Littlejohn, Buddy Scott, Luther Allison, Johnny Copeland, Fenton Robinson, Jimmy Rogers, and Jimmy Walker. The good news is that their work has been preserved on CDs and tapes for visitors to buy in the city. It is also encouraging that a number of young blues artists (none yet 50 by the turn of the millennium) have emerged to keep the traditions alive. This new guard includes such young lights as Deitra Farr, Fruteland Jackson, Wayne Baker Brooks, and Shirli Dixon Nelson, the daughter of Willie Dixon.

For visiting blues fans who seek out the music, an added benefit is the musicians, even the headliners, who typically mingle with the crowd before and after shows. They are often happy to have a chat and maybe a drink; more than any other music, the Chicago blues remain of and for everyday people, with all the highs and lows and worries of everyday life. ❑

YEAR ROUND PERFORMANCES

With drama in general enjoying a resurgence, one major theater, Goodman's Loop,
is expanding and another, Second City, is still turning out superb comedic actors

There is no slow season on the Chicago entertainment scene. Whether large theaters or small cabarets, whether lavish ballet and opera productions or one-man shows, Chicagoans are accustomed to a wide choice for a night out. They are also accustomed to seeing live people on stage; in much of the Loop and its neighboring downtown areas, it was easier until relatively recently to find a play or a music act on stage than it was to find a movie house. Cinema-goers would typically head for outlying residential areas.

Despite the January-to-October nature of Chicago entertainment, a few attractions are necessarily seasonal. Some of Chicago's 120 theater companies, for example, concentrate on summer stock or Shakespeare in the parks during June, July and August. Similarly, summer brings many concerts, day and night and often free, at the Petrillo Music Shell in Grant Park.

The Blues Fest in early June and Jazz Fest in late August or early September are enormously popular weekend events, attracting internationally known stars. Another summer highlight are the outdoor concerts, from big bands and touring symphonies to jazz and pop stars, at Ravinia in the North Shore suburb of Highland Park. The autumn cultural offerings include the Lyric Opera of Chicago and the Chicago Symphony Orchestra.

For many Chicagoans and visitors alike, however, the ultimate night out in the Windy City includes the theater and one of the handful of swanky nightclubs or cabarets that serve up sophisticated songs along with the nightcaps.

Stepping out

A few years ago a *New York Times* reviewer wrote: "What is the current state of the American theater? Illinois!" Because there is so much theater in Chicago at any one time, at any time

of year, it's best to plan ahead. Both major dailies, the *Chicago Tribune* and the *Chicago Sun-Times*, have extensive Friday entertainment listings for the weekend. In addition, there's a lengthy theater guide in the *Reader*, a free four-section Chicago weekly found by the entrances of numerous stores and coffee shops.

Theater bargains for those who don't plan ahead are available from Hot Tix booths. The booths are run by the League of Chicago Theaters, a trade association for theaters and theater companies in the Chicago area.

The Chicago booths are to be found in the Loop, at the corner of State and Washington Streets across from Marshall Field's, and at Tower Records, 214 South Wabash; at the Visitors' Center at 811 N. Michigan Avenue; and at Tower Records, 2301 N. Clark Street. Theater tickets are available the day of the performance at half price, and on Friday for weekend performances. Tower Records' Hot Tix booths accept cash only. The booths also sell full-price

PRECEDING PAGES: Edward Hopper's *Nighthawks*.
LEFT: waiting in wings.
RIGHT: the Second City performance features cabaret-style entertainment and drinks.

advance tickets for theater, concerts, sports and other events. Note that a service charge applies to all purchases.

The Hot Tix booths offer free copies of the *Theatre Chicago Guide*, with its current listings of productions, addresses and telephone numbers for member theaters and detailed maps of playhouse locations.

Long history

Many of the best known Chicago companies of the 1990s started in the 1960s and 1970s, but the city's stage history goes back more than 150 years. The first plays were presented in

create a community-based theater for Hull House, seeking a company in the city's heart, nurtured by neighborhoods. From among those artistic roots came actor Mike Nussbaum and playwrights David Mamet and Alan Bates.

Variety of venues

The Body Politic Theatre was created in the mid-1960s, offering theater games for actors to learn body language. Its executive director, Jim Shiflett, had been taught by the legendary improvisationist Viola Spolin. One of its first program directors was Paul Sills, Spolin's son and a master of improvisation in his own right.

1837, when Chicago was incorporated as a city. By the time Abraham Lincoln won the Republican nomination in Chicago in 1860, the city had several permanent theaters.

The waves of immigrants who came to a brawny Chicago brought with them spirited productions in their native tongues and the city was soon a port of call for an international roster of performers – a tradition that continues today with touring troupes from Broadway and London shows.

However, there's much more to Chicago theater than touring shows in Loop playhouses. In the early 1960s, controversial, avant garde director Bob Sickinger came to Chicago to

Sills had been a director of The Compass Players in 1955, a group that borrowed from *commedia dell'arte*, a Renaissance style in which actors improvised on scenarios. The Compass Players were characterized by an explosion of creative energy, rehearsing scenarios during the day, performing at night, then taking audience suggestions for more improvisations. From this group, which spawned the Second City improv group, came Mike Nichols, Elaine May, Shelley Berman and Barbara Harris.

By the mid-1970s, there was rich competition for the Body Politic. Victory Gardens Theater focused on Chicago playwrights and made a commitment to black and Hispanic theater. Wisdom Bridge Theater vibrated with youth, originality and inventiveness. The Evanston Theater Company, now the Northlight Theater, performed contemporary works, fresh interpretations of classics and forgotten plays with thought-provoking productions. And there was David Mamet's St Nicholas Theater Company, producing early, highly praised works by the playwright. There was also the irreverent Organic Theater, which created a living cartoon on stage with *Warp*, a campy, sci-fi serial.

The number of off-Loop theaters increased rapidly and by the time they exceeded 100, crit-

often been used interchangeably with the phrase "Chicago theater," this is not the case. And while the dramatic community still argues over a definition of "Chicago theater," its basic components consist of an energizing strength and a collective heart.

"Chicago theater artists were unable to succeed, and they were unable to fail. And both those things were blessings," wrote Robert Falls, artistic director of the Goodman and former artistic director of Wisdom Bridge. "You couldn't really fail, because it didn't really matter, whereas in New York or Los Angeles if you failed, that was it. In Chicago, people

ics were saying Chicago theater was becoming a major force. Emerging in the late 1970s was a distinctively gritty, visceral mode of performance and in-your-face directional style that came from the Steppenwolf Theater Company. Productions left audiences spent and critics raving. From this theater of realism have come the later writings of Mamet and the acting of John Malkovich and Glenne Headley.

While the Steppenwolf style of lean linguistic vernacular and intense acting has

LEFT: T-shirt display; *The Nutcracker,* Aire Crown.
ABOVE: pavement piper; Fernando Jones' tribute to Junior Wells.

approach it more as their work, as their art. They're continually writing, acting, designing and directing plays. They're interested in a body of work."

Second City

One of the things that makes the term "Chicago theater" so immensely difficult to nail down is that it must also include Second City, without doubt its most famous company. The city's theaters of realism and improvisation have links in language and situations.

They both make profound use of colloquialisms and of placing the common person in very uncommon situations. But whereas one plays for intensity, the other does so for more sophisticated laughs.

There's a full history of the homegrown genre available in the Chicago Theater Collection for reading and viewing at the Chicago Public Library. Open to the general public, it includes original scripts and videotapes of famous performances. Meanwhile there's plenty of live theater to enjoy.

Steppenwolf productions should not be missed. Victory Gardens and the Organic also

have reliable productions. There are also several noteworthy companies. The Court Theater in Hyde Park has a repertory which includes innovative productions of classics, rarely-seen masterpieces and significant works by contemporary authors. The season of the Pegasus Players in Uptown might include modern and classical productions, a musical and a new script.

For more traditional performances, there's the Shubert Theater, just off State Street in the Loop. Most of the Broadway touring compa-

> ### GRASS ACT
>
> Open air music venue Ravinia is renowned for its huge, sprawling lawn where "seating" never runs out and concertgoers are free to bring their own picnics.

SECOND TO NONE

The Second City theatre alumni list reads like a *Who's Who* of comedy. Although the Second City outposts in Toronto and Detroit have turned out their share of successful entertainers, Second City Chicago, a vibrant presence on the entertainment scene since the late 1950s, is still second to none when it comes to producing top-notch comedic actors and actresses.

Famous rib-ticklers who cut their teeth in Old Town include: former *Saturday Night Live* cast members Dan Aykroyd and the late John Belushi, who starred together in the Chicago-based comedy *The Blues Brothers*; James Belushi, John's younger brother, whose movie credits

include the Chicago-based comedy *About Last Night;* the late Chris Farley, another member of the Second City-to-*Saturday Night Live* pipeline and, like John Belushi, a master of slapstick; Bill Murray, a former *SNL* cast member with a long list of hit comedies to his credit; Brian Doyle-Murray, Bill's brother, who has played supporting roles in dozens of comedies; Joan Rivers, the comedienne and talk-show host; Jerry Stiller, a veteran actor best known for his role as George's father in the television sitcom *Seinfeld;* and George Wendt, known best for playing a bar regular on the sitcom *Cheers.* Book ahead if you want to be sure of getting a seat.

nies play here for longer runs. For shorter runs, of perhaps a week, they play the Arie Crown at McCormick Place. But unless you're absolutely dying to see the show, skip the Crown. Its huge size destroys the intimacy of theater and people have complained about the hall's acoustics.

There are several notable theaters in the round and dinner theaters within easy driving distance of the city. These include the Drury Lane Oakbrook, about a 30-minute drive from downtown, and, for fans of musicals, the Marriott Theatre in Lincolnshire, which is about 45 minutes away.

oldest and largest resident theater. Its stage has hosted the American premieres of David Mamet's Pulitzer Prize-winning *Glengarry Glen Ross* and Nobel Laureate Wole Soyink's *Death and the King's Horseman.* The Midwestern premiere of August Wilson's Pulitzer Prize-winning *Fences* was also performed at the Goodman. An annual sellout and Chicago tradition is *A Christmas Carol*, adapted from Charles Dickens. As a last resort, try going directly to the Goodman for occasional returns from season ticket holders or – for those with the time or with budget constraints – call the Goodman and offer to be a volunteer usher.

Tough tickets

Two on the city's "must see" list are usually among the toughest tickets in town to come by: the Goodman and Second City. Virtually any production at the Goodman Theater, located behind the Art Institute of Chicago on Michigan Avenue until its expansion and move to State Street in 2000, will be difficult for non-season ticket holders. Recent seasons were nearly sold out, but tickets are sometimes available through agencies and touts.

Opened in 1925, the Goodman is Chicago's

LEFT: John Lee Hooker at the Chicago Blues Festival.
ABOVE: Dizzy Gillespie at the Chicago Jazz Festival.

Also tough to get are seats for Second City, where improvisation became a household word. Located in Old Town, some of the country's best comedic talent developed here. The acting is called "improve" because current revues were put together with improvisations that came from audience suggestions after the regular show. The secret to good seats here is to go to performances during the week. Plan on staying for the late improv show, and moving up for better seats when the revue crowd departs. Then you too, if you like, can add your suggestions for the actors to tackle.

The Second City atmosphere is a pleasant one, with cabaret-style seating and drinks; the setting is a simple one. Six or seven actors work the stage with a few chairs and fewer props. They create topical sketches in a slice-of-life environment and throw in songs. The very first show in 1959 took on President Dwight D. Eisenhower, grand opera, the medical profession and the cultural pretensions of FM radio. The troupe never stopped breaking ground and television's *Saturday Night Live* might never have become so successful without the influence of Second City. Theater's future in Chicago looks bright. As well as the Goodman's planned move into a new theater complex several theaters are under construction.

Park West, at 322 W. Armitage Avenue, hosts both cabaret acts and rock groups; then there's ImprovOlympic, at 3541 N. Clark Street, which is a highly acclaimed improv club, and well worth the trip from downtown. And finally, because it's often one of the best ways to wind up an evening of theater or an elegant dinner, there's Pops for Champagne, at 2934 N. Sheffield Avenue and a short cab ride from Michigan Avenue. This elegant room has a rose and green motif with a low bar that forms a crescent around the raised stage. Upholstered chairs surround the bar, so patrons can relax without having their legs dangle from stools.

Cabaret

Sure-bet cabarets are more difficult to recommend in Chicago, not because they are few, but because they open and close like matchbook covers. The tiny cabaret where the willowy singer interpreted Gershwin may have closed because it was never discovered. The elegant room where long-familiar names were booked may have closed because its coziness meant they couldn't charge a big enough cover to pay the performers and still make a healthy profit. Again, check the newspaper listings and call the clubs for more information.

Meanwhile, three nightspots are worth mentioning, depending on the entertainment. The

The rest of the room is given to comfortable table seating. In summer there's a romantic outdoor garden.

Pops has a light menu and delicious desserts. Local performers take to the tiny stage nightly, weaving through the crowded tables to thank music lovers for coming. Sometimes it's a veteran jazz pianist, at other times a stylish blues vocalist. The giant bottles of champagne on display make it clear that the club is serious about bubbly – serious to the tune of 120 varieties on the menu, eight or so available by the glass. ❏

ABOVE: theatres try hard to be noticed in Chicago, with this one topping the bill.

Getting Into "Oprah"

George, the audience coordinator, has a question. "Do you know how to get on national TV?" he asks the crowd of about 200 people, mostly women, who want to do exactly that. "Act like you're very excited to be here, and hang on to the edge of your seat," he tells them. "See that cameraman? He's looking for interesting reactions. So ask a question. Look interested."

George works for Oprah. Further identification is rarely needed. Talk-show host Oprah Winfrey is known worldwide, an industry unto herself. While George loosens up the crowd, the TV lights go on to brighten the studio where *The Oprah Winfrey Show* is taped five times a week. By end of the 1990s the show – the most popular in history – was being seen in over 130 TV markets around the world and 208 US markets, covering 99 per cent of US TV households. But the increasingly raw emotions coaxed out of participants by it and its more extreme imitators made Oprah start questioning the future of the format.

The subject of today's taping is bachelor parties. Oprah, barely 5 feet (1.5 meters) tall, slips into the studio unnoticed, encircled by producers and assistants. She is busy scanning blue note cards when the audience sees her and claps. Oprah looks slightly embarrassed, smiles, makes a small wave and says, "How y'all doing?"

To her dismay, a makeup man dabs at her face with a sponge. "May I have some water, please?" she asks no one in particular. The bottle arrives and she sips through a straw while the audience watches intensely. "I hate water. I really do." They laugh, having suffered with her as she shed 65 pounds in a nationally-monitored diet and then regained most of it.

Now Oprah is ready. She clears her throat, the theme music plays and she starts reading from the teleprompter. "We'll talk to one woman who found out there were prostitutes at her husband's bachelor party," says Oprah.

The woman says she was seriously traumatized by the revelation. "It was a violation. I couldn't be intimate with him for a while," she says. Now Oprah runs up the aisle with her microphone to where three strippers have been planted in the audience. "I'm a performer and I'm not there to do anything else," one declares. "It's clean, dirty fun," another says firmly, to the obvious dismay of some of the wives nearby.

An hour passes quickly and the producer tells Oprah there is just one minute left. "Do you want the last word?" he asks. She doesn't. She opts instead to let her audience argue among itself as the credits roll. The producer thanks the audience and then invites everyone to shake Oprah's hand on the way out. Most take up the offer.

Oprah moved to Chicago in 1984 at the age of 30 to host a faltering local talk show called *AM Chicago*. By 1985, it was the top show in its time slot and had been renamed, appropriately, *The Oprah Winfrey Show*.

Oprah has leveraged her success in television to record a number of achievements and firsts. Her net worth soared past $415 million, making her the wealthiest black woman in the world and the only African-American on *Forbes* magazine's list of the wealthiest people in America. Admission to watch a taping of the Oprah Winfrey Show at Harpo, 110 N. Carpenter Street, is free. Reservations are required: call 312 591 9222. ❑

RIGHT: the First Lady of talk knows when to listen.

A CITY WITH ITS ART IN THE RIGHT PLACE

Sculptures aren't confined to museums – when it made a commitment to public art, Chicago turned its open spaces into one big art gallery

A 1978 City of Chicago law mandates that 1.33 percent of the cost of constructing or renovating municipal buildings is set aside for the commission or purchase of artworks. The result is a city graced with one of the finest collections of public art in the world. The Percent for Art program, as it is called, also stipulates that 50 percent of the art must be by Chicagoans. During the program's first 20 years, the City acquired over 150 works for permanent, public display: one of them is Claes Oldenburg's 1977 *Bat Column* (*above*), a giant baseball bat outside the Social Security office at 600 W. Madison. Percent for Art has been so successful that it has inspired over 200 similar programs across the US.

Chicago also owes its outstanding array of public art to other programs run by the Department of Cultural Affairs Public Art Program, such as the Public Art of Bronzeville program and temporary summer sculpture exhibits in Montgomery Ward Park.

△ **CHICAGO**
Joan Miró's *Chicago* (1981) was one of the artist's last major works. The 39-ft high sculpture is at 69 W. Washington.

▷ **TIN MAN**
Towering over Oz Park, the *Tin Man* was created by John Walter Kearney (1995) in honor of *The Wizard of Oz*.

▷ **DAWN SHADOWS**
Louise Nevelson's work of art (1983) at Madison Plaza is best seen from the El, which inspired it.

◁ FLAMINGO
Alexander Calder's five-legged *Flamingo* was unveiled in 1974. It greets visitors to the post office at Dearborn and Adams.

△ NUCLEAR ENERGY
Henry Moore's work (1967) at the University of Chicago honors Enrico Fermi's successful experiment with nuclear energy.

△ THE FOUR SEASONS
Marc Chagall's work at Dearborn and Monroe in the Loop (1974) is made of bits of marble, glass and stone.

▷ MONUMENT WITH STANDING BEAST
Jean Dubuffet's creation (1984) guards James R. Thompson Center.

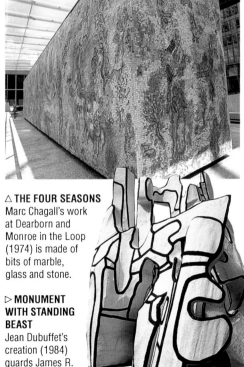

INTERNATIONAL TREASURES

A striking feature of Chicago's extensive public art collection is its international scope. The majority of the most famous outdoor sculptures in the city are the work of foreign nationals or artists who were not born in the US.

The list begins with the Spanish master, Pablo Picasso himself. Officially, his sculpture in Chicago (*above*) has no title, but unofficially it is known simply as "the Picasso." Built of Cor-Ten steel, the work was unveiled in 1967; it is now such a Loop landmark that the City runs a series of free public events in the plaza at its base called "Under the Picasso."

The work of another Spaniard, Joan Miró, the son of a Barcelona jeweler, is prominent in the Loop, and Henry Moore has four outdoor sculptures in Chicagoland, in addition to his *Nuclear Energy* at the university.

Claes Oldenburg, who gave the city the *Bat Column*, was a Swede who grew up in Chicago.

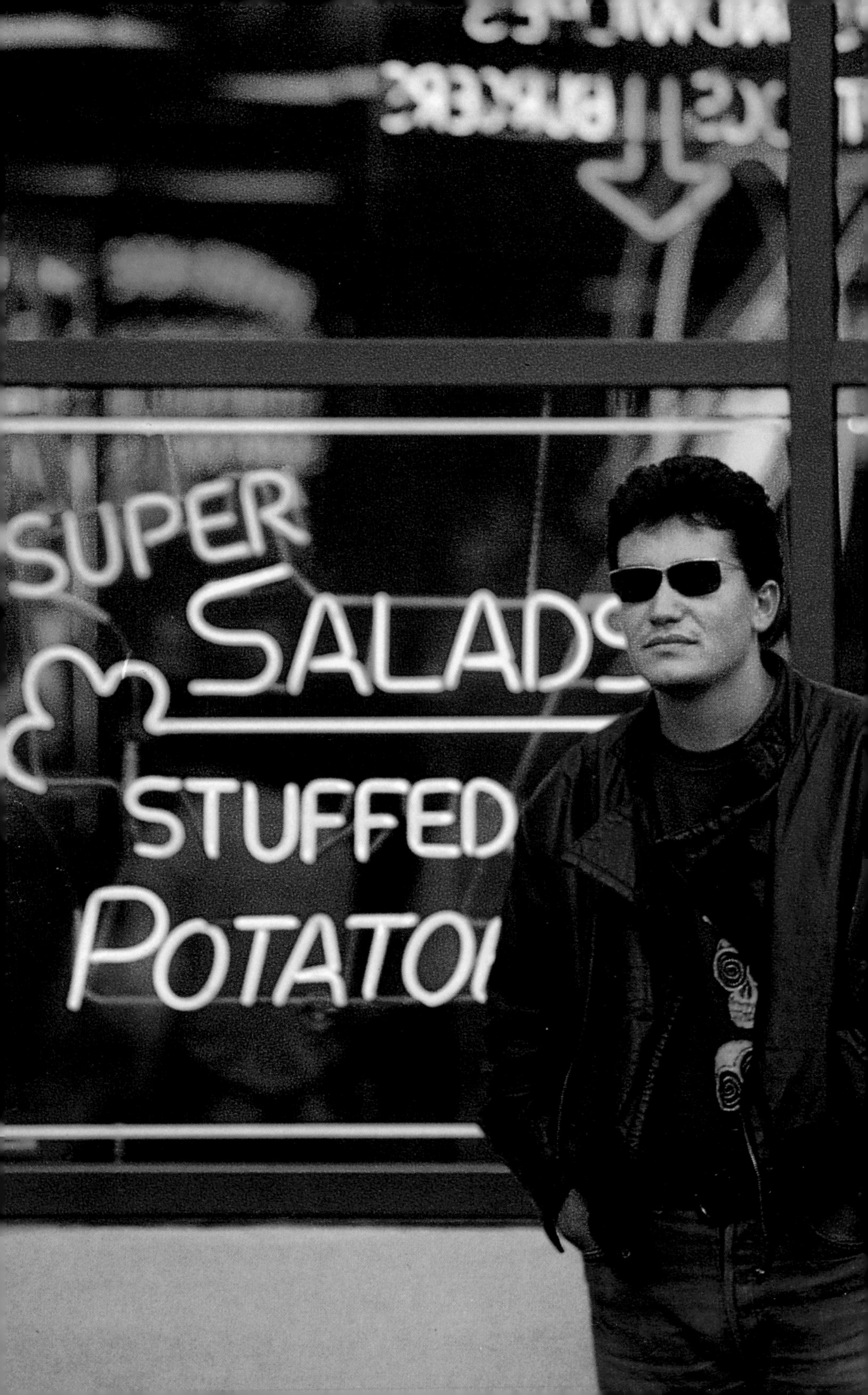
SUPER
SALADS
STUFFED
POTATO

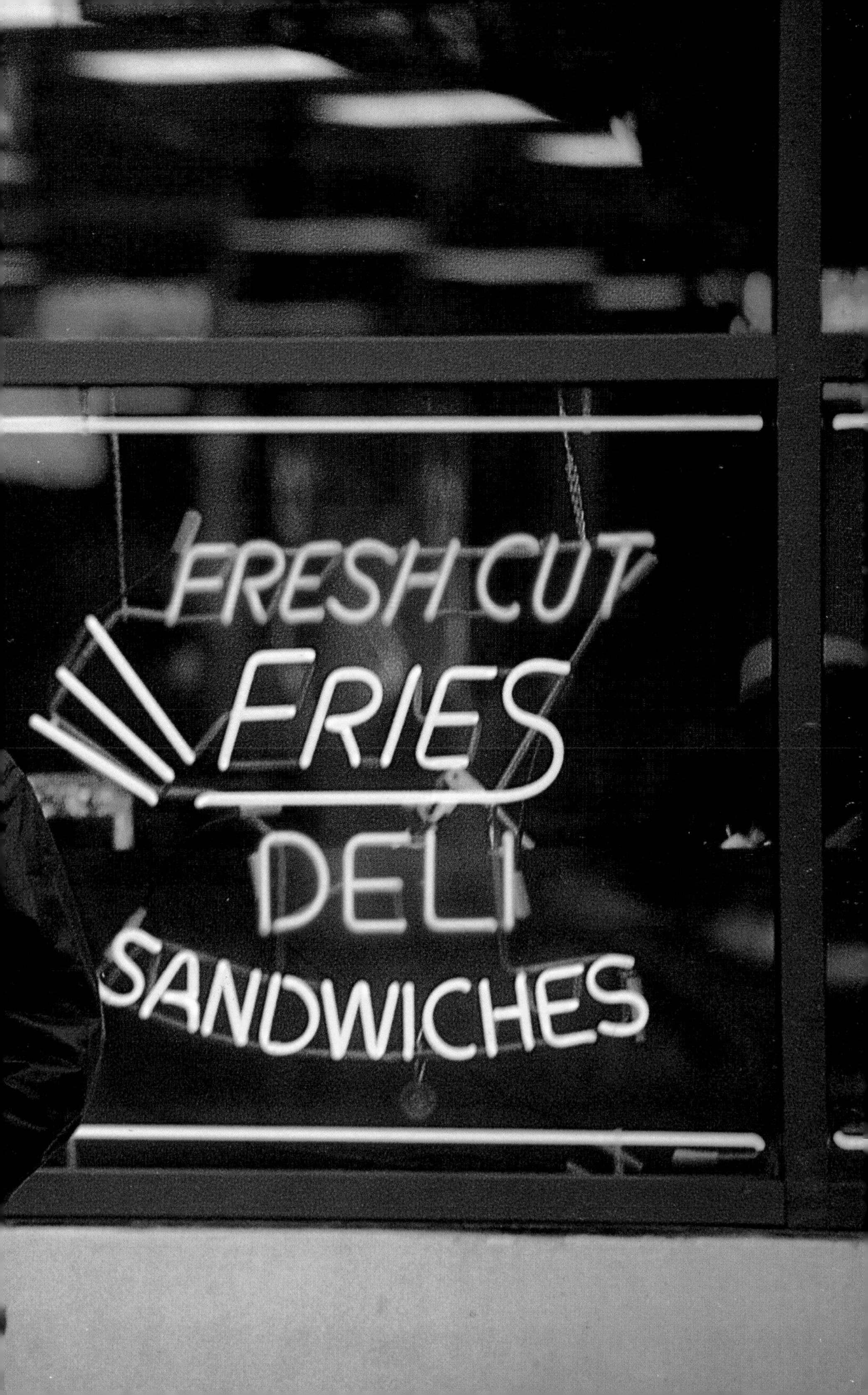
FRESH CUT
FRIES
DELI
SANDWICHES

TASTES OF CHICAGO

With every possible ethnic cuisine available, as well as numerous opportunities for both fine dining and simple American fare, food-lovers are spoilt for choice

Befitting a citizenry that considers eating out a serious business – it's right up there with sports and politics – Chicago is home to hundreds of unusual, interesting and just plain good restaurants ranging from elegant eateries to simple hot dog stands.

That's probably why Taste of Chicago is so popular. While it doesn't fall into the category of "gourmet" event, this annual downtown lakeside party, attended by hundreds of thousands of people, features dozens of restaurant booths in addition to live entertainment, allowing feasters to wander the grassy grounds sampling barbecued ribs, tempura, candied yams and frozen, chocolate-covered bananas. Taste, which runs from the end of June through July 4, is considered the largest food festival of its kind in the world.

When Chicago's stockyards were in their prime, the city was known as a steak town. Though today's diners are more diet-conscious, one restaurant that still prides itself on the perfect cut of beef is Morton's of Chicago. On Rush Street, the steak house takes its name from Arnie Morton, a colorful city restaurateur who founded Taste of Chicago and who is third of four generations in the Chicago wining and dining business. Morton's offers a clubby atmosphere, celebrity photos, white tablecloths and a heady aroma of grilled meats. Fork-tender porterhouse steak is the house specialty and the double fillet, charcoal dark outside, and moist red inside, is another favorite.

Fiesta

For Mexican food, the hot spot in town is the Frontera Grill, in the trendy River North area. They won't take lunch reservations for fewer than six, and dinners need to be booked several days in advance. Owners Rick Bayless and his wife Deann opened their tribute to South of

---

PRECEDING PAGES: so many options, so little time – figuring out what to have for lunch.
LEFT: submarine sandwich duty.
RIGHT: cooking at market.

the Border fare in 1987, simultaneously publishing a book, *Authentic Mexican: Regional Cooking from the Heart of Mexico.*

Don't lose confidence due to the couple's non-Hispanic names. The Baylesses spent eight years researching food in Mexico, and a taste of their cooking in the earth-tone restaurant wins

over any skeptics. They offer a full range of Mexico's grand cuisine: from Oaxaca, they serve a *sabaroso*, seared turkey breast in rich red mole, a sweetened chili sauce, while from Central Mexico comes charcoal grilled swordfish with a light cream sauce. The menu changes weekly.

Dining in style

For four-star gourmet fantasy, Chicagoland has its share, including the legendary Le Français in suburban Wheeling. But perhaps the most outstanding is Everest, which takes diners together with the food to elegant heights. Located in the city's financial district, Everest commands a spectacular, 40th floor view of Chicago's West Side. It is gorgeous at sunset and powerful at night, when cars on the Eisenhower Expressway create an expansive, twinkling vista.

Inside, the nationally acclaimed restaurant surrounds its guests in an ivory-toned ambience of understated elegance and attentive service that remains unobtrusive. The cuisine is inspired. Award-winning chef and owner Jean Joho has drawn on his Alsatian roots to present the magical and magnificent from his kitchen.

There may be light, Maryland crab salad in a thinly-sliced cucumber box; succulent Maine

lobster with Alsace Gewürztraminer and ginger; exquisite wild pheasant, wrapped in cabbage with basil; and flavorful venison medallions, served with huckleberry sauce.

Don't leave without sampling a dessert. Some recent favorites include cinnamon-spiced apple beignet with Kirsch ice-cream and the chocolate fantasy, an assortment that includes chocolate-honey sorbet in a molded, maple syrup basket.

Old timer

With restaurants opening and closing in Chicago like menu covers, an exception is the Berghoff Restaurant, which celebrated its 100th anniversary in 1998 with a week-long outdoor celebration. Located in the heart of the Loop, the Berghoff offers the city's best German food.

The huge dining rooms, with oak paneling and tables, are always crowded, no easy feat for a restaurant that seats 800 diners. Service? The term "hustle and bustle" could have been coined for the Berghoff waiters who always seem to be carrying several plates of tart *sauerbraten*, smoked *thuringer* with sauerkraut, tender *wiener schnitzel* and German pot roast, or delivering foaming steins of Berghoff beer.

The Berghoff serves some 2,500 meals plus 3,000 steins of their Dortmunder-style beer daily. Actually, it sold the beer first. Herman Joseph Berghoff, a German immigrant, opened an Indiana brewery in 1887 and brought his beer to the 1893 World's Columbian Exposition. It was such a hit that he opened the Berghoff and obtained Chicago Liquor License No. 1, now on display in the main dining room. The Berghoff also makes its own root beer.

EAT YOUR WAY AROUND THE WORLD

To experience Chicago is to explore its neighborhoods. Chicago is a melting pot of Chinese, Italian, Polish and Indian communities, to name just a few. The result is a diverse culture and a cornucopia of ethnic eating places. Here are some tried and tasted highlights:

☞ **Little India**: located between Kedzie and Western on Devon. Saris are the most common fashion statement and unless you speak Urdu or Hindi you won't be eavesdropping on too many conversations. Try Sari Niketan (2611 W. Devon, tel: 773-338- 9399) or The Indian Garden (2548 W. Devon, tel: 773-338 2929).

☞ **Little Italy**: south of the Loop, the Taylor Street neighborhood is home to some of Chicago's oldest Italian restaurants. Crusty loaves of bread, red wine, pasta and meatballs are menu staples and portions are large.

☞ **Chinatown**: Chicago boasts the fourth largest Chinese population in the United States. The hub of this thriving Chinatown is at Cermak Road and Wentworth Road. There are over 40 restaurants to choose from and a number of Chinese grocery stores.

☞ **Greek Town**: at about 200 S. Halsted Street Chicago goes Greek. Lamb, saganaki, suckling pig, Greek sausage and ouzo feature prominently on the menus. Dishes are reasonably priced.

Picking winners

In terms of newer restaurants, it's impossible to predict what will be trendy, or even open next month. Some chic spots have been packed one day and literally closed down the next. But if you had to pick, any venue owned by restaurateur Richard Melman would be a good bet.

Two of his restaurants, Shaw's Crab House and Shaw's Blue Crab Lounge & Oyster Bar, next to each other just off State Street, serve some of the best seafood in Chicago. The House offers white tablecloths and 1930s decor, with daily specials such as grilled mahi mahi and soft-shelled crabs. The Lounge puts diners

Twin-Anchors, which doesn't ordinarily deliver, to bring him plenty of ribs. Naturally, it was an offer they couldn't refuse.

Opened in 1932 in a former speakeasy, Twin-Anchors seems to get better with age. Many consider the ribs Chicago's best because they are picked with care, served as a slab that overhangs the plate and fall off the bone.

Exploring spice

For something completely different, Mama Desta's restaurant serves some excellent authentic Ethiopian fare not far from Wrigley Field. The savory food is that of the Amhara

on wooden stools for gumbo, chowder or stew. Fresh oysters and clams vary daily and the Maryland crabcakes are always moist.

Rib tickling

If you're looking for Chicago barbecue – meaty pork ribs slathered in a very messy and zesty sauce – Twin-Anchors Restaurant and Tavern had none other than "the chairman of the board" singing its praise. When the late Frank Sinatra came to his kind of town, he asked

and Tigrean peoples whose cuisine is among the most sophisticated in East Africa.

The more guests at a Mama Desta's table, the better to try more dishes. On each table is placed a pan covered with spongy bread called *injera*. Orders are then spooned on to the bread in a decorative arrangement. Diners tear some bread from a side serving, pinch the food with it, then eat with their hands. It's part of the fun.

Couples would do best to order the *Alitcha* combo and the hot combo. The *Alitcha* dish offers chicken, lamb and beef, cooked separately in a thick, mild green sauce. The hot combo has the same meats, but they are cooked in a spicy, red pepper sauce.

LEFT: a Chicago institution.
ABOVE: the Berghoff offers the best German food in the city.

Chinese choice

For Chinese food, also more enjoyable with larger parties, go to Chinatown. Cermak and Wentworth streets are the starting point. Walk through the ornate arch on Wentworth and take in the groceries, kitchen supply houses and souvenir shops. The aroma of garlic and ginger is intoxicating.

A local favorite that is all but unknown among tourists is the Three Happiness Restaurant on Cermak. It's a tiny storefront with a few Formica tables and cheap prices for, among other things, the best Singapore fried-rice noodles in Chicago. The noodles, which look like

spaghetti, are fried in a pan with Szechuan peppers and aromatic spices. Barbecued pork, shrimp and green peppers are added to this to make up a huge single serving. For those preferring Cantonese, Three Happiness offers plump *egg foo yong*, tasty chicken with pea pods and several good beef dishes.

Get along, little doggies

The best hot dogs can be found at Demon Dogs, under the Fullerton Avenue El stop. Owner Peter Schivarelli uses top-line Vienna beef hot dogs. The difference is that the better dogs come in a casing that keeps them from shrinking while they're being steamed. Besides the clearer flavor, there should be a slight crunch when that first bite breaks the casing. Chicago has many Vienna stands, but not all have the firmer, non-shrink casing.

A true Chicago dog must be loaded with "the works" – mustard, relish and onions. The tiny peppers are optional and very hot. Demon Dogs, named for the Blue Demon mascot of nearby DePaul University, sells 5,000 hot dogs a week. The french fries, cooked in vegetable oil instead of animal fat, are also excellent. Demon Dogs, opened in 1982, is regarded by many as the best hot dog stand in Chicago because it hasn't diluted its identity by adding salads or grilled chicken sandwiches to the menu. It also has free parking in a congested part of town. The decor is appealing: Schivarelli grew up with members of the rock group Chicago and has decorated his place with many of their gold and platinum records.

Deep dish pizza original

Chicago is famous for deep-dish pizza, a hefty concoction of chunky tomato sauce over a thick baked crust with plenty of mozzarella cheese. Add favorite ingredients, such as pepperoni, sausage, green peppers or mushrooms, and call it a meal.

A pizza war has been running in Chicago for decades among restaurants, critics and customers all claiming different winners. Visitors might want to begin their own research by returning to where it all started back in 1943. Pizzeria Uno, a couple of blocks from Michigan Avenue, is the birthplace of Chicago-style deep dish pizza. Pizzeria Due, established in 1955, is the sister restaurant and just as good. Creator Ike Sewell, the man most responsible

---

HIGH THREE

Put a different spin on *haute cuisine* and dine in the clouds. While, for a city that invented the skyscraper, Chicago doesn't exactly abound with lofty eateries, there are a few that will take you to dizzying heights.

For the bonus of an exquisite meal, reserve a 40th-story table at Everest (*see pages 99–100*). Those with higher aspirations can eat at Cité, 70 stories high, in Lake Point Tower. But the best view of all awaits the fiscally challenged – for just the cost of a lunchtime sandwich you can zoom to the 95th floor and the Signature Room in the Hancock. Arrive before noon to be sure of a window table.

for teaching Americans that pizza could be a meal rather than just a snack, makes pizza with a coarse, crunchy crust, a thick layer of mozzarella and a natural, perfectly seasoned sauce, a good foundation to build on.

No chips

A great burger and a correspondingly great character – or maybe it should be characters – are the attraction at the Billy Goat Tavern & Grill, a bar on lower Michigan Avenue that, with its convenient proximity to the *Tribune* and *Sun-Times*, is the city's hangout for newspapermen and women. They simply call it "the

roll. Take it over to the counter, load it up with pickles, onions, ketchup and mustard, and then survey the tavern's history on its walls.

Way before *Saturday Night Live* the place was famous for William "Billy Goat" Sianis, who opened the tavern in 1934 and welcomed sportswriters to drink there. One day a goat wandered in and was adopted as a mascot. Sianis, his goatee and goat made good pictures for the several daily newspapers of the day and many of those snaps are displayed along the walls of the tavern. The original Billy Goat's nephew, Sam Sianis, runs the place now and keeps the publicity going.

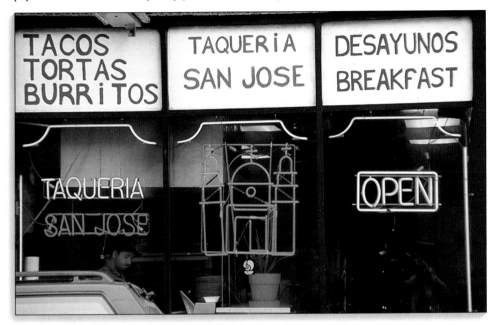

Goat" and their legions included the late Mike Royko, the Pulitzer Prize-winning *Chicago Tribune* columnist whom many saw as Chicago's conscience. Visitors often order cheeseburgers in groups, so they can hear the Greek grillman shout "cheezborger, cheezborger, cheezborger," as he slaps patties on the sizzling grill, as immortalized in the famous *Saturday Night Live* TV skits by the late John Belushi.

The burgers are juicy and excellent value. Try the double cheeseburger, served on a Kaiser

LEFT: Chicago-style barbecue lunch.
ABOVE: Chicago features a melting pot of different ethnic styles, including Tex-Mex.

The juice is loose

The best Italian beef sandwich – a Chicago classic – can be found at Mr Beef on Orleans. Thinly-sliced roast beef is slowly cooked in its own juices with a hint of garlic and packed into a fresh slice of Italian bread. On this, Mr Beef piles sautéed green peppers, hot peppers or both, and offers the choice of "wet," with extra juices, or "dry," without. Owners Dominic and Joseph Zucchero, who opened the beef stand years before the River North area got trendy, use fresh sirloin tip roasts. Fans include local and national celebrities alike, such as comedian Jay Leno, who once showed up on a nationwide talk show eating Mr Beef sandwiches. ❑

A SPORTS-MAD TOWN

It's a sports lover's paradise, from the Bulls to the Bears, the White Sox
to the Blackhawks, Chicago has a team and a ball game to suit every taste

Chicago is a sporting kind of town, from what people read in the morning newspaper and what they talk about during the day to what they do after work and where they eat and drink at night. In the city's poorer neighborhoods, many young people see a career in sports as their best hope of claiming a slice of the American dream.

Public officials recognize the importance of sports in Chicago, from the millions in tax money that helped build Comiskey Park, the new baseball stadium for the White Sox, to the late-night basketball leagues aimed at keeping kids off the streets and out of trouble between the hours of 10pm and 1.30am.

Chicagoans love their professional teams – baseball's Cubs and White Sox, football's Bears, ice hockey's Blackhawks and basketball's Bulls – but they love to play themselves, too. The South Side pick-up basketball games are known for their "no autopsy, no foul" style of rough play, and the lakefront is a haven for volleyball players as well as runners, rollerbladers, cyclists and bodybuilders.

Parks all over Chicago feature a popular local variation of softball, baseball's slower cousin, that features a balloon-sized 16-in ball compared with the 12-in regulation softball and the 9-in baseball. (It's probably fitting that since the players are fatter, the ball they use for their game should be, too.)

Back in time

For many visitors, and for many Chicagoans as well, the quintessential Chicago sporting experience is an afternoon baseball game at Wrigley Field, home of the Chicago Cubs. The Cubs rarely win a game, but their loyal fans have never cared about a small detail like that.

A Cubs game is a high priority for visiting Americans because it's a chance to savor the national game, to step back in time to the days

before World War II when all baseball games were played in the afternoon instead of at night, under lights. Wrigley Field is one of the oldest baseball parks in the major leagues, and fans revel in its ivy-covered walls where balls sometimes become lost and entangled in the vines, and in the way its erratic breezes can turn harmless fly balls into important home runs.

For foreign visitors, even those who know or care little about baseball or sports in general, a visit to a Cubs game at Wrigley Field is a prime opportunity for people-watching, for sizing up the style of these ruddy creatures who call themselves Chicagoans.

Perhaps more than any other big US city, the people of Chicago represent the great middle class of America – in size, shape, apparel, speaking voice, social behavior, eating habits, economic standing, political attitudes and social concerns – or lack thereof. And there is in all probability no better place than an afternoon baseball game at Wrigley Field to observe first-

---

PRECEDING PAGES: Bear-faced battle.
LEFT: Bulls' star Michael Jordan.
RIGHT: kicking kiddie, starting early.

hand folk who are so cheerfully, relentlessly, unabashedly American.

Wrigleyville is a middle-class, aspiringly gentrified North Side neighborhood of large, solid-brick apartment blocks and one-time family homes that have been largely carved into flats and unassuming duplexes. It is also not the most accessible place Chicago could have put a ballpark. But for many devoted fans – and they are indeed a fiercely loyal bunch – the El (elevated railway) ride to Addison, a short walk from the park – it never seems right to call this little bandbox a stadium – is as much a part of the game as hot dogs and popcorn and beer.

THE SNACK PACK

Before Bears football games, many fans "tailgate" in the parking lots near Soldier Field, setting up grills beside their cars and cooking hamburgers.

Safe at home

Most afternoon games are sell-outs, due to the remarkable allegiance that Cubs fans show for their long-suffering team. Yet tickets can be had, and usually for not much more than $5 to $20 above face value, depending on the location of the seats. Ticket scalping is illegal, but there are usually plenty of touts slyly making

COMISKEY PARK: WHEN BIGGER ISN'T BETTER

With its unique features and quaint surroundings, Wrigley Field has long been regarded by baseball fans as a national treasure. The same cannot be said of Comiskey Park, home to Chicago's other baseball team, the White Sox. Chicagoans have never warmed to the "new" Comiskey, a sterile, impersonal venue that opened in 1991 across the street from the site of "old" Comiskey, where the White Sox had played since the early part of the century.

The original Comiskey Park didn't have the allure of Wrigley Field, but at least it had the charm of an old-time ballpark. Old Comiskey was leveled when the new Comiskey opened next door. The new park – a stadium, really – is long on modern amenities but short on atmosphere. To its credit, Comiskey has wide concourses that make it easy to buy a hot dog between innings. It also has plenty of clean restrooms – a big plus considering that old Comiskey was notorious for its cramped, foul-smelling facilities. But Comiskey's upper-deck seats are outrageously far from the action, its loudspeakers are too loud, and the playing field has no unique features. Worst of all, the ballpark is located in a run-down part of the South Side, surrounded by urban wasteland. Like Wrigley, the best thing is the fans: on her first visit, the guide's project editor sat behind four raucously cheering, waving nuns.

deals across the street or around the corner from the official ticket windows.

Also, people without tickets can strike up a conversation with one of the Cubs' usher-guards outside the entrances; these guys have the uncanny ability to scan the entering crowd for people with extra tickets who will sell them at face value or even just give them away.

For visitors who just want to sample the atmosphere and look around a bit, the best bargain is probably a standing-room-only

LOUD CROWD

Blackhawks fans are different again. They have a tradition of screaming en masse throughout the singing of the national anthem at the games.

watching the game on overhead closed-circuit TV. For the worst view of the game but perhaps the most fun, adventurous fans prefer the outfield bleachers, where the infamous Bleacher Bums cheer maniacally, strip off their shirts at any hint of sunshine and typically end up soaked in beer, inside and out.

The real show at Wrigley Field is not the baseball on the field, but the fans themselves. Huge men bearing trays of beer and junk food carefully belly their way through the crowds. Bespectacled,

ticket, purchased even on sellout days for a few dollars from the regular ticket windows. These tickets do not guarantee a seat (though seats are often available due to no-shows) but they do afford decent views from the many aisles. Many people with standing room only tickets prefer to catch a couple of innings from the lower grandstand, a couple more from the upper deck and a couple more from the concourse, where they can munch nachos, pizza, bratwurst, burgers and other fast food while

LEFT: baseball buddies.
ABOVE: an afternoon Cubs game at Wrigley Field...
and all's well with the world.

serious young men concentrate on the game, scribbling in their scorebooks as they chart the action play by play. Seemingly oblivious to both the game and the cheers of young men, young women strut confidently in the aisles.

Local heroes

There are other sports heroes, of course, and they say a lot about Chicago and its makeup. In the 1950s, the baseball heroes were the Cubs' Ernie Banks and the White Sox's Minnie Minoso, a pair of black sluggers known as much for their sunny dispositions as their home runs. In the 1960s, the Chicago Blackhawks had two of the greatest ice hockey players ever,

Bobby Hull and Stan Mikita, both team-oriented players who were also prolific scorers and tough guys who comported themselves as gentlemen in a game known for its thugs. In the 1970s, the Chicago Bulls basketball team was led by a combination of smooth black players such as Chet Walker and Bob Love and hard-nosed, scrappy white players such as Jerry Sloan.

The heroes of the 1980s and 1990s have been the Cubs' white Ryne Sandberg and black Andre Dawson, both quiet sluggers known for their off-field charity work; the Bears' football player Walter Payton (rightly nicknamed "Sweetness") and the Bulls' ex-star Michael Jordan, whose high scoring and soaring slam-dunks have made him the most exciting basketball player of his era. All the above-mentioned stars have now retired.

> ### LUCKY NUMBER?
>
> The number 23 has become synonymous with former Bulls star Michael Jordan. Former Cubs second baseman Ryne Sandberg wore the same number.

Drinking in sports

The Chicago Bulls' former coach, Dick Motta, once used a backhanded reference to opera to describe his team's hope in the face of despair:

THE ALTERNATIVE WRIGLEY FIELD

The allure of a Cubs game is not confined solely to the "friendly confines" within Wrigley Field. It's possible to soak in the atmosphere of a Cubs game without ever setting foot inside the ballpark.

Perhaps the most coveted way to see a game is to watch from atop one of the apartments and flats just beyond the outfield walls. It's not exactly a close-up view, but fans who look on from the rooftops are able to enjoy a game and a cookout simultaneously. Getting such a perch can of course be a little tricky – most of the rooftops are reserved for building tenants or group outings – but not by any means impossible. Your best bet is to ask around at any of the nearby bars, many of which hold rooftop Cub parties throughout the summer.

Sharp-eyed observers will notice that at every game a small crowd gathers just beyond the left-field wall at the corner of Sheffield and Waveland Avenues, for this spot is a prime landing area for home runs. There are a few dozen regulars who patrol the area, socializing with each other, chatting up strangers and hoping to grab a ball that sails out of the park. For those who prefer guaranteed souvenirs, to keep and take home, Wrigley Field, needless to say, is surrounded by shops and stands that sell an array of Cubs trinkets and apparel.

"It ain't over 'til the Fat Lady sings." Nowadays, after the Fat Lady sings she is likely to be seen, along with other fans of both food and sports, at one of Chicago's many influential "sports" bars.

The sports bar, as originated in Chicago, was once merely a neighborhood tavern that had a TV installed so that afternoon customers could watch the Cubs in dark, air-conditioned comfort. Now, however, the sports bar has become an American "concept," much expanded and imitated across the country but

THE GOAT IS GUILTY

Fans believe the Cubs were forever cursed by Billy Sianis' goat after the owner of the famed Billy Goat Tavern and his goat were denied admission to a game.

of pay-per-play sports trivia games, miniature bowling, little basketball hoops and even indoor baseball batting cages. But what keeps people coming back to the most prominent sports bars are the large quantities of good food, mainly burgers and pasta dishes or pizza, served up from the kitchens.

The Black Sox

Chicago, of course, wouldn't be Chicago without its history of scandal, and that extends to sports, too. The Chicago "Black Sox" baseball

still not done anywhere as well as in its birthplace of Chicago.

Good food

The modern sports bar still has TV, but there are likely to be several large screens that may show taped highlights or past games when nothing live is being broadcast. Besides the usual theme decorations of sports equipment, photos and memorabilia from hats to bats, many sports bars offer participation in the form

LEFT: a summertime volleyball game in action in Grant Park

ABOVE: racing around the Loop.

bribery scheme discredited the national pastime and is still America's biggest sporting outrage.

In October 1919, the Chicago White Sox arrived in Cincinnati to play the first World Series – the annual championship between the winners of the rival National and American leagues – since the end of World War I. Baseball fans across the nation prepared to follow the games, play by play, as relayed by telegraph to rented halls.

The White Sox were the overwhelming favorites. Pitcher Eddie Cicotte had won 29 games, but the hero of Chicago was "Shoeless" Joe Jackson, an illiterate former cotton-mill worker from South Carolina who wielded a huge, fearsome bat he called "Black Betsy" and had a league-leading 356 batting average.

The bribery plot was initiated by White Sox first baseman Arnold "Chick" Gandil, according to Eliot Asinof, who wrote a book that was the basis for one of the several movies that have been made on the subject. Gandil met with a bookmaker in a Boston hotel three weeks before the series began. For $80,000 to be provided by a group of gamblers, he agreed to arrange for the White Sox to lose.

Gandil recruited Cicotte and five other White Sox players with the $80,000: third baseman George "Buck" Weaver; shortstop Charles

"Swede" Risberg; outfielder Oscar "Happy" Felsch; pitcher Claude "Lefty" Williams, and utility infielder Fred McMullin. Jackson demanded $20,000 for his participation and the gamblers agreed, bringing the total figure up to $100,000.

Ballplayers indicted

Rumors that Chicago was going to throw the series were so widespread that the dozens of gamblers crowding into the team's Cincinnati hotel room waved $1,000 bills at the players before the first game. Ultimately, the White Sox lost five games to three (the World Series was then a best of nine games, instead of today's

best of seven) in contests marred by bobbled catches and bad throws. The White Sox reportedly won their three games only out of anger when the gamblers were slow in making their bribe payments.

Gandil was eventually paid $35,000. Cicotte got $10,000 which he found under his pillow in the hotel the night before the first game. Risberg and Williams got $10,000 each, while Felsch and McMullin got $5,000 each. Jackson, too, only ended up with $5,000, despite his $20,000 demand. Weaver apparently decided not to help throw the games, and there is a strong argument that he in fact played to win. He was paid nothing.

The next year, under the relentless goading of newspaper reporters, a Chicago grand jury indicted the eight ballplayers on nine counts of conspiracy to defraud. The scandal devastated the baseball world. Team owners, under pressure to clean up the game, appointed Judge Kenesaw Mountain Landis as the first commissioner of baseball.

Say it ain't so

The scandal also triggered a wave of bitterness and cynicism. A Chicago newspaper reported that a young boy clutched desperately at Joe Jackson's sleeve as the fallen hero left the grand jury hearing and pleaded with him, "Say it ain't so, Joe. Say it ain't so."

"Yes, kid, I'm afraid it is," Jackson is said to have replied.

Like so many good Chicago newspaper stories of the era, this one turned out to be a fabrication by a reporter. But the bitterness was real. Chicago kids began to cry sarcastically, "Play ball!" to start sandlot games. The players were acquitted of the criminal charges, but Landis nonetheless suspended them from professional baseball for life. For a time they knocked around in semi-pro and "outlaw" leagues, sometimes taking the precaution of playing under pseudonyms.

For betraying the sport, and casting it into disgrace for several years until New York Yankee slugger Babe Ruth caught the fans' fancy, the 1919 White Sox have become forever known as the Black Sox. ❏

LEFT: baseball great Babe Ruth.
RIGHT: keeping feet on the ground and an eye on the ball.

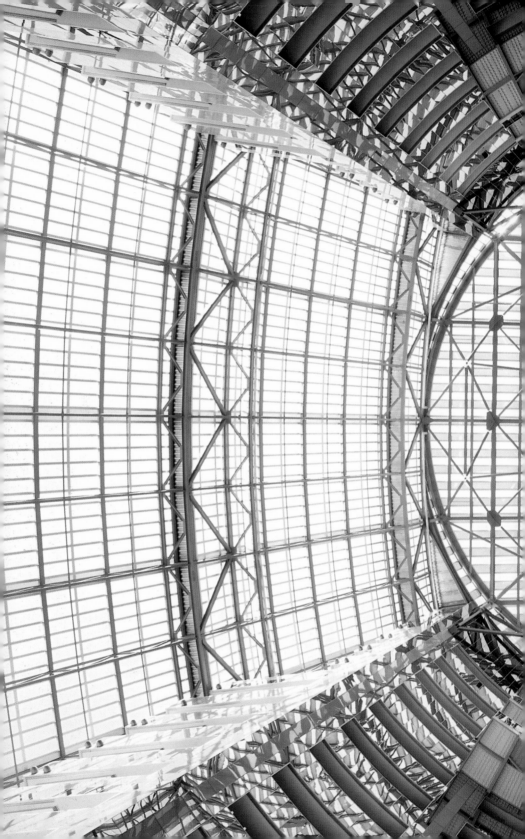

AN ARCHITECT'S PHOENIX

Despite the cavalier attitude of the city's powers-that-be towards preservation,
Chicago still boasts the world's first skyscraper, and some of its finest buildings

The collective psyche of Chicago has never recovered from the fire of 1871; one look at the city's architecture confirms it. One look up, that is. Those rows of skyscrapers, from the sinewy steel spires of the John Hancock Center to the illuminated turrets of the romantic 900 N. Michigan Building, might not be there but for the 1871 disaster.

Chicago has not looked back, or down, since that holocaust. The city gave the world the first skyscraper in 1885. That feat could not be achieved before that date because working elevators for such tall buildings were not yet invented. Today Chicago is home to some of the world's most magnificent buildings. The list includes the Sears Tower (the one-time tallest building in the world), Wacker and Adams, 1,468 feet (447 meters), 110 stories, built in 1974. There are also two of the world's largest buildings: the Amoco Building, 200 E. Randolph, 1,136 feet (346 meters), 97 stories, 1979; and the John Hancock Center, Michigan and Chestnut, 1,105 feet (337 meters), 97 stories, 1969. The urge to build bigger, taller and faster hasn't abated. Another fire, these giant buildings seem to say, won't wipe us out.

Long after other major American cities have gasped in horror at the faceless glass slabs lining once-pleasant boulevards, Chicago continues to be a place where few if any obstacles are put in the way of really big real estate developments. Los Angeles might make developers build art museums, Boston may insist on low-income housing and New York may champion the greater good of historic preservation, but here, builders are still sitting pretty – and high.

Scraping the sky

Considering the freedom granted to developers, it is a miracle that Chicago has any good buildings at all. The integrity of the cityscape

PRECEDING PAGES: the soaring atrium of the James R. Thompson Center. **LEFT:** the *Flamingo* has landed, courtesy of Calder. **RIGHT:** walking the tightrope on LaSalle: *Crossing* (1998) by Hubertus von der Goltz.

was ensured by the early marriage of big building to cutting-edge architecture: Chicago didn't just rebuild after the fire, it invented the skyscraper – the architectural form that was to define American cities.

From that day forward, good – or at least interesting – architecture has gone hand in hand

TALL TALES

Although it can no longer say it is the "world's tallest building," the Sears Tower still never ceases to amaze. It has 104 elevators, 25,000 miles (40,000 km) of plumbing, 16,000 windows, and 43,000 miles (68,800 km) of telephone wire. It took 76,000 tons of steel to construct its 110 stories. Each work day 11,000 people earn their living here. As many as 5,000 more come to enjoy the view from the 103rd floor Skydeck, still the world's highest observation deck. On a clear day you can see a distance of some 40 miles (64 km), meaning you can say you "saw" Wisconsin, Indiana and Michigan, even if you never left Illinois.

with big building. Ask Chicago developers why they hired famous architects such as Cesar Pelli, Helmut Jahn or Ricardo Bofill, and they'll look at you uncomprehendingly. The reason is self-evident: this is Chicago.

Perhaps no one epitomizes this phenomenon like local-boy-made-good Paul Beitler, a professional descendant of the men who rebuilt Chicago after the fire. Beitler started his career as a salesman before becoming a leasing broker and making the extremely rare leap to developer. He is one of the most powerful players in Chicago's real estate and architectural circles; by the late 1990s, as chief executive officer of

the property management firm of Miglin-Beitler, he controlled 30 Chicago buildings.

Suburban shadows

In 1987 Beitler built the only high-rise in the Chicago suburbs, a 31-story office building in Oakbrook, for which he engaged Helmut Jahn, one of the city's and the world's most famous and controversial architects.

"Tower" is a relative term in Chicago. Examples from the dawn of the skyscraper are clustered in the city's South Loop along Dearborn Street, a group of buildings fewer than 20 stories tall, with masonry facades. Here are the

THE SKY'S THE LIMIT

Could the Gulf War and a serial killer have anything to do with the fortunes of real estate development in Chicago? If you are Paul Beitler, yes. The Chicago real estate tycoon has become famous for his obsession with erecting the world's tallest building. The Miglin-Beitler Tower (or "Sky Needle") would stand 1,999 feet (609 meters) and 125 stories high. It would cost over $400 million to build.

Beitler conceived of it in the 1980s and since then various pesky obstacles have thwarted him. First the Gulf War broke out the year construction was to start. That precipitated a decline in the real estate market which made it much more difficult to fund the project.

Then there was the 1997 serial killer on the loose in the US. Among the victims of murderer Andrew Cunanan – who killed himself in the end – were Beitler's business partner (the other half of Miglin-Beitler) Lee Miglin. Miglin's untimely and gruesome demise not surprisingly had the effect of delaying Beitler's realization of his long-cherished ambition.

If Beitler's project does eventually succeed in getting off the ground it will take four years to finish. But it would secure once again for the United States the title of "the world's tallest building." Until, of course, the competition starts all over again.

protruding bays, the spare, unornamented surfaces, the penchant for expanses of glass that would characterize Chicago building for the next century. Here are the "Chicago windows," grouped in sets of three.

These proto-skyscrapers look squat and somewhat inelegant today, sooty and down on their luck. But these buildings embody the spirit of post-fire Chicago: no-nonsense, sturdy, and very dependable structures with a minimum of fuss. If more of their ilk have not been saved – and

SALVAGE LOVE

Architectural salvage firms sell pieces of former great Chicago edifices. Buy that door or elevator from Architectural Artifacts or Salvage One (*see Travel Tips*).

much the city has lost and continues to lose.

This is the double-edged sword of Chicago architecture: its go-for-broke mentality spurs architects and developers to stretch the limits of the skyscraper form, but also obliterates the city's history in its path.

Building history

Of course, many early buildings still stand. The 16-story Monadnock Building at 53 W. Jackson Boulevard, built in 1891 by John Root, has walls that are six feet (two meters) thick at the bottom.

Chicago has an appalling track record on historic preservation – it's because Chicago is much better at building new landmarks than preserving old ones.

For example, all that's left of the facade of one of the city's most famous landmarks, the Stock Exchange Building designed by Louis Sullivan, is the entrance arch, saved when the building was demolished in 1972 and resettled, sculpture-like, behind the Art Institute of Chicago. There it remains, a reminder of how

LEFT: shimmering skyscrapers.
ABOVE: shoulder to shoulder downtown, architectural contrasts.

Although constructed using outmoded technology, the building has a modern sensibility. The clean lines are what architecture critics call "honest," meaning the building doesn't pretend to be anything it isn't. Chicago architecture, if not its politics, is known for honesty.

Across the street along Dearborn are the Pontiac (14 stories, built in 1891), Old Colony (16 stories, 1894) and Fisher (18 stories, 1896) buildings, some of the earliest examples of the steel-frame skyscraper. Steel frames opened up the sky for architects, allowing them the freedom to design true high-rises.

Ironically, the Fisher Building is less modern-looking than the older Monadnock. It exhibits a nostalgia for old-fashioned forms, however, with an ornamented facade designed to disguise the swarthy steel construction beneath. The quintessential Chicago skyscraper is characterized by simplicity, a lack of "unnecessary" ornamentation; style is secondary to structure. These buildings aren't ashamed of the steel skeleton beneath the facade.

Early skyscrapers that flaunt their construction technology still stand on State Street, where the 15-story Reliance Building and the 12-story Carson Pirie Scott department store exude the confidence and the skill of Chicago's architectural pioneers.

Glass houses

The Reliance Building was built in 1895; Carson's, one of Louis Sullivan's most famous designs, in 1899. It is startling, given their age, that such a high percentage of the facades are made of glass. These are show-off buildings, bragging that so many stories can be held up by such thin tendons of steel. They are only a stone's throw in spirit from the glass towers of the modernists, for which Chicago architecture is probably best known.

It is no accident that Chicago, where the value of new construction has always come before the less tangible good of saving the old and treasured, was the refuge for Bauhaus architects fleeing wartime Germany. Ludwig Mies van der Rohe was the most prominent of these to settle in Chicago, which proved a receptive canvas for his daring new buildings.

Perhaps nowhere is Mies' glass and steel vocabulary better articulated than in his buildings here, from the famous 860–880 Lake Shore Drive apartments to the IBM Building at the Chicago River and Wabash Street. As these structures prove, his goal was an international style that didn't distinguish among residential, office, industrial or public uses. These are prisms, faceted jewels, beautiful in their craftsmanship and precision, but cold.

With Mies leading the way, Chicago developed an architectural style that can only be described as macho. The street grid is peppered with these monumental office buildings, and the major federal and city buildings are also cut from modernist cloth.

Modernist influence

Some of the city's best modernist buildings are the least famous – Time-Life at 541 N. Fairbanks, Inland Steel at 30 W. Monroe, First National Bank at Madison and Clark streets – and the idiosyncratic: Marina City (dubbed Corncob Towers by locals) at the river and Dearborn, plus the Metropolitan Correctional Center at Van Buren and Clark, a downtown jail with slits of windows splayed outward, so the prisoners get the maximum view.

Chicago's modernist buildings are energizing – dynamic and daring essays in construction. They provide a shimmering backdrop for

---

HOT PROPERTY

Helmut Jahn's balloon-like State of Illinois building was controversial from the start. Governor James Thompson (for whom the 1986 edifice is now named), declared to the dismay of office workers that it was "the first building of the 21st century." Matters weren't helped by the all-glass design, which turned the offices into greenhouses and brought disgruntled, sweating employees and television crews together faster than you can say "heatstroke," or by Helmut himself, who suggested to an overheated secretary that she find a new job. Today, better air conditioning and the magnificent atrium have restored tempers.

LEFT: sculptures are a big part of the city.
RIGHT: helicopter flies Sears Tower airspace.

the latest round of tower-building, in which this hard-edged city has acquired a slightly more romantic, certainly less masculine ambiance. Everything the modernists believed in has been turned on its ear by the post-modernists, and while Chicago was slow to acquire some of these new designs, it has caught up with a vengeance. The result: a skyline with a little less brawn and a little more grace.

The other nice thing about these new towers is the echo of an architectural aesthetic that made Chicago famous for its building. Details such as the tri-partite Chicago window, a 10-story cornice line along Michigan Avenue and a preference for rough-hewn stone at ground level are cropping up in these new designs as the architects pay homage to their building's local antecedents.

Architecture has always been one of the city's greatest exports. No more. New York architects, most notably Kohn Pedersen & Fox, have contributed some of the city's most magnificent

THE SHOWS GO ON

A significant part of Chicago history was revived in the 1980s and 1990s when the celebrated Chicago and Oriental Theaters were restored to their past glory.

BUILDING KNOWLEDGE

How is a Helmut Jahn building different from a Ricardo Bofill? What is the current ranking of the John Hancock Center among the world's tallest? Which buildings survived the Chicago fire? The Chicago Architecture Foundation, tel: 312-922 3432; www.architecture.org, exists to answer such Trivial Pursuits-type architecture questions and offers a wide range of architecture tours of the city by bus, river, foot and even bicycle.

There are nine core tours on offer and some 50 special interest tours, including "Movie Palaces by Bus," "Grand Hotels" and "Cemeteries!" Shopaholics might be tempted by the tours of Carson Pirie Scott and Marshall Field. (Just remember, though, that these are architecture tours, not docent-led shopping sprees.) Note that many of the tours are not available during the winter months.

Here's a taster:

☞ The Foundation's one-and-a-half-hour Architecture River Cruise is the best of all the river tours if you want to actually learn something. Over 50 sites are highlighted.

☞ The Loop walking tour, "Early skyscrapers," looks at the first buildings to rise out of the ashes of the 1871 fire.

Some tours require advance reservation; for others, such as the popular river cruise, advance reservation is highly advisable.

buildings in recent years; KPF's 333 W. Wacker Drive is one of the best buildings in the city. The 36-story office tower makes a virtue of its triangular site, curving along the bend of the Chicago River on its west facade and presenting a jutting, angular face to the rugged city to the east. The reflective glass, long a favorite of the modernists, is here transposed into a skin as warm as it is taut, lit up daily by the reflection of the setting sun.

There's no question that the out-of-town architects have effected a change in tone. Suddenly, for example, there's a skyline to light up. The flat tops of the Miesian buildings didn't

offer much in the way of drama. But the new round of towers – 900 N. Michigan Avenue, 123 N. Wacker, the AT&T Corporate Center (100 S. Franklin), NBC Tower (200 E. Illinois) – boast distinctive tops, often fanciful turrets or spires, that lend themselves to night lights.

Night skyline

Some of the old-timers are lighting up, too. The Chicago Board of Trade (Jackson and LaSalle) and 919 N. Michigan (formerly the Palmolive and then the Playboy Building) have joined the Wrigley Building and Tribune Tower, both located north of the river on Michigan Avenue, which have long been illuminated at night.

Chicago is lucky to have so many wonderful buildings, because it has precious few wonderful open spaces. The city has less parkland per capita than any other major city in America, and the relentless street grid precludes the grand vistas of European and East Coast cities. This is a place whose children would be startled by the sound of birds and for whom a special farm-in-the-park was built to show them where milk comes from.

While developers can produce great buildings, great spaces require planning, which necessitates putting the brakes on development. And the same zeitgeist that has nurtured the construction of tall buildings has stifled city planning in Chicago. American city planning was born here, with Daniel Burnham's 1909 plan, but it was a stillbirth. Planning may get in the way of development and, as such, has always been suspect.

Old clause

Planning in Chicago has almost always, therefore, happened by accident. For example, one would think the city's magnificent front yard, Grant Park, was the result of a grand scheme. In fact, it is the consequence of retailer Montgomery Ward's irritation in the late 1890s over plans to build a small city of public buildings – museums and the like – in Grant Park. The building would have obscured the lake view from his corporate headquarters on N. Michigan Avenue, so Ward dug up an old clause in the city code that decreed the lakefront should be "forever free and clear." Ward prevailed, preserving his view, and one of the city's great amenities, forever. Although Burnham's name is invoked regularly, very little of his ambitious city plan was ever implemented. The Buckingham Fountain made it, as did the layout for the museums along the lakefront. But there's no Civic Center, few of the tree-lined boulevards and not much of the system of lakefront lagoons and islands that Burnham envisioned.

Instead, it is the great planner's credo – "Make no little plans" – that is invoked, and that philosophy has shaped the city. Developers make no small plans, either, and by some magic the result is one of the world's great architectural mosaics. ❑

LEFT: downtown Chicago.
RIGHT: the Ferris Wheel at Navy Pier.

PLACES

A detailed guide to the city and surroundings, with principal sites clearly cross-referenced by number to the maps

Chicago is a city of extremes, from the weather to the politics to the architecture. Given its rambling, rambunctious history, it's not surprising that the city retains much of the spirit of individualism upon which it was built.

That individualism is reflected in the city's different districts, from the gloss of the Gold Coast and the Magnificent Mile to the dozens of neighborhoods that fan out from the city's focus, the downtown lakefront. Sociologists debate whether or not Chicago is America's "most segregated" city, but no one disagrees that it is the major city best defined as a collection of neighborhoods.

Many of the ethnic barriers of the old immigrant neighborhoods have broken down, but enough remain to make Chicago a living exhibit of the American melting pot. Fires, riots, booms and busts, strikes, atomic experiments – the landmarks of events that shaped America are literally underfoot throughout Chicago.

Another distinct aspect of Chicago is its North-South divide. The side of the river on which one is born has relatively little influence on future wealth and happiness, but everything to do with a lifelong disdain for people born on the other side.

Both North and South Siders agree, however, that the downtown lakefront is Chicago at its most extreme: a vast lake, tall buildings, great museums, popular beaches, glittering shops, renowned theaters, famous hot dog stands, classy restaurants and the Midwestern Americans who use these aspects of their city daily.

Chicago's sense of irony is reflected in the way that, after years of trying to shrug off the gangster legacy, there are now guided tours showing where who did what to whom.

Rush Street is Chicago's best-known district for night – time revelry, but today the action has spread much wider and is more varied. Comedy and cabaret clubs are a specialty, from the Second City troupe that has produced so many TV and movie stars to the smaller spots that feature local comics and singers.

Finally, Chicago offers more festivals and celebrations of music, food and people than perhaps any other city in the United States. Chicago is a town to be celebrated for what it is now rather than for its past, and Chicagoans are only too happy to do that kind of celebrating almost every day. ❑

PRECEDING PAGES: Loop skyline; rising moon; brassy bird.
LEFT: downtown clock.

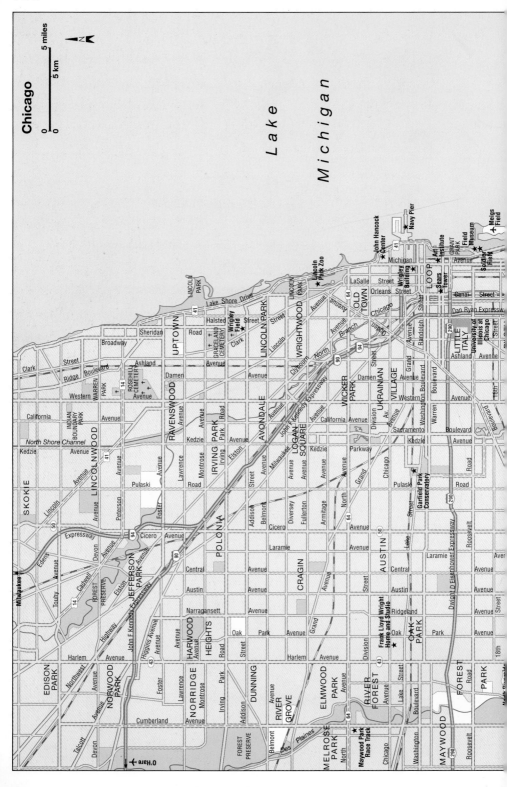

Chicago

5 miles
5 km

Lake Michigan

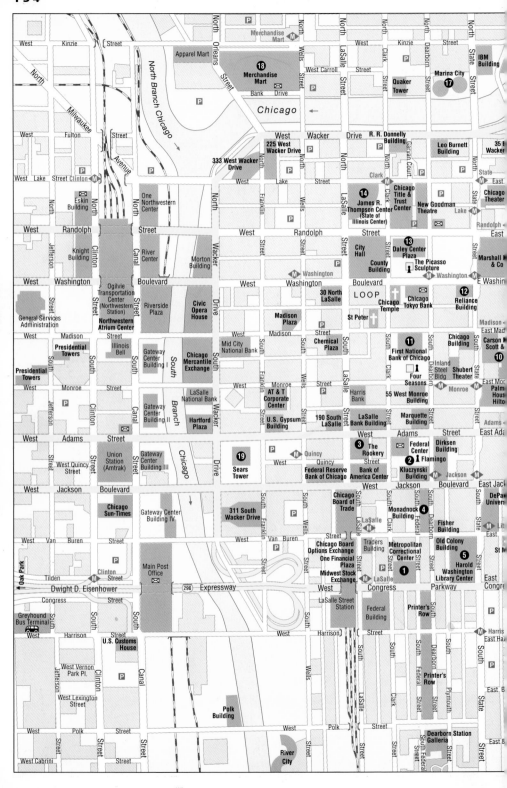

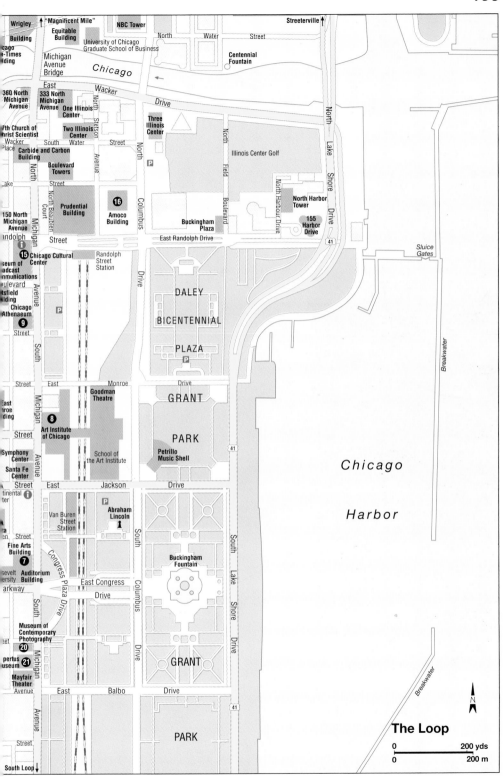

Wrigley
Building
cago
a-Times
ilding

"Magnificent Mile"

Equitable
Building

NBC Tower

University of Chicago
Graduate School of Business

Michigan
Avenue
Bridge

North   Water   Street

Centennial
Fountain

Streeterville

Chicago

East
Wacker

360 North
Michigan
Avenue

333 North
Michigan
Avenue

Drive

One Illinois
Center

7th Church of
hrist Scientist

Two Illinois
Center

Three
Illinois
Center

Place
Wacker

Carbide and Carbon
Building

South   Water   Street

Illinois Center Golf

North

Boulevard
Towers

North Field

North

Avenue

ake

North

150 North
Michigan
Avenue

Prudential
Building

16

Amoco
Building

North Beaubien Court

North Harbour Tower

North Harbour Drive

North Harbor
Tower

155
Harbor
Drive

North Lake Shore Drive

andolph

Michigan

Street

Columbus

Buckingham
Plaza

Boulevard

East Randolph Drive

Sluice
Gates

41

15

Chicago Cultural
Center

Randolph
Street
Station

Drive

seum of
adcast
nmunications
oulevard
tsfield
ilding
Chicago
Athenaeum

Avenue

P

9

Street

DALEY

BICENTENNIAL

Breakwater

South

PLAZA

P

Street   East   Monroe

Drive

East
roe
ding

Goodman
Theatre

GRANT

Michigan

8

Street

Art Institute
of Chicago

PARK

School of
the Art Institute

41

Symphony
Center

Avenue

Petrillo
Music Shell

Santa Fe
Center

Chicago

Street   East   Jackson   Drive

tinental
ter

P

Harbor

Van Buren
Street
Station

Abraham
Lincoln

a
en   Street

South

Fine Arts
Building

7

Congress Plaza Drive

Columbus

Buckingham
Fountain

sevelt   Auditorium
ersity   Building

East Congress

arkway

Drive

South

South Lake Shore Drive

Museum of
Contemporary
Photography

Michigan

Drive

eet

20

pertus
useum

21

GRANT

Mayfair
Theater

Avenue

East   Balbo   Drive

Breakwater

Avenue

41

The Loop

Street

PARK

N

0   200 yds

0   200 m

South Loop

THE LOOP

*The historic center of the city is rich in architectural splendor.
Choose from a variety of worthwhile tours or use this guide and
map to spend an afternoon exploring the area*

Map
on page
134

The Loop, a reference to the circumnavigations of the elevated train system, or the El, is the moniker given by Chicagoans to the historic heart of the city. The Chicago River, spanned by 10 bridges from Lake Shore Drive to Franklin Street, affords a good introduction to the Loop. Cruise boats, Chicago's answer to the *bâteaux mouches* that ply the Seine in Paris, dock at Navy Pier and Michigan and Wacker. One 90-minute Architectural Cruise chugs past Chicago's famous "corncobs," Marina City, the graceful trefoil curve of Lake Point Tower, the powerful steel-banded John Hancock Center, and the lopsided steel-and-glass, balloon-like James R. Thompson Center.

On another worthwhile cruise, a guide provided by the Chicago Architecture Foundation covers the city's famous downtown architects from Mies van der Rohe to Helmut Jahn, commenting on or pointing out some 100 notable structures in the course of the journey. Less scholarly but operating more frequently, non-specialist boat tours offer 60-minute, 90-minute and two-hour cruises throughout the day and into the evening, when the light-dotted cityscape is often silhouetted against a velvety sky.

Museum buses

Another way to get a sense of the Loop is to take one of the Chicago Motor Coach Co. bus tours. Tours start at the Sears Tower and near the Water Tower on Michigan Avenue and the buses stop at many of the museums and other significant sights in the Loop and Near North. It's a hop-on-and-off-as-you-please deal so culture vultures and their long-suffering companions may board the bus at one museum, get off to tour another and then catch a later bus to a third. Other tours buses like American Sightseeing and Gray Line take in a wider area.

As an adjunct to boat and bus, or just for its own flawed charm, visitors ought to consider a loop around the Loop via the El. It won't be a quiet experience. The wheels wring banshee shrieks from the tracks as they take the curves, teenagers scream deliriously into each other's rock-deafened ears, the motorman calls out stops over a muddy public-address system and the occasional lurching drunk or wacko extemporizes for the benefit of one and all. But that's Chicago, and the El is about as non-touristy as Chicago gets.

El on wheels

On the El, a good place to begin a Loop tour is at the Merchandise Mart between Wells and Orleans streets, north of the river. (To cross-reference sites with map, turn to page 140 where sightseeing begins for those on foot.) The Mart, closed except to the trade, wears a

PRECEDING PAGES:
fountain in
Grant Park.
LEFT: Dubuffet's
*Monument with
Standing Beast.*
BELOW: doormen's
changing of
the guard.

skin of limestone and terracotta ornamentals, but these do little to soften its brooding magisterial aspect. Those who board the southbound Ravenswood train one stop earlier, at Chicago, should keep an eye out for the "climbers" on the right, a startling sight even for seasoned riders. The **climbers** are life-sized models, a man and woman, dressed in business suits. They appear to be pulling themselves up or, possibly, letting themselves down the somber face of a building not much more than 30 ft (9 meters) from the passing trains. Each clutches a realistic briefcase in one hand, and a rope that trails from an overhead fixture in the other. A cartoon balloon sagging from the man's mouth declaims, "There must be an easier way in."

The tall buildings in the Loop can create a tunnel effect on particularly cold and windy winter days. At those times special ropes are set up to help pedestrians stay on the sidewalks.

It's worth a few minutes to leave the train and look around the El's **Quincy** station. Dating from 1897, it rises above the platforms like an art-deco bungalow. Back on the El, heading east on Van Buren, or equally good a place to start a walking tour, can be found an odd but dramatic triangular building, the William J. Campbell US Courthouse Annex, better known to its inmates as the **Metropolitan Correctional Center ❶**. This innovative 27-story building, designed for prison efficiency, maximizes the number of cells, each with its own window, in the given space. It also minimizes the hall space necessary to reach them. All in all, the center is a scientific rather than a humanistic exercise in incarceration.

Plaza art

BELOW: loop lines.
RIGHT: Met
Correction Center.

A couple of blocks north, on Dearborn Street, are the Dirksen Building and the Kluczynski Building and Post Office, together known as **Federal Center ❷**. Named after prominent native sons, they are frequently cited as two examples

of Mies van der Rohe's most successful designs. Alexander Calder's *Flamingo*, a series of deep-red arcs whose lightness and grace belie the work's 50 tons, occupies a large, open square between the two buildings. A block or so west at 209 S. LaSalle is **The Rookery** ❸, a magnificent redstone building designed in 1886 by Burnham and Root. The lobby was remodeled in 1905 by Frank Lloyd Wright and lovingly restored to its 1905 appearance a few years ago. Continue a couple of blocks east to 140 S. Dearborn for the **Marquette Building**, by Holabird and Roche, then double-back a couple of blocks to the 16-story **Monadnock Building** ❹, on Dearborn between Van Buren and Jackson. Built in 1891, it's the highest edifice ever erected using wall-bearing masonry construction instead of the modern metal-frame method of construction. Named after a picturesque mountain in northeast Vermont, the Monadnock Building remains a personal triumph for architect John Root, and one of the last great examples of a now obsolete technology.

Map on page 134

Chicago is organized on a grid system. Everything starts from zero, represented by the intersection of State and Madison Streets. Throw in the lake (always east) and navigating becomes a no-brainer.

Fizzy facade

Just down the street where Dearborn intersects Van Buren St is the **Fisher Building**, built in 1896 and extended in 1907. From the El, the building's facade, tiers of tall windows gathered into triplets by rounded masonry arches, appears to shimmer gently. Also on the left is a 1912 structure originally called the **Rothschild Building**. In 1936, the building became Goldblatt's department store. Since 1993, it has been renovated and is now home to **DePaul University**. This building may be of particular interest to music buffs. Commonly referred to as The Music Mart, it houses several music and instrument retail stores on the first and basement levels. Also on Van Buren taking up the entire block between

BELOW: the Rookery.

TIP

When you need to get away from the madding crowds head for an alcove desk on one of the higher floors of the Harold Washington Library at 400 S. State, where you'll find a restorative oasis of peace and calm. Treat yourself to a coffee on the way in or out in the first-floor coffee bar.

BELOW:
an engineering
dedication,
Daley Center.

State Street and Plymouth Court is the **Harold Washington Library Center 5**. (open daily except public holidays; Mon 9am–7pm, Tues and Thurs 11am–7pm, Wed, Fri and Sat 9am–5pm, Sun 1–5pm; tel: 312 747 430). The building, of neo-classic design, uses elements of ancient Greek and Roman structure, such as columns, arches and vaulted ceilings. The 756,000 sq ft (69,622 sq meters) library appears in the *Guinness Book Of World Records* as the largest public library building in the world.

As the train swings left entering Wabash on its northward run, or you walk a block east, you will pass the **CNA Plaza 6**, a deep, almost oxblood red pair of buildings supported on steel columns – Mies van der Rohe's influence. On the left are glimpses of students poring over books at DePaul University's Loop campus, and on either side office buildings flow by as, through the windows, draftsmen move T-squares across boards, dancers spin, and typists punch.

Unless you are determined to complete the loop, exit at Adams and Wabash, head a block east to Michigan, then south to the granite-and-limestone **Fine Arts Building 7**. Originally a showcase for the Studebaker Carriage Co., it now produces artists such as Jackson Pollack and Virgil Thomson. Further south, on the same block, the **Auditorium Building** once housed a hotel and offices as well as a theater. The theater and its magnificent tiered ceiling remain, but **Roosevelt University** has taken over the rest.

Heading north again, the nearby **Santa Fe Center** building houses the Chicago Architecture Foundation's Shop and Tour Center. This bookstore-cum-gallery is devoted to the history of Chicagoan architecture. The Foundation offers more than 50 tours of architectural highlights in and around Chicago. Two blocks on is **Symphony Center**, home to the Chicago Symphony Orchestra

since 1904. Across Michigan Avenue is the **Art Institute** ❽ (open daily Mon, Wed, Thurs and Fri 10.30am–4.30pm, Tues 10.30am–8pm, Sat 10am–5pm, Sun 12–5pm; entrance free Tues; tel: 312-443 3600). Inside, the Art Institute offers a wide range of exhibits, including ancient Chinese bronzes, neolithic Ban Chiang pottery from Thailand, Arthur J. Rubloff's eye-popping collection of paperweights, some of America's choicest examples of French Impressionists and Post-Impressionists, arms and armor, textiles and pre-Columbian pottery as well as hugely popular temporary exhibits.

Founded in 1879, the Art Institute moved to its present French Renaissance-style quarters in 1892, just in time for the 1893 Columbian Exposition.(*see page 150*) In January 1986, when the Chicago Bears went to American football's Super Bowl, the lions found themselves in oversized football helmets fashioned from barbecue kettles.

Glorious protests

Extensive renovations and additions to the Institute over the past 15 years have added a new 1,000-seat auditorium, plus the entire **Trading Room** from the now dismantled Adler and Sullivan's Chicago Stock Exchange, which dates back to 1893. In recent years, the School of the Art Institute has been the center of considerable controversy. One student gained national attention when his painting of the late Mayor Harold Washington, decked out in bra and panties, was unceremoniously yanked from the wall by a group of irate aldermen.

In 1989, another student placed an American flag on the floor, leading some unconcerned museumgoers to walk on it. Protesters crowded the front steps, and motorists, invited to "honk if you love Old Glory," created a cacophony of

The El – a Chicago mover 'n' shaker.

BELOW: Mao by Andy Warhol, Art Institute of Chicago.

Save money by using
public transportation
with CTA unlimited
rides visitors' passes.
A day pass is currently
$5, 2-day $9, 3-day
$12 and 5-day $18.
You can buy passes
ahead of time. They
are available at
currency exchanges
and train station
vending machines.

BELOW: street artist
and his work.

patriotism on Michigan Avenue. Some legislators threatened to revoke public
funding, but the furor eventually flagged and died down. The Art Institute
regularly offers special exhibits and lecture series. It is also associated with the
Goodman Theater, which most nights presents classical and contemporary
drama, along with new works and training for would-be playwrights and actors.

At 6 North Michigan Avenue is the **Chicago Athenaeum ⑨**, a museum
aimed at showing how design can positively impact the human environment in
architecture, industrial and product design, graphics and urban planning (open
Tues–Sat 11am–6pm, Sun 12–5pm; entrance fee; tel: 312-251 0175). The
museum maintains a collection of graphic design, industrial design,
photographic and film archives and many more holdings.

Walking a block or so west along Madison will take you to **State Street**.
"That great street" has been known since the 1870s for its concentration of
premier department stores and world-class architecture. Widened for its
renaissance as a mall, the street gained stalls selling popcorn and fruit. But
major retailers such as Wieboldt's, Lytton's, Goldblatt's, Steven's, and
Montgomery Ward pulled up stakes in the 1980s, leaving a swath of schlock
storefronts advertising cheap electronics and kitsch.

Today the street enjoys a great rebirth. In 1996, Mayor Richard Daley
demonstrated his dedication to the maintenance of the city's historic districts and
reconstructed the street making it look as it did in the early 19th century.
Complete with globe-shaped gas lights, replicas of the ones President Coolidge
switched on when he opened the street in 1926, and black steel-gated entrances
to the subway, the street again invites shoppers and strollers. Much of the
shopping has returned as have additional sights such as free outdoor winter ice

skating at the corner of State and Washington and year – round street music provided by Chicago's most innovative struggling musicians.

A few oldtimers remain. Evans, selling women's clothing just south of Madison, tries to ignore the occasional anti-fur picketers. **Marshall Field's** is still an anchor of the street, along with rival department store **Carson Pirie Scott & Co ⑩**. Designed by Louis H. Sullivan and built by Daniel Burnham, the Carson Pirie Scott building retains the architectural tension and grace which made it revolutionary at the turn of the century. Wide, light-embracing windows on the terracotta facing rise above cast-iron reliefs that lend strength to the lower floors. The grill on the southwest corner recreates, in metal, swirling floral fantasies reminiscent of Art Nouveau calligraphy. Across the street, at 7 W. Madison, is the **Chicago Building**, another design of Holabird and Roche, and one that typifies their contribution to the Loop's architecture.

Scraping skies

The tallest bank building in the world, the **First National Bank of Chicago ⑪**, soars in a gentle, pale-gray arc above a plaza that opens a few steps down from street level in the fibrillating heart of Chicago's commercial center on Dearborn and Madison. Around noon, on sunny days, the plaza around the **Hamal Fountain** rapidly fills up with crowds of downtown office workers, lunching al fresco. On the Dearborn Street side, Marc Chagall's *Four Seasons* mosaic mural, 70 ft (21 meters) of multi-colored marble, glass and stone, squats uncomfortably and is best visited at night when it's illuminated

A block north at 32 N. State is the **Reliance Building ⑫** designed by Daniel Burnham and erected in 1895. Until recently in a state of disrepair, this building,

Shop till you drop in the Loop – the Carson Pirie Scott building.

BELOW:
arty student.

with its extensive use of glass and whose style predated Chicago's famous glass towers, had a facelift in 1995. Meanwhile, at the **Daley Center Plaza** ⓭ 162 tons of rusted steel rise 50 ft (15 meters) high. Known only as **"the Picasso,"** it has been the butt of jokes and the subject of criticism since it was first erected in 1967. What is it? The consensus says a woman, though some say a bird, a dog or a range of obscene suggestions. Kids on the other hand have never had a problem deciding what it is, and happily slide down it for hours. On the south side of Washington Street, directly across from the *Picasso*, stands **Joan Miró's** ***Chicago***, a highly-stylized female figure formed from steel-reinforced concrete. Her skirt is a lively mosaic, and she shows no signs today of the red spray paint with which vandals greeted her controversial arrival in 1981.

Stand with your back against one of the sloping pillars of the First National Bank and look up. Does it seem like the building is falling over? Or is that you?

On the hot track

Across Clark Street are **County Building** and **Chicago City Hall** and, another block north, the **James R. Thompson Center** ⓮ (State of Illinois Center) which opened on May 6, 1985 amid negative publicity, escalating costs and many design and maintenance problems. Some called it designer Helmut Jahn's homage to megalomania. Others merely noted that 17 stories of glass encircling a huge rotunda topped by a shortened glass cylinder could be expected to play havoc with internal temperatures. And in the early days it did. Office workers on upper floors, forced to wear sunscreen and dark glasses on bright days, suffered from temperatures in the high 90s F during the steaming summer months, despite an air-conditioning system working to capacity. And when the air-conditioning broke down, the building had to be virtually evacuated.

BELOW: the view from Sears Tower.

More than 50 state agencies are housed in the center, as well as three levels of restaurants and shops. An art gallery exhibits primarily Illinois artists and artisans, and is well worth a visit. So is the building itself, despite its drawbacks as a place to work. A glass-enclosed elevator provides a thrilling, stomach-lurching ride to the top floor, not recommended for acrophobes. A tour of the building may be had by asking at the information booth. Outside, at the main entrance, Jean Dubuffet's *Monument With Standing Beast*, 10 tons of white fiberglass outlined in black, stands guard.

The theater district

The Harris Theater and the Selwyn Theater, built in 1922, have been saved from destruction and in the process the Chicago theater district reborn. The Goodman Theater Group, previously housed in Grant Park, is renovating these historic theaters to be part of their new theater producing major shows. By the fall of 2000 the **New Goodman Theater**, the newly renovated **Oriental Theater** at Dearborn and Randolph, and the **Bismarck Palace Theater** west on Randolph will complete the theater district where as many as 9,000 seats could be filled on any given night.

A brief detour will take you to the **Leo Burnett Building** before you head south to the **Chicago Cultural Center** ⓯ (open daily; Mon–Wed 10am–7pm, Thurs 10am–9pm, Fri 10am–6pm, Sat 10am–5pm, Sun 11am–5pm; closed holidays; entrance free;

tel: 312-744 6300), which flaunts Tiffany mosaics and domes resplendent with stained. Vast public spaces connected by vaulted arches and sweeping staircases create a satisfying interior. The Center offers programs and exhibits in the performing, visual and literary arts; architectural tours are available.

Going back towards the river, check out the **Amoco Building** , the **Prudential Building** and the **Carbide and Carbon Building**. Built in 1973, and clad exotically in extra-thin marble at the insistence of the then company chairman, the Amoco exterior had to be replaced at exorbitant cost some years later when the marble began falling off. The distinctive **Marina City** ⓱, built in 1967 on the north bank of the river, is both residential and commercial as well being home to the newer House of Blues. A few blocks west is **Merchandise Mart** ⓲, originally built for Marshall Field & Co. and later purchased by the Kennedy family. Tours of the wholesale – mainly interior design – showrooms are available. The first two floors are occupied by retail stores. Across the river, on the south side where it curves, is **333 West Wacker Drive**, a distinctive green building cleverly designed to fit snugly on the bend.

On LaSalle Street, roughly between Madison and Jackson but spilling over onto Wacker Drive, is a financial district that could well be called Wall Street West (see next chapter). The Lyric Opera's home on Wacker Drive, the **Civic Opera House**, is nicknamed Insull's Throne, so-called for both backer Samuel Insull and its fancied resemblance to a chair of monumental proportions.

Sears soars

In describing the world's second tallest office building, one is tempted to borrow from Alexander Pope, who wrote that he "lisped in numbers for the numbers

Map on page 134

Carbide and Carbon Building.

BELOW: rollerblading in the Loop district.

RIVER REVERSAL

The sewage system of early Chicago was primitive. With waste being dumped into the river, that flowed into Lake Michigan, the source of the city's drinking water, people were becoming seriously sick. In 1854, a cholera epidemic swept the city, taking the lives of over 5 percent of the population.

First the Water Tower and Pumping Station was constructed in an attempt to supply clean water via a tunnel from the lake, but the sickness continued. Then the Illinois and Michigan Canal was made deeper so that the river would change course and flow away from the city, but this just shifted the problem to outlying communities.

Deaths from water polluted by human waste brought about a state of emergency by 1886, when fatalities caused by typhoid were 174 per 100,000 persons. In 1900, using a series of locks and channels, a bold engineering feat was successfully completed – the permanent reversal of the Chicago River so that it would no longer run into Lake Michigan. A 28-mile (45-km) canal was built between the south branch of the river and Lockport. Chicago had built the first of its own rivers to dispose of waste waters.

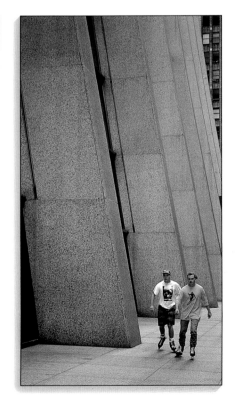

Map
on pages
134–5

Along for the ride.

BELOW: Chicago photographed by NASA.

came." Completed in 1974, the 110 stories of **Sears Tower ⓲** soar 1,454 feet (443 meters), enclose more than 4 million sq feet (371,612 sq meters) of floor space and accommodate some 16,500 people daily. From the 103rd-floor Skydeck, (open daily; March–September 9am–11pm, October–February 9am–10pm, entrance fee) 1,353 feet (412 meters) above the ground, you can see four US states on a clear day (a rarity in Chicago).

Roughly 16,000 bronze-tinted glass windows and 28 acres of black anodized aluminum cover a framework of 76,000 tons of steel – and enough concrete for a 5-mile long (8 km), eight-lane highway. There is only one set of buildings in the world, the Petronas Towers in Kuala Lumpur, which stands taller, at 1483 feet (452 meters).

On Michigan Avenue, south of the Loop, are the **Museum of Contemporary Photography ⓴** (open Mon–Wed, Fri 10am–5pm, Thurs 10am–8pm, Sat 12–5pm; closed Sun and all of August; entrance free; tel: 312-663 5554) and the **Spertus Museum ㉑** (open Sun–Wed 10am–5pm, Thurs 10am–8pm, Fri 10am–3pm; entrance free Fri; tel: 312–922 9012). The former, a Columbia College project, takes light-sensitive emulsions – not to mention 19th-century coated glass plates and contemporary electronic adjuncts – seriously. Special exhibits usually complement the internationally-respected Permanent Collection and Print Study Room. The Spertus has a split personality. Part of the collection celebrates the survival of the Jewish people as embodied in their art. The rest of the collection mourns the horrors of the Holocaust.

Those in need of sustenance might like to mosey on over to **Printer's Row**. A spiffy, up-and-coming area it would be churlish to brand yuppified, Printer's Row offers the young and affluent a neighborhood to call their own.

Chicago in the movies

The human drama, comedy and crime of Chicago, along with a cityscape ranging from lakefront and skyscrapers to ghettos and stockyards, has been a fertile playground for American filmmakers.

The play *The Front Page* by Ben Hecht and Charles MacArthur described the comic rough and tumble of Chicago newspaper life in a style that has spawned several movie versions along with a tradition of adapting Chicago's experimental theater for the big screen.

One of the most successful examples was local playwright David Mamet's modern romance-comedy of manners, *Sexual Perversity in Chicago*, the basis for the 1986 movie *About Last Night*. That film provided springboard roles for several rising young actors, including Demi Moore, Rob Lowe, Jim Belushi and Elizabeth Perkins, and provided a vivid picture of yuppie life in Chicago.

Perhaps the quintessential Chicago movie, however, has been *The Blues Brothers*, the 1980 comedy starring John Belushi and Dan Aykroyd as Jake and Elwood Blues. The story is corny but the two stars shine and some classic music scenes are provided by Aretha Franklin, James Brown and Ray Charles.

Other popular movies filmed in or around Chicago in the 1970s and 1980s included *Silver Streak* in 1976, *Looking for Mister Goodbar* in 1977, Robert Altman's *A Wedding* in 1978, and *Somewhere in Time* and *My Bodyguard* in 1980. *Ordinary People*, the film directed by Robert Redford that won an Oscar for best picture in 1980, was filmed in Chicago and its North Shore suburbs.

Risky Business made a star of Tom Cruise in 1983, and John Hughes' *Ferris Bueller's Day Off* used Chicago locations well in 1986. Also filmed in Chicago were *The Color of Money*, the Paul Newman-Tom Cruise sequel to *The Hustler*, and Cruise-vehicle *Top Gun* in 1986; a rare John Hughes non-teen comedy, *Planes, Trains and Automobiles*, in 1987; *The Untouchables*, a 1987 blockbuster depiction of crime fighter Eliot Ness's battle against the Capone mob; *Major League*, *Uncle Buck* and *Music Box* starring Jessica Lange in 1989; and another Jessica Lange film, *Men Don't Leave*, released in 1990.

Movie-goers around the world saw a lot of Chicago scenes in 1993's *The Fugitive*, starring Harrison Ford, but then there was a sudden drop in the number of movies shot in Chicago. That spurred the Chicago Film Office and unions to make the city competitive as a movie location, an initiative that worked. Recent box office successes filmed in Chicago include *My Best Friend's Wedding*, with Julia Roberts, *While You Were Sleeping*, starring Sandra Bullock, and *Chain Reaction*, starring Keanu Reeves.   ❏

RIGHT: Dan Aykroyd, left, and John Belushi in *The Blues Brothers*.

SOPHISTICATION AND STYLE

Chicago, usually known for its matter-of-fact style, has contrived over the years to cultivate one of the world's most sophisticated art collections

The Art Institute of Chicago has not only an extensive and varied art collection but also a school, where young talent is groomed. In 1879, when Chicago was only a half of a century old, a group of prominent businessmen joined together around the common cause of establishing an institute of art. Their goal was to preserve and exhibit art of all kinds. The collections at the early Art Institute were a mixed bag, including sculptures, prints and drawings. Over the years, through acquisition and private donation, the collection grew. Charles Hutchinson, son of one of Chicago's premier businessmen of the time, was the institute's first president.

RARE FINDS

With his friend Martin Ryerson and backed by the fortunes of Chicago's elite, Hutchinson traveled the world searching for rare finds. They raced to Tuscany by train and carriage to convince an heiress, a member of a European royal family who had squandered her inheritance, to sell them part of her treasures, which included Rembrandt's, *Young Girl at the Open Half-Door*.

Bertha Palmer, the wife of Potter Palmer (Chicago's merchant king), gathered a vast collection which, over time, she donated to the Art Institute. A personal friend of the American impressionist painter Mary Cassatt, Bertha acquired works by Monet and Renoir as well as by Cassatt herself.

At its 101st anniversary, the institute held an exhibition honoring some of its former students, who included Georgia O'Keefe, Grant Wood, and Red Glooms.

▷ **MULL SHIRT**
The mull shirt, a precursor to metal armor, is a body shield made by interlocking a network of rings.

COLLECTION FROM ALL CORNERS

It is the works of French Post-Impressionists such as Georges Seurat (1859–91) that make the Art Institute of Chicago so famous.

Seurat's masterpiece, *A Sunday on La Grande Jatte* (*above*) shows a group of people relaxing at a suburban park on an island in the Seine called La Grande Jatte. The brilliance of the artist's work is in his technique, and if you want to learn more about the subtleties in Seurat's methods, you can take a special tour with one of the curators.

Although the president of the Art Institute no longer dashes off to buy art on the cheap from the crumbling monarchies of Europe, the museum does host traveling exhibitions. Monet and Van Gogh, as well as Seurat, have all been featured in sell-out shows. But the insititute also exhibits textiles as well as paintings and drawings from every region of the world.

△ DRAWING ROOM
Glimpse at the Thorne Miniature Rooms and see various elements of European interiors from the late 16th century to the 20th century. There are 62 tiny rooms.

◁ PROUD LIONS
These lions stand guard at the main entrance to the Art Institute.

▷ PAPERWEIGHT
Paperweights are known as the crown jewels of glass-making. Flowers and swirling colors often to dominate paperweight design, but the Institute also has unique designs such as this silkworm.

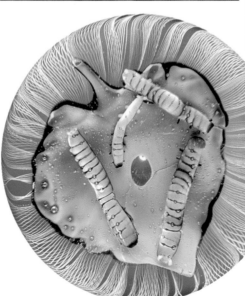

THE FINANCIAL DISTRICT

Map on page 156

Chicago remains the world center for futures trading, and the Chicago Board of Trade and Mercantile Exchange are well worth a visit for their views of the trading floors

Chicago's financial district is best known for its colorful, raucous futures markets. Amid the seemingly manic action of the trading pits, world prices are set for corn, wheat, soybeans, pork bellies and live cattle, to name just a few of the commodities involved. These century-old markets have become increasingly sophisticated and now include financial instruments such as US Treasury bonds, foreign currencies from Japanese yen to German marks, Eurodollars, stock options and stock indexes.

LaSalle Street is Chicago's answer to Wall Street, lined by somber bank buildings and glistening skyscrapers that are filled with brokerages and law offices. The financial district runs from roughly Madison Street on the north to Jackson Street on the south, where LaSalle stops at the foot of the towering **Chicago Board of Trade ❶** (viewing gallery open Mon–Fri 8am–2pm; entrance free; tel: 312-435 3590) to form an architectural canyon. The district has been expanding westward to Wacker Drive, where the **Chicago Mercantile Exchange ❷** (open to visitors Mon–Fri; upper gallery 7.15am–2pm, lower gallery 8am–3.15pm; entrance free; tel: 312-930 8249) occupies a newer 40-story twin tower. A block north of the Board of Trade, on South LaSalle, is Chicago's oldest bank, the Continental Illinois Bank and Trust Building, now the **Bank of America Center**. This massive block-square building's "classic" design is said to be copied from early Roman baths. Across the street from it is the **Federal Reserve Bank of Chicago ❸**.

It makes sense that commodity trading was invented in Chicago, which grew up as a transportation crossroads nestled in the Midwestern breadbasket. In the 1800s, wagons, oxcarts, barges, canal boats and railroads hauled crops here from fields across the prairie. At harvest time the streets and waterways were choked with loads of grain as local farmers scrambled to find buyers. Often there were surpluses in which case spoiled grain was frequently dumped into Lake Michigan. The exchanges evolved to provide an orderly marketplace for agricultural commerce.

Pit bulls

With the growth of financial futures, futures trading has spread to New York, Tokyo, London, Hong Kong and other international cities. But Chicago remains the industry's center. Traders are easy to spot, their bright-colored trading jackets unmistakable in the financial district's bars and coffee shops.

Inside the exchanges, traders and brokers gather in octagonal, stair-stepped rings called "pits," which allow buyers and sellers to see one another. Each pit is for a specific commodity and the biggest are crammed with hundreds of traders who at first glance

PRECEDING PAGES: Chicago Mercantile Exchange. **LEFT:** Chicago Board of Trade. **BELOW:** financial area skyscrapers.

seem to be simply jumping up and down, frantically waving their arms and shrieking at each other. The activity looks chaotic, but there's method to the madness. Fortunes are at stake here and millions of dollars have been made and lost in a split second.

This fast-moving game lures high-rollers: a seat on the Board of Trade, for example, costs about $400,000. But the prospect of a big score has attracted players from practically every background: ex-cops, waiters, football players, lawyers, teachers, doctors, even professional gamblers have tried their luck in these trading pits. The number of Jaguars and Porsches parked in surrounding lots attest to the success of many. The unlucky lose their seats and sometimes, literally, their shirts.

On the exchange floors, there are legendary tales of brash traders who won or lost huge sums trying to corner the markets. Traders still tell stories about the time the action in the soybean pit got so crazy that a trader's leg was broken – and no one noticed him writhing on the floor in pain until after the closing bell had sounded, ending trade for the day. Or the one about the time a fire broke out on the Chicago Mercantile Exchange floor and the traders refused to stop buying and selling.

Crying out loud

The physical commodities – wheat, corn and so forth – don't actually change hands. Instead, trading takes place in the form of futures contracts, which are agreements to deliver or take delivery of a certain commodity during a specific month at a price agreed upon in the pit.

It all happens under the open-outcry method, a free-form auction in which

TIP

Try to visit the Board of Trade visitors gallery where the action of the pit can be seen first hand while a recording explains the action on the floor.

BELOW: interior of the Board of Trade building.

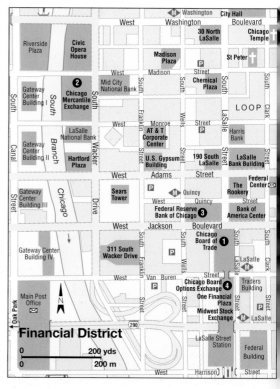

Financial District

0   200 yds

0   200 m

Map on page 156

each trader shouts out a bid or offer, often red-faced and screaming to be heard over the din. They bellow in pit lingo unintelligible to outsiders: "Ten July at a quarter!" To attract other traders' attention as they try to make themselves understood, they gesture with hand signals symbolizing their prices and the number of contracts they want to buy or sell. Traders stand in specific areas of each pit according to the contract delivery month for which they're trading.

Surrounding the pits are banks of telephones operated by brokerage houses. Most trade orders originate from customers outside the exchange and are phoned in. They are recorded by order-takers, time-stamped and then rushed by floor runners to brokers in the pits.

Though it seems little more than a game of dice, the daily hysteria performs a necessary economic function. Traders are buying and selling futures contracts on farm products that may not yet have been planted or harvested. The business is largely speculative and highly risky. But futures trading makes it possible for farmers, processors and wholesalers to lock in a price for their products; they can sleep soundly at night knowing they are protected against damaging price swings regardless of drought or flood.

Rising stars.

Future money

Since the 1970s, the biggest growth has come in the area of financial futures, now accounting for more than half the futures exchanges' business. Stock-index futures, used by traders to speculate on general stock market trends rather than specific share prices, came under the spotlight of controversy during the Wall Street market crash of 1987; some pundits argued that the futures' pessimism made the crash worse than it might have otherwise been. Today, the relationship

BELOW:
Continental Illinois
Bank Building.

between futures trading and stock market volatility is still a subject of energetic debate among experts.

To accommodate their enormous growth, the Chicago exchanges have built shiny new trading floors with video and electronic signboards enabling traders to monitor developments in stock, bond and futures markets around the world. Despite the high-tech surroundings, floor trading practices actually have changed little since the 1800s. But historic changes are in the making. The exchanges are developing automated systems so that trading can take place via computer screens as well as in the pits, a contemporary development which may have unforeseen effects on transactions.

At the heart of the district, at 141 W. Jackson Boulevard, lies the venerable Chicago Board of Trade, the world's oldest and biggest futures exchange, founded in 1848 by a group of local businessmen. Even for those bored by financial matters, this landmark Art-Deco skyscraper is worth a look. Designed by Holabird & Root and built in 1930, its lobby elevator doors are graced by golden bundles of wheat. Just off the lobby is the Ceres Café, a bar and restaurant where traders gather to drown their sorrows, celebrate their profits, or simply take a break, their eyes glued to the commodity prices flashing by on electronic boards punctuating the walls.

The 32-ft (10-meter) tall statue of Ceres, Roman goddess of grain, which sits atop the Board of Trade building, is faceless. Perhaps sculptor John Torres thought a statue 309 ft (94 meters) above the ground would not be discernible from below.

Night trading

The Board of Trade is one of the few exchanges open at night. Evening trading sessions are held Sunday through Thursday, catering to businessmen in the Far East dealing in US Treasury bond contracts, and agricultural futures and options.

The Chicago Mercantile Exchange, established in 1919, began life as a tiny

BELOW: hailing a cab that never comes.

MARKET FORCES

During the Wild West days at the Chicago Board of Trade, before heavy regulation, Joe Leiter, son of millionaire department store founder Levi Leiter, went to the Chicago Board of Trade and attempted to squeeze the wheat market. It was 1897. There was war in Turkey and famine in India. Anticipating the world's need for food Leiter started buying all the wheat he could, knowing demand would drive the prices sky high at which time he could sell his wheat for a huge profit.

Phillip Armour, Leiter's opponent in the commodities market, thought wheat prices had gone too high and sold all the wheat he could. In December crisis hit. Armour had to deliver 9,000,000 bushels of wheat to Leiter. This seemed next to impossible because the Great Lakes were blocked with winter ice and the wheat was stored in grain elevators all over the country. In a superhuman show of will, or ego, Armour assembled a fleet of grain boats at the head of Lake Superior. Led by ice-breakers, they dynamited passages through the ice and, by December 31, Armour made delivery of the wheat.

After a few more similar crises, the Board of Trade established a self-regulatory body to ensure no single trader could corner or own the entire market.

butter and egg market and developed into the world's largest trading center for livestock and foreign currencies. In 1972, it was the Mercantile Exchange that pioneered financial futures, used by banks and investors to manage risk. Its stock-index market, which is founded on the Standard & Poor's 500, is the industry's biggest.

Several years ago the Merc moved to a new, glitzier home on South Wacker. In a corner of the exchange, butter and egg prices are still recorded, though only out of nostalgia. The brass spittoons once used by cattle traders are now gone. But the jargon of the pits lives on: a popular gathering spot at the Merc is the Limit Up bar, its name taken from the traders' term for a big swing in price that causes a market to temporarily shut down.

Just south of the Board of Trade on LaSalle and linked by a bridge is a red, polished-granite complex known as **Exchange Center**. This houses the city's two securities exchanges, the **Chicago Board Options Exchange ❹** (visitor's gallery open Mon–Fri 8.30am–3.30pm; entrance free; tel: 312-786 5600) and the **Midwest Stock Exchange** (gallery open Mon–Fri 8.30am–12.30pm and 1.30pm–3.30pm; entrance free; tel: 312-663 2980).

The Chicago Board Options Exchange is a mere youngster compared to the city's other exchanges. Founded in 1972 as an offshoot of the Board of Trade, it is the birthplace of stock options trading. Some traders maintain that trading options to buy and sell shares requires more tactical finesse and knowledge of mathematical theory than the futures game. Traders in the pits can be seen clutching notes outlining complicated strategies devised by computer.

Compared to the rollicking commodities markets, the 104-year-old Midwest Stock Exchange is almost church-like. ❑

Map on page 156

Plates to go.

BELOW: the trading floor in action.

TRADING PLACES IN CHICAGO

In inventing the concept of "futures," the Midwest capital established what would become the world's principal institution for futures exchange

The Chicago Board of Trade, the Chicago Board of Options, the Mercantile Exchange and the Mid West Stock Exchange – these are the world-famous financial institutions all located in the heart of Chicago's financial district, in and around LaSalle Street. This is where the city's founders – men such as John Kinzie and Benjamin Hutchinson – invented the "forward" contract that is known today as a "future." This was a whole new way of fixing grain prices so that farmers could depend on them and thus reduce their risk. Before the invention of futures, surplus grain that became unusable was routinely dumped in Lake Michigan.

These are the institutions that put Chicago, a rural outpost until the late 1800s, on the international map as the world center for futures trading. It is hard to believe that the chalkboards in the small vaulted room of the old Mid West Stock Exchange provided anything close to the tight efficient markets today's players demand.

The old Stock Exchange, legendary among Chicago traders because this is where stock trading began in the Midwest, was a central place for businesses, brokers and speculators to gather and trade. The floor where traders once used the "open outcry" system to communicate (with lots of yelling and gesturing) to buy and sell futures and cash contracts, is now full of the computers of Chicago's modern stock exchange.

In an effort to preserve the city's history, the original stock exchange, demolished in 1972, was re-created at the Art Institute of Chicago as it would have looked at the end of the 19th century.

△ **OPEN OUTCRY**
The Mercantile Exchange, the world's leading exchange in cattle and Cheddar cheese, still uses open outcry trading.

▽ **THE CHICAGO BOARD OF TRADE**
At the end of LaSalle Street, the Chicago Board of Trade is the center of the financial district.

HOW THE SEED WAS SOWN

The importance of farming to the early growth of Chicago can still be seen in its art and industry. In the early days of farming, the threshing of the crop was very much a community experience. The thresher – a machine made up of pulleys and belts and run with coal and then steam – was used to pull seeds from corn.

In those days, the threshing machines were large and also very expensive so they were often shared between farms.

Threshing time is remembered through both stories and art as a time when the community of farmers joined together to help each other complete the harvest of their crop. After all, Chicago was built on agriculture.

The Board of Trade was started as a central trading post for farmers who often traveled vast distances to sell their crops in exchange for seed and other goods.

△ **REMAINS OF THE DAY**
The frenzy is over, everybody has left the floor, and all that remains is the debris. Savoring the solitude, a trader ponders on the results of his day.

△ **OLD STOCK EXCHANGE**
Chicago is usually much more enthusiastic about putting up new buildings than preserving the old. But the former Stock Exchange can be seen today at the Art Institute.

◁ **MONEY TALK**
Clerks and traders rely on a complex set of hand signals, representing specifics of a contract, such as quantity and price, to communicate with each other.

THE MAGNIFICENT MILE

*Enjoy a leisurely stroll along Chicago's most glamorous avenue,
where shopping malls, art museums and fine dining are just a few of
its attractions, and Old Town is a hop and a skip away*

Map
on page
166

Chicago's Magnificent Mile, the city's premier high-class shopping and strolling street, stretches along N. Michigan Avenue between the Chicago River and Oak Street. The mile earned its nickname largely because of the array of shops that are the match of any upscale retail area: Tiffany, Cartier, Elizabeth Arden, Ralph Lauren, Chanel and Gucci to name a few. Within five blocks are five of the world's top department stores: Saks Bloomingdale's, Fifth Avenue, Neiman Marcus, Marshall Field's and Lord & Taylor, and a branch of Nordstrom's is planned for 2000. In winter, the white lights on the branches of the leafless trees give the avenue a warm holiday feeling, and in the summer the petunias and flowering cabbages create an urban garden.

A little history

Start with some history at the **Michigan Avenue Bridge**, over the Chicago River. Near the northeast pylon of the bridge is a plaque commemorating the passage through the Chicago River in 1673 of the first white men – Jesuit missionary Father Jacques Marquette and Canadian-born explorer Louis Jolliet. On their way north from their explorations on the Mississippi River, they entered the Des Plaines River. There, friendly Native Americans guided them through the Chicago Portage, a stretch of mud that the explorers realized connected the Great Lakes with the Mississippi River and the Gulf of Mexico.

Across the street a plaque near the bridge's southwest pylon notes the passage in 1681 through the Chicago River of Cavalier Robert René de La Salle and Henry Tonty on their way to the Mississippi River and the Gulf of Mexico. During that trip they claimed the Mississippi Valley for France, naming it Louisiana after their king, Louis XIV. On the north bank of the river and the east side of Michigan Avenue the city's first non-native settler built his cabin in 1781. He was Jean Baptiste Point DuSable, a French-speaking black man. He established the city's first commercial enterprise, a river trading post.

Set in the sidewalks on the bridge's south end, across Wacker Drive, are markers outlining the site of Fort Dearborn, the first US Army garrison in Chicago, which was built in 1803. In 1812 the fort was destroyed, and about two-thirds of its settlers and soldiers were killed by Indians incited by the British army during the War of 1812. A bas-relief on the southwest bridge pylon commemorates the event. The three other pylons have bas-reliefs commemorating Jolliet and Marquette, fur trader John Kinzie and the rebirth of the city after the Great Fire of 1871.

The Magnificent Mile was originally a dirt path called Pine Street, used primarily by lumber wagons

PRECEDING PAGES:
Lake Shore Drive
skyscrapers.
LEFT: magnificent
smile.
BELOW: waiting
for a strolling
companion on
the Mag Mile.

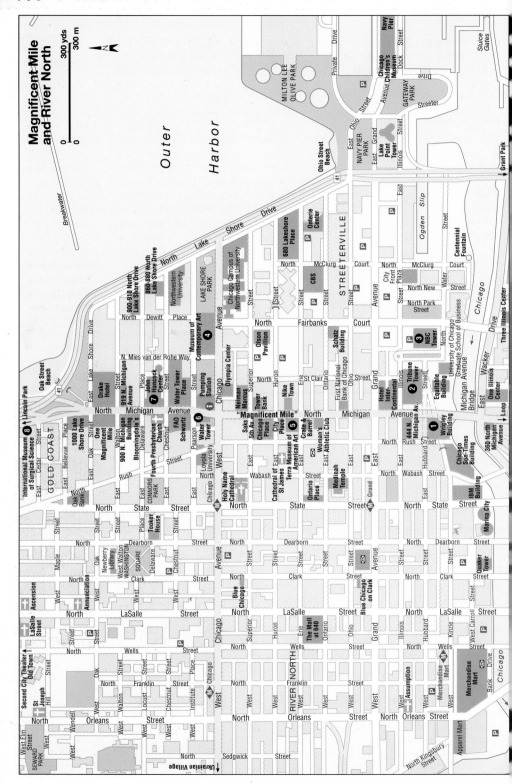

that loaded at the Chicago River. Once lined by warehouses, by the 1880s the area farther north of the river had become a popular building site for merchants' large homes; the streets were lined with wooden paving blocks. Today, the grand historic buildings mixed with the opulent extravagance of the stores ranks Michigan Avenue as one of the world's great shopping districts.

Map on page 166

Bridgeworks

The building of the Michigan Avenue Bridge, accomplished with great civic fanfare in 1920, ignited the spectacular growth of the street, by then attached to Michigan Avenue and thus renamed. The bridge itself is a fine example of the double-leaf trunnion bascule bridge. This style, so common over the Chicago River, is known internationally as a "Chicago style" bridge. "Bascule" is from the French for "see-saw," which is what a bascule bridge does. Its two halves rotate up and down on a pair of horizontal shafts called trunnions. The movement of the two sides, or leaves, can be accomplished with a relatively small motor because the weight of the leaves is precisely balanced by iron or concrete counterweights sunk into a pit below street level. The double-decker Michigan Avenue Bridge's leaves weigh 6.7 million pounds (3 million kilos) each. The counterweights are balanced so finely that they must be rebalanced every time the bridge is repainted.

Engineering aside, the bridge is a stellar attraction when it is raised and lowered, a frequent occurrence around midday during the spring and summer, enabling tall-masted sailboats to pass to or from their winter storage yards up the river. The sight of the roadbed hovering at nearly a 90-degree angle is astounding to visitors, though office workers hurrying to or from lunch find the wait to cross to the other side infuriating.

West of the bridge, at 330 N. Wabash, is Mies van der Rohe's **IBM Building**, erected in 1971, while standing sentry at the south end of the Magnificent Mile are two landmark buildings constructed at the same time as the Michigan Avenue Bridge. On the west side, just north of the river, is the **Wrigley Building ❶**, built in 1921 with an annex added in 1924. Its lacily decorated white terracotta facade, modeled after the Giralda Tower of Seville Cathedral, is floodlit at night, making it resemble an ornate wedding cake.

Pressing business

Across Michigan Avenue to the east is the **Tribune Tower ❷**, a Gothic revival skyscraper complete with a topping of flying buttresses. Built in 1925, its design was chosen by a nationwide competition held in 1922. It houses the offices of the *Chicago Tribune*, but the printing plant is along the north branch of the Chicago River, at Chicago Avenue and Halsted Street. To see the giant presses rolling, cross Michigan Avenue, pass between the two Wrigley Building halves and enter the home of Chicago's other major daily newspaper, the *Chicago Sun-Times* **Building**, where a glass-walled corridor overlooks the press room.

The Tribune Tower offers a marble lobby inscribed with quotations from famous personages ranging from

Wrigley's, based on the west side north of the river, originally manufactured soap, and later baking powder. As a sales incentive the company began giving away two packets of chewing gum with every can of baking powder – and they discovered the gum was more popular.

BELOW:
Tribune Tower.

Euripides to the powerful former *Tribune* publisher Robert R. McCormick. And the sides of the building are studded with hunks of famous buildings and historical sites around the world, gathered by *Tribune* foreign correspondents at the request of McCormick, who reportedly asked them to pursue only "honorable means" in acquiring them.

Just east of Tribune Tower is **NBC Tower** ❸. Its similarities to Rockefeller Center in New York are no coincidence. The architect Adrian Smith, of Skidmore, Owings and Merrill, studied the Art Moderne-style complex, along with nearby Chicago buildings including the Tribune Tower, before designing the NBC Tower. The result, wrote architecture critic Paul Gapp, is "the best-looking masonry-clad skyscraper constructed in Chicago since the 1930s."

Historical sites immortalized in the exterior wall of the Tribune Tower include Westminster Abbey, the Parthenon and the Taj Mahal. Each fragment is duly labeled.

A pier-less detour

Descend the stairs just north of the NBC Tower, and walk three blocks on Illinois Street to **North Pier**, a complex of restaurants, shops, and leisure attractions that is currently reinventing itself as River East Plaza. North Pier/River East Plaza has looked like the poor cousin of the bigger, smarter Navy Pier for years, and it remains to be seen whether the new enterprise, due to open its doors in the summer of 1999, succeeds.

North of Illinois, between Grand and Chicago Avenues, bounded by St Clair Street and the lake, is the area known as **Streeterville**, named for George Wellington Streeter, who claimed squatter's rights here for over 30 years. Streeter and his wife were excursion boat operators whose boat ran aground in 1886 in the lake south of Chicago Avenue. Instead of freeing the boat, they filled up the lake around it. Streeter "sold" some of the real estate to other

BELOW: leafy lunch on the Mag Mile median.

squatters, and it was not until 1918 that he was forced out by court order. Today, Streeterville is restaurants, offices and home to the **Museum of Contemporary Art ④** (Tues, Thurs and Fri 11am–6pm, Wed 11am–8pm, Sat and Sun 10am–6pm; closed Mon; entrance fee; first Tuesday every month free; tel 312-280 2660). The museum occupies an exhilarating building designed by Josef Paul Kleihues.

Map on page 166

Elder citizens

The Magnificent Mile has seen such a dizzying pace of development in recent years that it is difficult to picture what it looked like in more genteel, bygone times. Among the new construction, a few elegant buildings remain featuring mansard roofs and neo-classical detailing. Built in 1929 on the west side of N. Michigan Avenue as the Medinah Athletic Club, the **Hotel Inter-Continental** features a gilded onion-shaped dome and a floor-by-floor history of the world in interior design, from the Assyrian lions carved into marble balconies on the second floor to the 13th-century Florentine mosaics in the stairwell to the Renaissance paintings above the elevators on the fifth floor. The **Terra Museum of American Art ⑤** (open Tues 10am–8pm, Wed–Sat 10am–7pm, Sun 12–5pm; closed Mon; entrance free every Tues and first Sun each month; tel: 312-664 3939), which specializes in 19th-century paintings, is another example of a classic Chicago design. This narrow building, with a marble facade, houses a compact museum of American paintings from the collection of industrialist Daniel J. Terra, who opened the museum in 1987.

Chicagoan shoppers beat the cold.

Continuing north, from Viacom Entertainment Store on Michigan Avenue and Ontario Street on the west side to Nike Town on the east at Erie, the street

BELOW: playing for passers-by.

is packed with specialty retail stores. At the four-story Crate and Barrel you can furnish your home with the trendiest designs. Or stop in Tiffany or Cartier to find the perfect little diamond. Craving a new gadget? The Sony store will sell you electronics from palm-sized computers to wall-sized televisions. For several floors of stores visit **Chicago Place** at 700 N. Michigan Avenue.

Great Fire survivor –
The Water Tower.

A block north of Neiman Marcus, 737 N. Michigan, is the **Water Tower** ❻, an elaborate, pseudo-Gothic tower surrounded by crenellated medieval turrets, and one of Chicago's most famous landmarks. Oscar Wilde, on visiting Chicago in 1882, called it a "castellated monstrosity with pepper boxes stuck all over it." Perhaps he would change his tune if he saw it today set in a beautifully manicured park amid the thriving shopping district. The tower was built to conceal a standpipe that equalized the pressure of the water pumped from the **Pumping Station** to the east, a less elaborate structure made of the same yellow Joliet limestone. Both structures were built two years before the devastating Chicago Fire of 1871, and are among the few buildings in the area that survived the fire. The tower is used for art exhibits, and the Pumping Station still functions as it was intended and also serves as a **visitor information center**. Just beyond the Water Tower at Michigan and Pearson is Borders, a three-level book lover's paradise.

Good views

BELOW: hangin' out
on the Mag Mile.

North of the Water Tower, between Pearson and Chestnut streets, is **Water Tower Place**, renowned as an upscale downtown shopping mall. Just north of Water Tower Place is the **John Hancock Center** ❼. The third-tallest building in Chicago (and sixth-tallest in the world), it is a tapered black tower marked

CRIME ON THE COAST

The murder in 1997 of a Chicago businessman drew international attention. Lee Miglin, a real estate developer, was found in his Gold Coast garage stabbed and slashed to death. Police quickly linked Andrew Cunanan, described by his mother as a high-paid homosexual prostitute, and already being sought for murder, to the Miglin case when Cunanan's car was found nearby and Miglin's Lexus missing. The Lexus later turned up in a cemetery parking lot in Pennsville, New Jersey, where cemetery worker William Reese had been killed.

Cunanan, who also later shot dead Italian fashion designer Gianni Versace at his Miami Beach villa, was finally cornered on a Miami Beach houseboat where he shot himself to death before he could be arrested, leaving many questions unanswered. But among the documents found in a vehicle used by Cunanan after the Versace murder was one linking him to the Miglin murder.

Miglin's relationship to Cunanan, if any, remains a mystery. *Vanity Fair* magazine reported that Cunanan had informed a friend that he planned to start up a business with Miglin's son Duke. After Cunanan's suicide police swiftly closed the case, claiming his intention was to commit a random robbery when he murdered Miglin.

with external X-shaped braces that support the building against wind. At 1,105 ft (337 meters), the John Hancock offers a lower observation deck (open daily 9am–midnight; entrance fee; tel: 312-751 3681) than that of the 1,468-ft (448-meter) Sears Tower. Some aficionados prefer the view from the Hancock for it includes vast panoramas of the lake. On a clear day, visitors can see the states of Wisconsin to the north, Indiana to the south, and Michigan straight across the lake. In addition to the observation deck the Hancock Center has shopping and comfortable, inviting dining.

At the junction of Michigan Avenue and Chestnut Street is **Fourth Presbyterian Church**, an elegant Gothic church built in 1912. Featuring a cloistered walk and a quiet courtyard with a stone fountain, the church often has classical concerts. Check the information board on the Michigan Avenue side for information. Farther north are some of the more spectacular examples of recent North Michigan Avenue development. The **900 N. Michigan Building** houses Bloomingdale's and a six-level mall which includes elegant shops such as Christofle, purveyors of fine silver, and Gucci accessories and clothes. As the namesake of the street, **One Magnificent Mile**, at the corner of Michigan Avenue and Oak Street, is not to be outdone and has several shops and fine, somewhat expensive restaurants.

Once a guiding light

For a blast from the past, there's the former Playboy Building, now known as the **919 N. Michigan Building**. This 37-story Art Deco-style skyscraper was built in 1930 with a revolving beacon on top that was used to guide airplanes until taller buildings rendered it obsolete. At the northernmost foot of the

Map on page 166

TIP

One of the best views of Chicago by night is from the women's restroom in the Signature Lounge, the 96th floor bar of the Hancock Center.

BELOW: window shopping for the kids.

Shopping Centers

Once you've got them by the malls, their hearts and minds are sure to follow. Indeed, nowhere has the "malling" of America been more apparent or more welcome than in the shopping centers of Chicago.

To those who study such trends, the American mall is variously seen as a shrine to the national urge to acquire, or the new "town square," where elderly people walk, teenagers loiter and people with causes set up table.

There is no doubt, however, that most Americans see the mall as a place to explore. Studies show that more and more families regard shopping as a leisure activity. So a trip to the mall is a "day out" for the family, especially as malls add skating rinks, cinemas, and amusement centers.

Within Chicago, the crown jewel is Water Tower Place. This popular

shopping emporium features seven levels with 125 boutiques, salons, eateries, and cinemas in a dazzling array of steel, glass and marble.

The best way to tackle Water Tower Place is to take one of the glass elevators to the top floor, and then work down by escalator: jewelry by Christian Bernard; shoes by Browns; gifts by Chiasso.

Across Michigan Avenue, Bloomingdale's bestows its aura on over 50 shops. A huge colorful mural adorns the atrium and the Four Seasons Hotel looms 58 stories tall in the same structure as this elegant mall.

Nearby, at 700 N. Michigan Avenue, is glitzy Chicago Place. The 80 shops, spread over eight levels, include stalwarts such as Saks Fifth Avenue and high-ticket emporia such as Louis Vuitton. An eighth-floor food court wraps around an indoor garden. The barrel-vault dome and Prairie School-inspired trappings provide visual relief.

Northwest of the city, the suburb of Skokie offers the Old Orchard Center, an outdoor, low-slung, neatly arranged set of boutiques and department stores. A pool, stone islands, delicate Japanese bridges, flower beds and welcoming benches add a cool touch during hot summer months. Arcades protect shoppers from the elements and the whole complex is kept scrupulously clean. Old Orchard's 60-plus shops include Saks Fifth Avenue and Marshall Field.

Farther north, Northbrook Court is a grande dame of malls – enclosed, bi-leveled, unmistakably tennis-set suburban. The 144 stores arrayed around broad intersecting aisles and plazas with modernist sculpture, include Neiman-Marcus, Circle Gallery, and Mark Shale.

Finally, for the truly dedicated who don't mind the trek, there's Woodfield Mall in Schaumburg, a granddaddy of US malls containing a whopping 235 shops. During the summer, up to 200 buses a day bring customers from a four-state area to shop at Schaumburg's stores. ❏

LEFT: multilevel parking at the mall.

Magnificent Mile, at Michigan Avenue and Walton Street, is the **Drake Hotel**, built in 1920. The Drake faces the lake and Oak Street Beach on the north, and offers the weary walker a lobby in the manner of the grand hotels of Europe.

On its north side, the hotel anchors **E. Lake Shore Drive** – a one-block street said to be the single wealthiest block in Chicago, and one of the wealthiest in the world. Some of the amenities in the elegant buildings, constructed between 1912 and 1929, include bedroom vaults for furs at 209 E. Lake Shore Drive; a turntable on the garage floor of the Drake Tower, just east of the Drake Hotel, to allow incoming cars to turn around swiftly so they can drive right out again; and refrigeration for garbage at the Mayfair Regent Hotel, lest it develop a smell. Advice columnist Ann Landers lives here. TV personality Oprah Winfrey lives here. Nancy Reagan lived here as a girl. Abra Wilkin, a granddaughter of John D. Rockefeller, lives in the Drake Tower penthouse, and once hired helicopters to bring up materials for a redecorating job.

Walk east, then turn back south on Lake Shore Drive to see 860 and 880 N. Lake Shore Drive, two apartment buildings designed in 1952 by Mies van der Rohe. To reach **Oak Street Beach**, double back to the southeast corner of Michigan Avenue and E. Lake Shore Drive, and duck down the pedestrian underpass. Return to the underpass, this time veering right to the west side of Lake Shore Drive. Emerge at the corner of the drive and Oak Street for a stretch of high-fashion shops.

Rushing out

At the end of the block is **Rush Street**. Once known as Chicago's nightclub district, the area is still popular with suburban revelers who pack taverns near

Map on page 166

TIP

If your budget doesn't stretch to a night or two at the Drake Hotel, treat yourself instead to afternoon tea in the sumptuous lobby.

BELOW: taking a break.

Map on page 166

TIP

For the best people-watching in Chicago, grab a window stool in Starbuck's on Rush Street at Oak.

RIGHT: finding your bearings outside one of the malls.
BELOW: modern Lisa.

Rush, State and Division streets. Rush Street itself is more elegant, with intimate restaurants, cafes and quaint boutiques. West of N. Michigan, between the river and Chicago Avenue, is one more example of an old industrial Chicago neighborhood turned condo. Filled with new developments and restaurants amid old warehouses turned lofts, **River North** offers housing for young professionals, with quick access to the Loop.

Gold Coast

Just north of Division Street, on State Parkway, is a charming Art-Moderne apartment building constructed in 1938 with glass blocks wrapped around its curved corners. This area along Lake Shore Drive is known as the **Gold Coast**, a preserve of wealth and elegant architecture. One block west is Astor Street, and the **Astor Street District**, the heart of the Gold Coast.

At the northwest corner of Burton and Astor streets stands the district's largest building, **Patterson House**, a Renaissance revival home designed by New York architect Stanford White, commissioned in 1892 by *Chicago Tribune* publisher Joseph Medill as a wedding gift for his daughter and son-in-law. Also notable are the **James Charnley House**, at 1365 N. Astor Street and designed by Frank Lloyd Wright; the James Houghteling houses at 1308–12 N. Astor, designed in neo-Elizabethan style by architect John Wellborn Root in 1887, as well as the 1922 French Renaissance revival Joseph T. Ryerson House at 1406 N. Astor.

There is also the Art-Deco **Edward P. Russell House** at 1444 N. Astor Street, designed by Holabird and Root in 1929, and two Art-Deco apartment buildings at 1301 and 1260 N. Astor Street. At the northern end of Astor at **North Boulevard** is the earliest house on the block, a large Queen Anne mansion

designed by Alfred F. Pashley in 1880 as the residence for the Roman Catholic Archbishop of Chicago. Around the corner, at 1524 N. Lake Shore Drive, is one of the city's more unusual museums. The **International Museum of Surgical Science ❽** (open Tues–Sat 10am–4pm; closed Sun and Mon; entrance fee; tel: 312-642 6502) tells the history of surgery, with a gruesome variety of surgical instruments.

Heading back west, do not miss the lovely, lacy apartment building at **1550 N. State Parkway,** designed in 1912 by Benjamin Marshall and Charles E. Fox.

Old Town

Walk west on North Boulevard, which becomes North Avenue. One block past La Salle Street is Wells Street and the heart of **Old Town**, a neighborhood that has veered from wealth to seediness and back up to wealth again. The side streets north and west of the intersection are lined with pretty townhouses. Old Town has become a bridge between the elegant Gold Coast and yuppie **Lincoln Park**.

Just north of North Avenue, on Wells Street, is the home of **Second City**, the innovative comedy club that served as a training ground for such stars as Elaine May, Alan Arkin, Joan Rivers, John Belushi and John Candy. Wells Street south of North Avenue, once a hippie haven, is now a strip of fancy shops, bars and restaurants. ❑

CHICAGO
■ P L A C E

◆ SAKS FIFTH AVENUE ◆

THE LAKESHORE

Lake Michigan is the jewel in Chicago's crown, and the lakeshore a source of fun activities and attractions, from Navy Pier and the Children's Museum to the Shedd Aquarium and Lincoln Park Zoo

Map on page 180

Nothing defines Chicago more than its lakefront. **Lake Michigan** is the city's front yard: an urban vacationland, outdoor sports playground and important cultural center. Chicago is situated at the southern tip of Lake Michigan, one of the five freshwater Great Lakes formed by melting glaciers at the end of the last Ice Age. With the coming of the European explorers in the 17th century, the site quickly became a trading center because of the transportation crossroads formed between the lakes and nearby inland rivers.

More than 900 ft (274 meters) deep in places, 300 miles (480 km) long and 118 miles (189 km) across, Lake Michigan is the second largest of the Great Lakes. It has a profound effect on the city's weather, acting as a sort of insulating blanket that keeps lakefront neighborhoods cooler in summer and a bit warmer in winter. It unleashes fierce winds that come sweeping down over the water, picking up moisture and sometimes dumping "lake effect" snow on the city.

Leisure by the lake

In the minds of Chicagoans, the city's 29-mile (46-km) lakeshore is the third coast of the US. Visitors are surprised by its breadth and beauty. Other cities may boast waterfronts that are in fact more stunning, but Chicagoans will argue, with good reason, that none beats theirs for fun.

Chicagoans make the most of hot summer temperatures by flocking to the lake for a day of play. Even in the coldest weather, when steam rises eerily from the icy water, some hardy souls regularly bundle up for a stroll. In the chill of spring, smelt fishermen along the shore huddle to keep warm.

Weather permitting, Chicagoans can lie on a beach, sail, visit a zoo, picnic, windsurf, hear a concert, see a play, watch a ballet, hit a bucket of golf balls, play chess, eat brunch, jog, roller skate, ride a bike or see an airshow, all within a few square miles.

Architect Daniel H. Burnham in the early 1900s was the first to visualize the lakefront's possibilities as a recreational center. He rejected the typical waterfront development pattern which was dominated by shipping and other industrial users. The immense scale of the lake inspired Burnham to draw an ambitious plan for a chain of parks, beaches, cultural facilities and pleasure boat harbors along the shore.

A trip along **Lake Shore Drive**, a thoroughfare skirting the shoreline on one side and skyscrapers and parks on the other, is a glorious way to take in the lakefront and city skyline. The drive stretches 124 blocks from Hollywood Avenue on the north to Jackson Park on the south.

But better yet, those with the time should take a walk or a bike ride. The lakefront is laced with

PRECEDING PAGES: waiting for a ship to come in. **LEFT:** pier approval. **BELOW:** married on the beach.

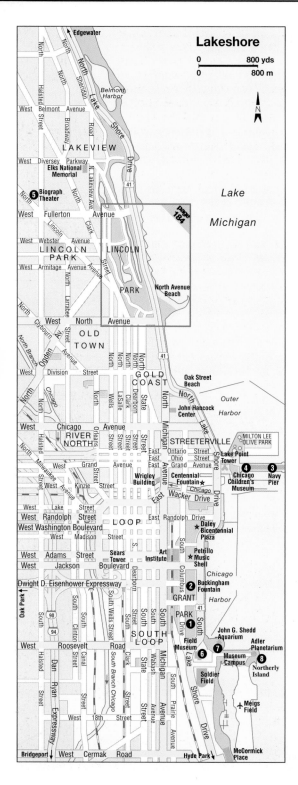

Lakeshore

0   800 yds
0   800 m

jogging paths and bicycle trails scenic enough to entice even the most dedicated couch potato into exercise. There are many museums, harbors and historic points along the way.

The bike path pretty much parallels the course of Lake Shore Drive on its east side. But beware: bike paths and beach areas often become dangerously crowded in the summer. It will take a little practice to avoid all the rollerbladers, runners and cyclists. The best time to escape the mob scene is early morning or late afternoon.

Another picturesque way to enjoy the lakefront is to view it from the water itself. There are a half-dozen or so good **boat tours** of the city, including several offering lunch or dinner cruises. They leave from Navy Pier at Grand Avenue and the lake, and from the Chicago River, next to the Wrigley Building (410 N. Michigan Avenue).

On the edge of the Loop, **Grant Park ❶** is home to several of the city's famous museums: the Art Institute, Field Museum, Shedd Aquarium and Adler Planetarium (*see page 143 for more on the Art Institute*). The center of the violent 1968 antiwar riots during the Democratic National Convention, Grant Park's biggest crowds these days come to the Petrillo Music Shell (Columbus Drive and Jackson Drive) for its lively array of free concerts.

The **Grant Park Symphony** performs on weekends during the summer. Its weekend-long music festivals – the **Blues Fest** in early June and **Jazz Fest** in late August or early September – draw fans from around the world. Thousands of picnickers enjoy the music, dance and savor one of the finest views of the city's skyline.

In the week and a half leading up to the Fourth of July, scores of local eateries sell their Chicago-style and ethnic cuisine at the **Taste of Chicago** festival. On Independence Day itself, fireworks light up the sky and the symphony plays a rousing version of Tchaikovsky's 1812 Overture. Another nearby attraction is **Buckingham**

Fountain ❷ which, each summer evening at 9pm, throws jets of water as high as 135 ft (41 meters). At night, concealed lights turn the jets yellow, pink, blue and green, creating one of the lakeside's more spectacular kinetic effects. Modeled after a fountain at Versailles, it was given to the city by heiress Kate Buckingham in memory of her brother, Clarence, a director of the Art Institute. Outdoor concerts are a pleasant feature of the nearby **Petrillo Music Shell**.

Towards the north end of Grant Park is the **Daley Bicentennial Plaza** where, from November to March, there is an excellent, free skating rink. Just north of the river, **Centennial Fountain** entertains passersby with an entrancing display on the hour from 10am to 2pm and from 5pm until midnight. Just east of North Pier, past Lake Shore Drive, is **Lake Point Tower**, a curving, three-lobed condominium building whose architects took their inspiration from a 1921 Mies van der Rohe proposal for a Berlin skyscraper.

Varied past

To the north, at Grand Avenue, **Navy Pier** ❸ stretches almost two-thirds of a mile into the lake. Its tip provides what some people claim is the best lakefront vantage point in the city. A multi-million dollar facelift begun in 1990 changed dilapidated to dazzling. The city spruced up the pier's image with picnic tables and flowers. Art classes and free concerts under the canopy are included in the pier's expanded summertime programs. Cyclists, skateboarders, roller skaters and fishermen are welcome. There's a **Ferris wheel**, a carousel, and, in the summer, a large paddling pool that becomes a skating rink in the winter. Parents traveling with fidgety children will find the nearby **Chicago Children's Museum** ❹ (open Tues–Sun 10am–5pm, and Mon during summer; entrance

Map on page 180

Making music on the street.

BELOW: an artist at work at Buckingham Fountain.

free Thurs 5–8pm; tel: 312-527 1000) a godsend, with exhibits aimed at children of all ages. They can explore the Climbing Schooner, have fun putting their ideas into practice with the Inventing Lab, solve lots of puzzles, create paintings and ceramics, or join a studio "television panel" and see how they performed in the videotape afterwards.

Olive Park, surrounding the city water filtration plant at Ohio Street, has a small but good beach and tree-shaded area for lounging on the grass. It was named for a soldier, Pfc. Milton Olive Lee, who died in Vietnam in 1966 by throwing himself on a hand grenade to save the lives of four friends.

It's easy to see why the Lincoln Park neighborhood is so popular: on the east side residents enjoy the park and lake, and to the west they have tree-lined streets, a huge choice of eating-places, and interesting shops to browse in. There isn't a wealth of landmarks in Lincoln Park, but the **Biograph Theater ❺**, where gangster John Dillinger was famously betrayed and shot dead in 1934 (*see page 38*), is on Lincoln Avenue and the **Elks National Memorial** occupies the southwest corner where Diversey and Lake View Avenue meet.

Sports by the lake

The park has something to offer sports enthusiasts of all kinds. At Diversey, west of Lake Shore Drive, is a driving range for golfers. The **golf course** itself is just north of Addison Street. The Chicago Park District maintains more than two dozen sandy beaches along the lakefront, bordering some of the city's richest and poorest neighborhoods. They are officially open (that is, manned by lifeguards) from mid-June, when public schools let out for the summer, to Labor Day. But hardy swimmers can plunge in at their own risk any time the weather

BELOW: "mum" display, Lincoln Park Conservatory.

TOURING THE LAKE

The boat tours that depart from Navy Pier offer a marvelous view of the Chicago skyline, and there is a variety of tours aimed at suiting all tastes. The *Odyssey* and *Spirit of Chicago* both offer lunch and dinner cruises all year round. For a romantic atmosphere, check out the *Odyssey's* midnight cruise, operating in the summer months only.

Hearty souls who crave a truly nautical experience should climb aboard the *Windy*, a schooner with ample deck space. The ship's friendly crew members offer information about the boat and the lake, and passengers are invited to help trim the sails or even take the helm. As the boat heads further away from shore, a panoramic view of the city unfolds, and passengers can see the city's south side and north side at the same time.

Those for whom a boat tour isn't a boat tour without the opportunity to have a drink in hand should try the *Ugly Duck*, a bright yellow cruiser that is essentially a floating nightclub. Deck space is somewhat limited, but passengers can sit at tables inside, order cocktails, partake in a buffet, dance or listen to music and view the magnificent skyline while avoiding lake breezes that can chill bones even at the height of summer.

allows. The beaches are free, easy to find and very accessible – they are usually named for the nearest cross-street. On peak summer days, finding parking may be hard, so walking, taking a cab or using public transportation is wise.

Map on page 180

The city's most famous stretch of sand is **Oak Street Beach**. Located across Lake Shore Drive from the posh high-rises of the city's Gold Coast neighborhood and only steps from Oak Street's exclusive boutiques, this is where the beautiful people go. There is also some serious beach volleyball played here. To get to the beach, use the pedestrian underpass at Michigan Avenue and Oak Street. Other popular beaches at **North Avenue** and **Fullerton Avenue** are frequented by the youthful, arty and sophisticated residents of the nearby Lincoln Park neighborhood. A bit south of the North Avenue beach house (hard to miss because it resembles a steamship) is an open-air chess pavilion. Farther north, Foster Avenue Beach, popular among urban youths, is known for its pick-up basketball.

The most crowded weekend of the season is in mid-August, when Chicago holds its yearly air-and-water show. Hordes of spectators jam the beaches to view the aerial parade featuring daredevil stunts and aircraft of all kinds.

Freewheelin' through summer.

The museum district

South of the formal boundaries of the Loop, the Field Museum of Natural History, Shedd Aquarium and Adler Planetarium, which are collectively known as **Museum Campus**, draws travelers and scholars. The **Field Museum ❻** (open daily 9am–5pm; entrance free Wed; tel: 312-922 9410) contains more than 20 million artifacts. Named after Marshall Field I, one of the principal benefactors, the museum was built in 1921 from a Daniel Burnham design, and

BELOW:
chess pavillion in Lincoln Park.

is regarded as one of the best museums in the world for anthropology, botany, zoology and geology.

An enormous dinosaur, a brachiosaurus, welcomes visitors to the high-ceilinged entrance hall, along with a pair of African elephants that, for many Chicagoans, are a symbol of the museum. One of the most spectacular exhibits, the life-sized tomb of Unis Ankh, scion of the Fifth Dynasty Pharaoh, has been carefully reconstructed, down to two original tomb chambers excavated in 1908. The labyrinth's display cases merge into a human-scale model of an ancient Egyptian village. Gem lovers gravitate through the extensive array of precious stones to gawk at the Chalmers Topaz, resplendent in all its 5,890 carats. The jade room has a superb collection of Orientalia, tempered by a small sampling of ancient jade. This stone comes not only in green but also in rich ox – blood red, mustard-seed yellow and white flecked with carmine.

In the swim

Nearer the lake, in the **Shedd Aquarium ❼** (open daily 9am–5pm, weekends 9am–6pm weekends; discount Mondays; tel: 312-939 2438), 90,000 gallons (340,000 liters) of sea water provide a home for sharks, eels, sea turtles and other denizens of the Caribbean deep in the world's biggest public fishbowl. Divers swim among the creatures two or three times a day, doling out food as spectators crowd around, cameras ready to snap a hammerhead shark or moray eel literally eating out of a diver's hand. The Shedd Aquarium's Oceanarium duplicates a Pacific Northwest environment for whales, dolphins, sea otters and seals.

The **Adler Planetarium ❽** peers up at the heavens from the northern point of Northerly Island, a five-minute walk from Lake Shore Drive via Achsah

BELOW:
blowing bubbles
by the beach.

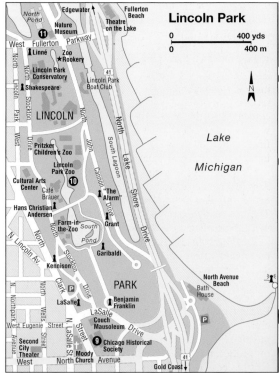

Lincoln Park

Bond Drive. The planetarium (open daily 9am–5pm, Fri 9am–9pm; entrance free Tues; tel: 312-922 7827) project pictures of the night sky as it was when Tyrannosaurus Rex roamed the Midwests Cretaceous swamps and forests.

Friday nights, weather permitting, which, unfortunately, it seldom does, the show culminates with a closed-circuit TV panorama of the sky through a direct feed from the 20-in (50-cm) Doane Observatory telescope. There's also a three-story museum that includes a moon rock collected by the Apollo 15 astronauts, and the telescope through which Sir William Herschel first sighted the planet Uranus. More recently, a 60,000-sq-ft (5,600-sq-meter) addition was opened, featuring the StarRider Theater. The new addition also offers panoramic views of the sky, Lake Michigan and the Chicago skyline and visitors can enjoy casual dining with a tremendous view in the Adler's new cafe. Just south of Grant Park are two of the city's most-visited facilities: **Soldier Field**, home of the Chicago Bears football team, and the enormous **McCormick Place** (tours available; tel: 312-791 7000), convention capital of the world. Small children may enjoy checking out the planes coming into nearby **Meigs Field**.

**Maps:
Area 180
Park 184**

Zoo star with stripes.

Lincoln Park

Farther north, the 1,000-acre **Lincoln Park**, Chicago's largest park, borders the lake between North and Hollywood avenues. The park has been called Chicago's Central Park, and in fact the two were designed by the same landscape architect, Frederick Law Olmstead. It's a fine grassy park suited for strolling and picnicking, complete with rambling walks, lagoons and ponds, footbridges, gardens, bronze statues, two museums, a zoo and several cafes.

At Lincoln Park's southern tip, at North Avenue and Clark Street, sits the red-brick **Chicago Historical Society 9** (open daily 9.30am–4.30pm, Sun 12–5pm; entrance free Mon; tel: 312-642 4600). Its exhibits highlight the city's colorful history and characters, including pioneer life, Fort Dearborn, the Chicago Fire and the gangster era. Especially good are its collection of materials on Abraham Lincoln and the Civil War. Nearby, half hidden by shrubbery, is the **Couch Mausoleum**, a reminder of the days when the park was a municipal cemetery. At the time of the Chicago Fire, the city was moving coffins to private cemeteries. When the fire roared north, families took refuge here, climbing into open graves to escape the blistering inferno.

The park's best-known attraction is **Lincoln Park Zoo 10** (open daily 9am–5pm; entrance free; tel: 312-836 7000) The fact admission is free is remarkable. The zoo is famous for its great ape house, with a world-renowned collection of gorillas.

The **Farm-in-the-Zoo** consists of several big red barns that offer visitors a sample of rural life, including cows being milked and chicks hatching. The zoo Rookery provides a peaceful respite for a variety of land and water birds that come to feed and nest. Located near the regular zoo's west entrance is a children's zoo, open most days during the summer months. Just north of the zoo, on the northwest corner of Fullerton Parkway and Cannon Drive, is the **Nature Museum 11** of the Chicago Academy of

BELOW: the US national symbol, the bald eagle, in Lincoln Park Zoo.

Maps:
Area180
Park 184

Sciences, scheduled to open in the fall of 1999, where visitors can learn more about wildlife and the environment. The park is also home to some of the city's nicest gardens: the **Lincoln Park Conservatory** (open daily 9am–5pm; entrance free; tel: 312-742 7736) lush with ferns, palms, and other plants; and the **Grandmother's Garden**, between Stockton Drive and Lincoln Park West.

Not far away is an interesting, if somewhat age-worn, Viking ship. Dating from the Columbian Exposition of 1893, it is a copy of a 10th-century ship built by Norway for the exposition and sailed across the Atlantic by a crew of 12. At Fullerton Parkway, right on the lakefront, is the **Theater on the Lake**, which stages Broadway plays in the summer months. Strictly community theater, it's nonetheless delightful on a warm evening under the stars.

Shipping

Visible out in the lake just north of Grant Park is the system of locks that enabled engineers to reverse the flow of the Chicago River (*see page 147*). A massive digging project diverted its flow into the Illinois River and downstream to the Mississippi. Today, most shipping is done by rail or air. But the lake remains a vital part of the city's life. Most important, Chicago pumps its drinking water from the lake through intake cribs located two miles offshore. Bulk commodities still move through Chicago to ports around the world.

The **Port of Chicago** is located near the steel mills of the industrial southeast side at the Calumet River. The St Lawrence Seaway connects the Great Lakes to the Atlantic, making the city a mid-continent port for ocean-going vessels. Inland, barge traffic on the Illinois and Mississippi rivers links Chicago to the Gulf of Mexico. ❏

BELOW: Navy Pier entertainers.

Studs Terkel

Studs Terkel is best known for his five books of oral history including Working *and* The Good War *and his radio interviews on* WFMT. *Here, speaking into someone else's tape recorder for a change, he talks in his inimitable style about his adopted city.*

Chicago is the double-headed city. Our god is Janus, the two-headed god. Nelson Algren, of course, spoke of that often, most eloquently in *Chicago: City on The Make*. He spoke of the city of the night and the city of the day. He wrote of the winners and the losers, of the Jane Addamses and the Al Capones.

The myth, the legend, of course, is that after the fire they – all the people of Chicago – worked together. Nonsense. The fact is there was a split, a big split. Why, the Haymarket Riot came just 15 years later.

Chicago has always been split. The first fur traders – prototypes for our great robber barons – were gypping the Pottawattomies. It was a new land, a new country.

Then John Kinzie and his Anglo-Saxon Protestant crowd came here from back East, and the immigrants shortly after that, and everybody was stepping on the next guy. The Germans had a tough battle against the WASPS, fighting for Sunday beer. And the Irish had it tough – No Irish Need Apply.

Who came to Chicago? Hands. I call Chicago a city of hands. Hands is an old-time word for working person. And yet a crazy thing happened here with the rich men and their wives at the turn of the century. Mrs Potter Palmer and the other wives longed for culture. Whether or not they knew what it was, they wanted it. And so Chicago became a center for culture because of the wives of guys who were meatpackers.

So what's to see in Chicago? Well, let me tell you. You've got to see the lake, the goddam lake, so magnificent.

And just stand on the corner of Oak and Michigan, where you've got this crazy juxtaposition. You've got this magnificent lake, and right next to it are these crazy buildings where Xerox copies of things are being made.

There is no other city that has a lake, this natural wonder, right in the heart of it. And there's the beach, a common beach, a democratic beach. The poor, the middle class, blacks and whites – they're all on the beaches. And the Art Institute. Go there. And look at the goddam buildings, the architecture. Isn't it remarkable?

You know, I was born in New York City and I had asthma as a kid. But I was cured of asthma when I got to Chicago. We had a rooming house at Ashland and Flournoy. And I could smell the south wind from the stockyards. I just needed something, I think, and Chicago had the energy I wanted, and the feeling.

And then it got exciting. ❏

RIGHT: Chicago institution Studs Terkel.

THE NORTH SIDE

Trendy espresso bars, fine dining, great jazz, a baseball game at Wrigley Field and the chance to explore New Chinatown – the North Side's appeal lies in its diversity

Map on page 192

T he fattest madam in the 1860s on Chicago's North Side was Gentle Annie Stafford, who weighed 300 pounds (136 kilos) and liked to put on airs. So successfully did she drill her prostitutes in proper manners and refined conversation that, at the opening-night party of a new brothel, one backslapping girl bellowed at every man she met: "Who's your favorite poet? Mine's Byron."

More than 130 years have passed since Gentle Annie's day, but the North Side remains Chicago's classy side of town flush with restaurants, nightclubs, galleries, theaters, concert halls and people who like to put on airs. Naturally, this tends to grate on South Siders who talk about North Siders the way some Canadians talk about Americans – all the time, with great emphasis on the "us" and "them," defining themselves by the contrasts. North Siders, on the other hand, talk about South Siders the way Americans talk about Canadians – almost never. They forget the South Side exists.

Diverse lifestyles

But, if truth be told, Chicago's North Side is by no means a uniform world of wine snobs and effete theatergoers. To think so is to think like a South Sider. The North Side is a collection of diverse neighborhoods, ethnic groups and lifestyles, from the third-generation bungalow dwellers of the far Northwest Side to the Vietnamese of Argyle Street to the Koreans of Lawrence Avenue to the Poles of Milwaukee Avenue.

One good way to tour Chicago, especially north of Lincoln Park, is to follow old Indian trails. Most of the major diagonal streets, such as Clark and Milwaukee, run along the former trails. Because they are among Chicago's earliest roads, they bisect many of the city's oldest and most interesting neighborhoods.

The first neighborhood as you venture north of Lincoln Park is **Lakeview** ❶, one of Chicago's most trendy residential areas. Bounded by Diversey Parkway and Irving Park Road, the neighborhood is home to mostly young white-collar professionals, and filled with fashionable espresso bars and kitschy restaurants. Clark Street serves up an array of tantalizing taste sensations including Thai, Japanese, French, Ethiopian and good ol' American treats.

The cultural heart of Lakeview is the baseball park **Wrigley Field** and surrounding area, **Wrigleyville** ❷, which is filled with houses, apartment buildings and bars with rooftop decks for a bird's-eye view of the ballgames. Local sports bars such as Hi-Tops Café and Murphy's Bleachers appease those without game day tickets. One of the best bars in Wrigleyville is Sheffield's Wine and Beer Garden at 3258 N. Sheffield. This bar somehow manages to strike a

PRECEDING PAGES: North Side churchgoers. **LEFT:** Wrigley Field lights up. **BELOW:** casual weekend elegance on the North Side.

pleasant and improbable balance between the yuppie need for fancy bottled beers and jazz music and the old neighborhood's traditional informality.

During the off-season, business booms as locals and visitors alike cheer on their favorite college or professional football or basketball team as well as any other sports venue which happens to be televised.

For more than a decade, a majority of Wrigleyville residents fought all efforts by the *Chicago Tribune* Co. – owners of the Cubs – to bring lights and night baseball to the old ball park. They worried that drunken fans might rock the night with noise, urinate on lawns and tie up traffic.

Cubs crazy.

They feared, at bottom, the Great Wrigleyville Revival might falter. As it happened, the *Tribune* prevailed, and night baseball came to Wrigley Field in the summer of 1989. It did, indeed, create a good deal of noise, rowdiness and gridlock. But the Great Revival never missed a beat. Property values continue to soar. The 3700 block of North Clark Street is one of Chicago's most avant garde. Check out Cabaret Metro for cutting-edge rock music, or the Ginger Man for its big pool tables and exotic imported beers. The "restaurant row" of Lakeview is N. Southport Avenue.

Victoriana

A block north of Wrigley Field is a one-block stretch of Victorian England, incongruously out of place and out of time. **Alta Vista Terrace** ❸, listed on the National Register of Historic Places, is a narrow side street of 40 striking houses, built in 1900 and modeled after a street in London. The ornate facades of the houses are paired, one on each side of the street.

BELOW: dual focus.

Northwest of Wrigleyville is an area called **Lincoln Square**. This stretch of

Lincoln Avenue remains predominantly German with imported beers and bratwurst available at the Chicago Brauhaus, 4732 N Lincoln Avenue. Merz Apothecary boasts homeopathic remedies since 1874. Delicatessen Meyer at 4750 N Lincoln has an Old World charm and ethnic treats abound. The **Old Town School of Folk Music** relocated to 4544 N Lincoln in 1997. Their new folk center features a concert hall, classrooms, gallery, music store and cafe. Housed in the old Hild Library building, the renovation combines treasures of old and new. It's definitely worth a visit – a real toe-tapper!

Back east to the old Indian trail, at Clark Street and Irving Park Road, lies **Graceland Cemetery ❹**, Chicago's most stately and historically significant resting-place. You can pick up a map at the front office and walk through Chicago's past. (Foreign visitors should not confuse this Graceland with the Memphis mansion of the same name, which is the final resting place of its former owner, Elvis Presley.)

The tombs at Chicago's Graceland include those of John Kinzie (1763-1828) the city's most prominent early settler, farm-machinery inventor Cyrus H. McCormick, meatpacking mogul Phillip D. Armour, retailing giant Marshall Field, architects Louis Sullivan, Daniel Burnham and Ludwig Mies van der Rohe, as well as civic planner and builder Charles Wacker. Near **Lake Willowmere**, in Graceland stands perhaps the most impressive monument in the cemetery, the intricately detailed **Getty Tomb**, designed by Sullivan and built in 1890. The limestone monument is considered by many to be a landmark of modern architecture.

Home of the stars

Graceland's elegance stands in dramatic contrast to the shabbiness of the community immediately to the north: **Uptown ❺**. Until about 1950, Uptown was one of Chicago's most exclusive communities. Wealthy businessmen lived in spacious Victorian, Prairie, Queen Anne and Georgian-style homes in Uptown's most exclusive lakefront neighborhoods. Movie stars of the silent era, including Charlie Chaplin, Gloria Swanson, Douglas Fairbanks and Mary Pickford, worked at the Essanay Film Studio on West Argyle Street. Big Band-era stars such as Tommy Dorsey, Glenn Miller and Frank Sinatra performed regularly in the famous **Aragon Ballroom**, 1106 W. Lawrence.

But Uptown's glamorous image was cruelly shattered by a post-World War II housing shortage. Many of its finest homes and apartment buildings were converted into low-rent rooming houses. The community was flooded with penniless newcomers, including Appalachian coal miners and Native American Indians. Uptown today remains synonymous with winos, the immigrant and migrant poor, flophouses for the homeless and half-way houses for the mentally ill.

Uptown has been rediscovered of late by the forces of gentrification – real estate speculators, housing rehabilitators and young professionals. The Aragon, serving up professional wrestling for many years, is

Map on page 192

Good sports are always welcome.

BELOW: Graceland Cemetery.

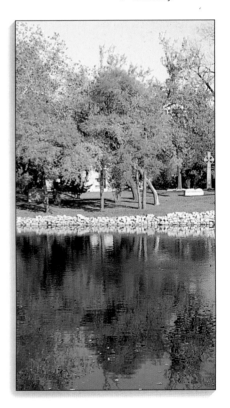

once again a hot concert and dance hall. And the nearby **Riviera Theater** also hosts an array of pop and rock concerts. The lakefront neighborhoods, particularly, are luring back a moneyed crowd. Former Illinois Governor James Thompson, for one, makes his home here. Thanks to gentrification and the recent arrival of thousands of remarkably ambitious immigrants from the Far East, Uptown is making a comeback. One Uptown neighborhood in particular stands out: **New Chinatown** ❻.

Until 1920, Chicago was the movie capital of America, and Argyle Street the home of a major film studio. Then, news got around about a great Californian land deal in an area by the name of Hollywood.

New Chinatown

This two-block stretch of Argyle Street, bounded by Broadway on the west and Sheridan Road on the east, pulsates with the verve and entrepreneurial spirit of Vietnamese and Cambodian refugees, a majority of whom are ethnic Chinese. Vietnamese and Chinese restaurants, grocery stores and clothing stores line the street. Thousands of Asian customers, ignoring seedy Uptown drifters, pour into the area on weekends for the good prices on 150-pound (68-kilo) bags of rice among other things, and the authentic smells and sights of home.

Argyle Street is a microcosm of the American immigrant experience. After the Vietnam War, Vietnamese and ethnic Chinese living in Vietnam fled to America and Chicago, choosing to settle on Argyle because rents were cheap. They pooled their meager resources and opened small stores and restaurants. Thousands now live in Uptown's tenements. A few have moved on to better city neighborhoods and the suburbs.

BELOW:

jazz clubs entertain in Chinatown.

Trung Viet Grocery offers a wide selection of traditional Vietnamese foodstuffs. The store was started by a family that came to Chicago from Saigon more than 20 years ago.

Map
on page
192

The other Chinatown, first settled by Chinese immigrants around 1912, is centered on Cermak Road and Wentworth Avenue and continues to serve as a Midwestern receiving area for immigrants from mainland China.

Around the corner from Argyle Street is one more Uptown treat – the **Green Mill Jazz Club**. The Green Mill, at 4802 N. Broadway, is a legendary Chicago late-night jazz and jam-session bar once owned by "Machinegun Jack" McGurn and frequented by Al Capone. In the 1940s, when Big Band musicians and torch singers finished a job at the Aragon or the Edgewater Beach Hotel, they would shed their tuxes and jam till dawn at the Green Mill. Among those who sat in were Frank Sinatra, Billie Holiday, the drummer Gene Krupa, trumpeter Roy Eldridge and drummer Claude "Hey Hey" Humphrey, who later died homeless, frozen in a grocery store parking lot in Uptown.

The Green Mill went sour in the 1960s and 1970s, when Uptown was at its seediest, but it has come back strong. It offers excellent jazz on almost every night except Monday, when the Poetry Slam is featured. The Slam is a Green Mill original where local poets with strong constitutions take the stage and serve up their best verse for the mixed crowd of locals and tourists. When they're good, the crowd cheers. When they're not, the crowd jeers.

A taste of New Chinatown.

Swedish models

Centered at Foster and Clark streets, just north of Uptown, **Andersonville ❼** is Chicago's last Swedish community and a fast-disappearing one at that. Swedish bakeries, delis and restaurants still dot Clark Street, but have been joined by Japanese, Thai, Korean and Assyrian establishments. When Andersonville celebrates *Midsommarfest* nowadays, blocking off Clark Street for an all-day

BELOW: focused on the road ahead.

Old Country summer fair, it assumes something of an international flavor. Strolling through Andersonville is a highly relaxing experience – walking down Clark, you can nibble on Swedish meatballs, Assyrian falafel or Turkish baklava, washed down with Thai iced coffee.

At one time Chicago had more Swedes than Stockholm. They settled in five neighborhoods, founded more than 50 churches and printed several daily newspapers. But their grandchildren moved to the suburbs. Now, by some estimates, as many as 50,000 Chicago-area residents – including former Governor Thompson – can claim predominantly Swedish ancestry. But relatively few still live in Andersonville. It is quite probable that Andersonville will eventually entirely shed its Swedish identity.

When touring the neighborhood – as the king and queen of Sweden did in 1988 – stop by Svea Restaurant, at 5236 N. Clark Street, an Andersonville landmark known for its authentic Swedish pancakes with lingonberries, herring salad, limpa bread and boysenberry cobbler. The 5300 and 5400 blocks of Clark Street have many Swedish landmarks such as Wikstrom's Scandinavian American Gourmet Foods at 5247 N. Clark, which features a spicy potato sausage called *potatis korv*, and The Swedish Bakery, known for its cinnamon raisin bread and marzipan cakes.

A hip place to relax and browse for travel books, maps and wearables – many from Third World countries – is Kopi, A Traveler's Cafe, at 5317 N. Clark in Andersonville. It has a full espresso bar and offers the weary tourist a selection of snacks, hearty soups and fresh-baked desserts which you can enjoy while sitting at a hand-painted table.

The best stop-off for souvenirs in Andersonville might be the gift shop of

BELOW: hurrying home for lunch.

DANCING TO ANOTHER TUNE

The number of dancers who descended on the Aragon Ballroom in its heyday in the 1920s, 1930s and 1940s often exceeded 18,000 a week. The owners, the brothers Karzas, had already opened the Trianon Ballroom on the South Side in 1922, and, encouraged by its success, opened the doors of the $2 million Aragon six years later, on July 15, 1926. For sheer elegance and opulent decor there was nothing else to touch it. The new dance venue, in Uptown on the North Side, immediately drew the crowds, many coming from outside the city.

The dancers loved the ballroom itself, which held 8,000, and was designed to look like a Moorish castle courtyard with palm trees and "stars" in the ceiling, and they liked too the fact that the men were required to show up in jackets and ties and the ladies were expected to wear evening dress. On the opening night – a lavish event attended by a host of politicians and celebrities of the day and reported in the next day's newspapers – the first ticket was bought by ex-mayor "Big Bill" Thompson.

Alas, the advent of television began to drive the number of dancers down and the last of the regular dances was held on February 9, 1964. Today the Aragon is mainly used for concerts and sometimes dances.

the **Swedish American Museum** (open Tues–Fri 10am–3pm, Sat and Sun 10am–3pm; small entrance fee; tel: 773-728 8111) at 5211 N. Clark. The museum features a permanent exhibit illustrating, through pictures and artifacts, the Swedish contribution to the building of Chicago.

For those last-minute gifts, head to The Landmark of Andersonville at 5301 N. Clark, a cooperative with three floors of shops selling country kitsch, clothing, ethnic crafts and collectibles.

Devon divide

Devon Avenue ❽, two miles to the north, is perhaps Chicago's most culturally diverse – not to say confusing – strip. To walk down Devon between Oakley Boulevard and Kedzie Avenue is to wander through another land. Represented are the shops of the New Guard – Indians, Pakistanis, Greeks, Turks, Palestinians, Syrians, Lebanese and Filipinos, as well as the Old Guard – Eastern Europeans and Russian Jews.

The best time to visit Devon Avenue is on a Sunday morning, when the sidewalks are jammed with crates of produce and men in *yarmulkes* and women in saris. In summer, the air is spiced with the intermingled odors of the Arab fruit markets, Jewish bakeries, tandoori chicken, hummus and espresso. For urban romantics, there is no better place to be.

Jews were among the first and last immigrants to settle on Devon. The first wave came from Eastern Europe in the early decades of the century. The most recent poured in from Russia in the 1980s, when the Soviet Union relaxed restrictions on immigration.

Asians began settling along Devon in the early 1970s. Devon is known

Map on page 192

Rock around the clock at the Hard Rock on North Side .

BELOW: Chinatown twins.

informally as Sari Row because it is lined with stores carrying Indian saris, fabrics, chiffon scarves and jewelry. Taj Sari Palace, at 2553 W. Devon, is one of the largest.

Devon also boasts quite a few Jewish and Arab butcher shops. Miller's Meats and Poultry sells meat that has been slaughtered and prepared in accordance with Jewish kosher law. Sawzi Suleiman and his brothers, the proprietors of Farm City Meats, supply fellow Arabs with meat butchered according to Islamic dietary law. In the 2900 block of W. Devon, the New York Kosher Market claims a cult following for its kosher hot dogs and salami. Patel Brothers Groceries at 2610 W Devon sell special Indian spices unavailable anywhere else. All the stores sell items unavailable in regular supermarkets.

If you have children, consider venturing a few blocks further north to **Indian Boundary Park**, at 2500 W. Lunt. The 13-acre (5.3-hectare) park has a terrific playground and its own small zoo which features alpacas, yaks, reindeer, swans, and goats, among other animals.

Poles apart

A second old Indian trail in Chicago, **Milwaukee Avenue**, starting west of the river outside the Loop and cutting diagonally through the city in a north-west direction, embodies the history of the single largest ethnic group in the Chicago area, Polish Americans. An estimated 1 million Poles and people of Polish descent live in the six-county Chicago area, the greatest concentration of Poles outside of Warsaw. Within the city, they have tended to settle in five geographically dispersed areas; the largest number historically have made their homes on or around Milwaukee Avenue.

BELOW:
a Milwaukee
Avenue restaurant.

The heart of America's Polish diaspora, **Polonia ⑨**, is on Milwaukee Avenue from Belmont Avenue to Central Park Avenue. Here, in an area called Jackowo, live Chicago's newest Polish immigrants, the best-educated and most sophisticated in the city's history. They love jazz and never learned to polka. Typically, these people may be certified accountants who are often forced to work as janitors.

The intersection of Milwaukee Avenue and Division Street, immediately northwest of the Loop, was called Chicago's **Polish Downtown** after the first Poles moved into the area in the 1860s. Unskilled laborers, they worked in the tanneries and factories along Milwaukee and the banks of the Chicago River. As Scandinavians and Germans worked their way northwest up Milwaukee Avenue, moving on to better lives in better neighborhoods, the Poles followed them through the neighborhoods. Today the old Polish downtown is gone. Second and third-generation Polish-Americans still live along Milwaukee, but in suburban-style neighborhoods on the far edge of town and beyond.

The biggest Polish restaurant on Milwaukee – and in all the Midwest – is in suburban Niles. Przybylo's White Eagle Banquet Hall, at 6845 N. Milwaukee (tel: 847-647 0660), claims that it can handle seven wedding receptions at one time, and is frequently put to the test. The new Polish Downtown is the **Jackowo** business district. Polish bakeries, bars and restaurants crowd the streets. Jackowo (pronounced *yahts-koh-voh*) is Polish for "hyacinth neighborhood." It takes its name from **St Hyacinth**, the local Roman Catholic Church. The Orbit, at 2940 N. Milwaukee, is a popular and boisterous restaurant in Jackowo known particularly for its pirogi. The **Polish Museum of America** hangs on in the old Polish Downtown, at 984 N. Milwaukee (*see page 212*). ❑

Map on page 192

BELOW: a Polish neighborhood bakery.

TIME TO CELEBRATE CHICAGO'S FESTIVALS

Chicagoans like getting together for a good time, and the city's numerous neighborhood and downtown festivals provide plenty of opportunity

Chicago is known as the City of Big Shoulders, but it could equally be known as the City of Big Parties. Throughout the year, Chicago residents flock to the city's numerous festivals to enjoy food, drink, entertainment, company and conviviality. Most of these joyous occasions are held on weekends or holidays, and many of them are held during the summer, but Chicago's festival season is actually 12 months long.

The city is home to a dazzling array of annual music festivals, food festivals, street festivals, ethnic festivals and art festivals. And the city likes to host the occasional parade as well. For a listings of events, see pages 278–9 in Travel Tips.

A CITY WITH TASTE

The king of the festivals – and the biggest and most popular of the many annual lakefront celebrations – is the annual Taste of Chicago, a massive food frenzy in Grant Park that takes place in late June and early July. As well as an abundant supply of food, there is also music and entertainment galore. Dozens of the city's restaurants set up stands for the 10-day gorge-fest, and over 4 million hungry people descend on them.

▷ **GENTLE WINDS**
An Andean musician forgoes pigging out in favor of playing pan pipes at the Taste of Chicago festival.

▽ **SWEET STREET**
A vendor sets up shop at the Belmont Street Festival, a popular neighborhood event held on the city's North Side.

▷ **LABOR LIBERTY**
The Statue of Liberty works a holiday, as a float bearing its likeness makes its way through the annual Labor Day Parade.

◁ **KIDS ON THE MARCH**
A group of excited young children clasp hands and precious balloons as they get ready to participate in the city's annual Columbus Day Parade.

△ **SHOWING CHARACTER**
Giant floats are a big attraction at the Christmas Day Parade. Here, a giant "Olive Oyl" is escorted down Michigan Avenue.

▽ **JAZZED UP**
A saxophone player belts out a number during the annual Jazz Festival, one of the city's most popular music events, held in Grant Park every summer.

GOING UP WITH A BANG

You might think that the inhabitants of a city which was once nearly destroyed by a fire would be rather wary of pyrotechnics. And yet fireworks are extremely popular in Chicago, and many of the city's festivals end with fireworks displays.

The White Sox, one of Chicago's two professional baseball teams, set off fireworks after some of their home games – sometimes even when they lose. But the city's most spectacular fireworks displays take place during the summer over the shores of Lake Michigan. One of the better vantage points from which to view these lakefront fireworks is Navy Pier, and the tour boats that dock there offer special fireworks cruises.

For the Fourth of July, which features the biggest display of them all, some fireworks fanatics reserve choice spots by pitching tents and camping out long before the show.

THE WEST SIDE

Map on page 206

This colorful collection of ethnic neighborhoods, much of it easily reached by public transportation from downtown, gives a fascinating insight into the marvelous melting-pot that is Chicago

Lacking a true center, Chicago's West Side offers students of urban development different focuses. Taylor Street at times resembles Lower Manhattan, complete with street eats and a carnival atmosphere each June when Taste of Italy erupts for a three-day gastronomic orgy of pizza, pasta, zuppa and vino. Wicker Park's perennial dilemma is whether to yuppify its aging frame house and gray stone ambience and set itself up as Newtown South, or to become a nest for the artistically and culturally dispossessed.

Greektown and Ukrainian Village are remnants of an ethnic Chicago that, urban renewal notwithstanding, retain some of their original color and character. Haymarket Square played a pivotal role in the early struggles of the American labor movement. Cabrini-Green is a failed experiment in public housing.

The University of Illinois at Chicago nibbles away at the surrounding community. The university began operating in 1946 at Navy Pier as a collection of temporary classrooms catering primarily to returning veterans. The move into the nucleus of today's campus at Harrison and Halsted, something akin to Godard's *Alphaville* or one of the more extreme Wagnerian stage sets, took place in 1965 amid hopes of creating "a Harvard of the Midwest." The reigning pundits recruited a crop of promising young scholars to make it happen.

Dominated by an inverted ziggurat that houses administrators and some faculty, the campus is a hodgepodge of structures. The **Behavioral Science Building** spirals like a labyrinthine concrete bunker, leading one professor to remark that he always expected a pellet of food to appear when he found his way to his office. Suspended walkways connecting the ziggurat, **University Hall**, with modular classrooms were supposed to provide cover during wet weather. As in so many Chicago projects, politics intervened. Substandard materials caused the walkways to leak water from the beginning.

PRECEDING PAGES: a Hispanic neighborhood. **LEFT:** backyard boogie. **BELOW:** leg men.

Settled in

Amid the stylistic mishmash, **Hull House ❶** (open Mon–Fri 10am–4pm, Sun 12–5pm; closed Sat; entrance free; tel: 312–413 5353) seems an oasis of dignity. A square brick 19th-century home now in the shade of the university, its gabled two stories rising over white colonnades, Hull House started life at 800 S. Halsted. Jane Addams and Ellen Gates Starr converted the stately edifice into a settlement house in 1889. Now a museum, Hull House unfolds the history of the West Side's ethnic population, from Jews at the turn of the century, through the enclaves of German, Bohemian and Irish immigrants, all of whom have contributed to the area's colorful melting pot.

West of the university, the thoroughfare of Taylor

Street is known as **Little Italy**. Italian ices can be bought on the sidewalks in summer and fine Italian food can be had year-round at some of the 30 restaurants spread through this community of about 8,000 Italians. Two of these are Rico's Restaurant at 626 S. Racine Avenue and the Rosebud Cafe at 1500 W. Taylor Street. There's another cluster of superb Italian restaurants in a dining area nearby, around 24th and Oakley.

Street shopping

Maxwell Street Police Station has enjoyed at least its 15 minutes of fame: the building's exterior appeared at the beginning of every episode of the "Hill Street Blues" television series.

Say the two words "Maxwell Street" in Chicago and an image of ethnic urbanites haggling over prices comes to mind. The original Maxwell Street Market was located off S. Halsted Street with its nucleus at Halsted and 14th streets. Less a location than culture, the Maxwell Street Market began as a push-cart produce market that miraculously survived the Chicago Fire of 1871. Maxwell Street has been home and shopping district to many nationalities and ethnic groups. In the late 1880s, immigrant Russian Jews provided the most pronounced ethnic flavor to the area. By the 1930s and 1940s, the Market began to take on the look and feel of a Southern farmer's market. It again recreated itself in the 1940s and 1950s as the proving ground for aspiring musicians.

Now at Canal Street and 15th Street, **New Maxwell Street Market ❷** is worth a walk-through, particularly on a Sunday morning, if only to watch a grassroots laissez-faire economy transcend racial and cultural barriers. From behind stalls and out of doorways, blacks and whites, Jews and Greeks, Latinos and Latvians conduct business.

BELOW: Maxwell St blues band.

Though bargains may exist, *caveat emptor* rules. The gold chain may well be 24-carat, as claimed, but the gold isn't likely to be more than a few microns

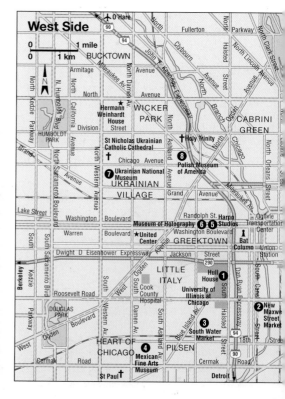

deep, and the "Rolex" or "Patek Phillipe" watches lining a hairy forearm are almost certainly from a Korean or Taiwanese factory. Locals and nostalgic suburbanites shop for kitchenware, garden tools and other stuff of daily life. Lounging policemen add their bit to the scene at Jim's Hot Dog Stand, 1320 S. Halsted, a stopping-off point for cheap franks or a Polish sausage traditionally washed down with orange soda or root beer.

Map on page 206

Hard underbelly

The belly of Chicago, **South Water Market** ❸, extends from 14th to 15th streets between Miller and Racine. Bays for refrigerated trucks, called "reefers," face each other across a boulevard-wide space where produce distributors take delivery of Georgia peaches, Maine cranberries, Texas and Florida oranges, Chilean grapes, lettuce and almonds from California, and broccoli, green beans and asparagus from all over the country. While primarily wholesalers, some distributors are not averse to a quick cash transaction, and early morning visitors often trudge back to their cars clutching a tray of dew-glistening raspberries or a 100-pound (45-kilo) sack of new potatoes.

Beat the blues.

Bohemia

Neighboring **Pilsen**'s mostly Bohemian population contributed significantly to Chicago's history during the freewheeling period of labor unrest in the 1870s. Today, the **Pilsen East Artists Colony** at 18th and Halsted provides a quieter avenue of expression for artists, sculptors, actors and writers, who hold regular individual exhibitions and hit the streets in October for their annual art fair.

Walkers will also find Mexican culture in contemporary Pilsen, notably at

BELOW: a Ukrainian Village wedding.

STREET WISE

In the city that created a blues style in its own image, one of the best places to hear the music is on the streets. Some say blues really got started during the Golden Era of Maxwell Street in the 1940s and 1950s, a proving ground at that time for aspiring artists.

In the late 1940s, artists such as Muddy Waters, Little Walter, Homesick James, Jimmy Rogers, Jimmie Lee Robinson and Eddie Taylor got their starts there, setting up along the streets and playing for tips.

There was also gospel, folk, jazz and polka. Daddy Stovepipe played country western and folk and Little Walter played waltzes and polka. You could walk down Maxwell Street and hear St Louis Blues, Beer Barrel Polka or the Tennessee Waltz. It was blues that made the most money, however.

As time went on, the University of Illinois at Chicago wanted the land around the Market. Many people felt Maxwell Street was an institution that should be saved , but it was not to be. When the market moved out, the blues moved into the clubs and bars.

Downtown street corners play host to the blues too, when individual performers and sometimes whole bands set up to play for donations from passersby.

BELOW: freight train on the move.

Casa Aztlan, 1831 S. Racine. Over a three-year period, Ray Pattan painted an exuberant panoply of Mexican themes halfway up the building's face. The best of Mexican art can be found in a more formal setting at the **Mexican Fine Arts Museum ❹** (open Tues–Sun 10am–5pm; closed Mon; entrance free; tel: 312-738 1503). But it is **St Paul Church** that makes the strongest impression in this essentially residential area. Buttressed, vaulted, and topped by five needle-fine spires, Henry J. Schlacks' Gothic fantasy at 22nd Place and Hoyne Street embodies a vision more usually associated with Gaudí or Horta than a 19th-century Midwestern church architect. Heading north towards Little Italy will take you in the direction of **Cook County Hospital**, the publicly funded safety net for the health insurance-less and inspiration behind the popular television medical drama series *ER*. It may be an old building, but the staff are top-notch and it would be hard to find a better emergency care facility anywhere.

Rail, post

Nearer the lake, in a corridor bounded east and west by Wacker and Clinton, are Union Station on Adams and Ogilvie Transportation Center, better known as Northwestern Station, used by Metra at Washington.

Union Station was intended to form the foundation of a high-rise, but the project never got that far off the ground. The station is worth seeing, however, for its exterior arcade supported by massive stone columns beneath a facade of rectangular windows and its somewhat seedy waiting room where the steel truss-and-plaster vault soars above to combine grace with grandeur in mid-air.

The **Ogilvie Transportation Center (Northwestern Station)** on West Madison is a relatively new replacement for the old Chicago and North Western

Railway Terminal, an architectural landmark where the classical portico and tesselated barrel vaulting in the main waiting room gave dignity to the whole idea of rail travel. In contrast, the present structure acts merely as a place for trains and passengers to meet. If you are near either station, and have the time to kill, check out the **Bat Column**, the towering sculpture in the form of a baseball bat that adorns the entrance of the Social Security office at 600 W. Madison. A few blocks west, then a block north, Oprah fans can worship at the seat of the chat show queen, **Harpo Studios** ❺ (*see page 93*). A couple of blocks to the west again is the **Museum of Holography** ❻, showing holographic art from around the world (open Wed–Sun 12.30–5pm; closed Mon, Tues; entrance fee; tel: 312-226 1007).

Greek eateries

Nearby **Greektown** lies north of the University of Illinois. For immigrants working in the markets on Randolph Street, Greektown offered a comfortable enclave of coffee houses, compatriots, shops dealing in Greek Orthodox vestments, candles, sacred images, Greek books and newspapers, but most of all a lively group of restaurants that remind them of their former homes.

Visitors today often seek out those restaurants, a dense patch along Halsted where the Dan Ryan and Eisenhower expressways wind about each other like fishing line before continuing their headlong flight into the suburbs. In restaurants with names like the Parthenon, Greek Islands and Rodity's, food and "neo – classical" theater mix well and customers join with waiters in celebrating the joys of eating, and smashing crockery, in good company.

Saganaki, Greek cheese doused with brandy and set aflame, is extinguished

Map on page 206

TIP

If you're running late for a train from Northwestern Station, you can pay for your ticket after you board, but it will cost a little more.

BELOW: annual Greek-American parade.

Feast for the eyes.

by lemon juice squeezed at the table, eliciting a loud shout of "Opaa!" in unison from staff and clientele. Most restaurants offer a family meal for four at very reasonable prices. Staples include *taramasalata*, a tangy pink fish roe spread; Greek olives and marinated eggplant; lamb braised with string beans or cauliflower, or baked; *pastitsio* and moussaka, noodle and potato-eggplant casseroles, respectively; and, finally, walnut-studded, honey-soaked *baklava* or rosewater-scented *galactoboureko* washed down with tiny cups of sweetened Greek coffee. Along the way, of course, there'll be ouzo, the anise-based aperitif that prepares the palate for the feast – or, some say, deadens it to the assault. Retsina wine, young and bracing, and spiked with resin, is a common dinner drink, along with the frankly sweet Mavrodaphne for the faint of heart. There'll also be lots of talk and smoke, perhaps some singing and once in a while even some spontaneous dancing and plate-smashing.

Bows to Kiev

Another holdover from the past, **Ukrainian Village**, occupies a chunk of territory in the vicinity of Chicago Avenue and Oakley Boulevard south of Wicker Park. Pride of place in the community goes to the **United Center**, home of Chicago **Blackhawks** hockey team and National Champion Chicago Bulls basketball team. The stadium, which has brought attention and investment to the community, serves as one more example of Chicago's prosperity. With capacity for 20,000 people, it is also used to hold concerts and was the site of the 1996 Democratic National Convention.

BELOW: a Pilsen neighborhood bar.

Pride of place in the community used to go to **St Nicholas Ukrainian Catholic Cathedral** on Rice and Oakley, an exotic, Byzantine construction

among the humdrum wood-frame and brick family houses that predominate in the area. The cathedral, built in 1913, is surmounted by a fanfare of ornate cupolas modeled on a Kiev original. The Milwaukee corridor, a onetime Indian trail that waves of immigrants gradually turned into a bustling mercantile microcosm of the developing city, leads northwest to **Wicker Park**, an island of gray stone buildings saddled with the description "mansion" by their original owners. A magnificent example of "gingerbread," the **Hermann Weinhardt House**, has been impressing passersby at 2137 W. Pierce since 1893.

The Wicker Park Association has touted its turf for a decade or so as an integrated, socially advanced center for alternative lifestyles. Yuppies buy and renovate buildings along Logan Boulevard to live in or to rent out, while blue-collar workers and the young unemployed gather in bars on Leavitt, Wabansia and Concord Place. Wicker Park today has been described by the *The New York Times* to be like Paris in the 1920s. The once Puerto Rican neighborhood has found its niche in Chicago's hip scene and today is peppered with galleries, antique stores, contemporary furnishing stores and eclectic art stores and cafes.

Just north of Wicker Park is an up-and-coming neighborhood known as **Bucktown**. Sharing many of Wicker Park's characteristics, Bucktown is home to Mexican families, artists and professionals. The same street in Bucktown is likely to have both a family-run Mexican restaurant and a French bistro.

Polish pride

A mile from Wicker Park, **St Stanislaus Kostka Church** is called "the mother church of all Polish Roman Catholic congregations in Chicago." Considering that Chicago's Polish population reputedly has been – and still may be – second

Map on page 206

Film producer Michael Todd, who was married to Elizabeth Taylor and died in a plane crash, grew up in Wicker Park.

BELOW: out for lunch.

only to Warsaw's, that's no small matter. Like St Nicholas, St Stanislaus reflects an Old World prototype, in this case a church in Krakow. Noble Street is also home to **Holy Trinity Church**, the focal point of fights, physical in more than one case, among parishioners of St Stanislaus and Holy Trinity over parish rights, as well as the German Catholic **St Boniface Church**.

Chess Records, the premier label for blues music, was the brainchild of two Polish-born brothers, Len and Phil Chess. The company was originally called Aristocrat Records.

Although burritos and pizza are now more common street food than kielbasa, two prominent repositories of Slavic culture fit comfortably into the neighborhood. To the west, on Chicago Avenue, the **Ukrainian National Museum** ❼ (open Thurs–Sun 11am–4pm; Mon–Wed by appointment only; small entrance fee; tel: 312-421 8020) displays the intricately-colored Easter eggs and folk costumes that Ukrainians remembered and recreated in their new homes. Documentary photographs of the life they left and the life they found in the New World promote a sense of unified cultural history that gives life to Ukrainian customs and provides a context for the folk art.

Reversing on Milwaukee and stopping at Augusta, the Polish Roman Catholic Union of America shares a building with the **Polish Museum of America** ❽ (open daily 11am–4pm; small entrance fee; tel: 773-384 3352). Here, special exhibitions and film festivals explore and help maintain the sense of ethnic identity shared by Chicagoans of Polish ancestry. A library of archive material draws historians of diverse interests to this scholarly cubbyhole just off the Kennedy expressway.

Riot history

BELOW: after pumping iron.

A few blocks south and east of the museum, **Haymarket Square** straddles Jefferson Street. The square was the site of an 1886 bomb blast that killed 10 people, including seven policemen, and provoked Chicago's most sensational and agonizing display of civic unrest before the 1968 Democratic National Convention and the Days of Rage. The Haymarket Statue, however, having twice (in 1969 and 1970) been knocked from its pedestal by student radicals, no longer adorns the historic patch of ground. The old statue, a likeness of policeman Thomas Birmingham, left hand raised in an age-old gesture of admonition, with helmet and belted coat reminiscent of London's bobbies, now holds court at the Police Training Academy on Jackson Boulevard.

Historically, Chicago finds itself in the middle of major movements from labor strikes to political chaos. Today it has found equilibrium. There was no better sign of this than the 1996 National Democratic Convention. Afraid the violence of the 1968 convention would be repeated, the city held its breath. It was a peaceful week and the city was able to start over with a clean slate.

Urban failure

The housing project **Cabrini Green**, condemned since 1993, must be included in any survey of the West Side. This urban nightmare began life in the early 1940s as a two-story project when it was leased mainly to returning servicemen and war workers. Black and Italian families, fairly representative of the neighborhood, also rented apartments in Cabrini Houses, as the complex was originally named. Robert Taylor, Chicago Housing Authority (CHA) chairman at the time, strongly argued for integration. Poor black neighborhoods were the chosen sites for most of the projects. The Cabrini Extension high-rises and William Green housing project were linked in the early 1960s, creating an island of low-income, chronically unemployed and underemployed tenants. The surrounding area, defined roughly by Division, Halsted, Chicago and Wells, deteriorated into a segregated slum that was regarded as one of the worst neighborhoods in the United States.

The quality of life in the ghetto continued to worsen as a result of several factors: the West Side riots in 1968, following the assassinations of Malcolm X and Dr Martin Luther King Jr; the development of gang fiefdoms; the isolation of the homes from nearby residential communities by a series of small stores and the commercial-industrial properties to the west on Halsted. Former Mayor Jane Byrne's two-week stay in the Cabrini Green projects during the early 1980s had no effect on the problems, though it amused some tenants and garnered national publicity for the mayor. The area deteriorated further and, by the time the project was condemned, police were no longer rushing into Cabrini Green when shooting was reported. Instead, they closed off the area until the gunfire stopped and then went in to tally up the dead and the wounded. The CHA made plans to turn the slum into a mixed-income community.

The result has been uneven. Many residents felt a genuine sense of community in the project, others feared the city's efforts would be half-hearted. Also, because of its proximity to the Gold Coast, Cabrini Green is attractive to developers and the fight to keep public housing in the area has been a tough one. ❑

Map on page 206

The majority of Chicago Housing Authority projects were built during the reign of Mayor Richard J. Daley (1955–76), and occupied by low income minorities. Huge urban ghettoes were the unsurprising result.

BELOW: watching baseball through the fence.

THE SOUTH SIDE

Map on page 218

This is where the renowned University of Chicago, the Museum of Science and Industry and Chinatown rub shoulders with grand old houses, ghostly steel mills, and an historic industrial village

Chicago's South Side was the home of the "Mickey Finn," the doctored drink that Michael Finn, the unscrupulous owner of the long-defunct Lone Star Saloon and Palm Garden, used to serve unwitting patrons in the 1890s so that he could rifle their pockets after they passed out. No need to worry though as visitors to the South Side today have a considerably better chance of remaining alert.

Such is the thinking on the South Side. As with any neighborhood rivalry or urban turf war, the roots of this north-south division are tangled in the past. t's difficult to explain the North-South friction in Chicago, but it dates back at least to 1839. That's when Chicago's first South Side pioneers settled in what is now downtown Chicago. They did this to be near the safety of Fort Dearborn and the trade of the Chicago River. Most of the early settlement was on the south bank of the river, west of what is now Michigan Avenue, making, for argument's sake, the first settlers South Siders.

PRECEDING PAGES: a daycare convoy. **LEFT:** Chinatown shop. **BELOW:** waiting for the tooth fairy.

Troubled waters

In 1831, the city fathers thought it would be a good idea to put a bridge across the Chicago River. The bridge was designed to open commerce to the North Side, an idea that the South Siders immediately deemed senseless. Since it was repeatedly rammed by boats trying to navigate the narrow river, the City Council eventually ordered it to be dismantled in 1839. Pioneer South Siders were jubilant and splintered the bridge with axes before North Siders could organize to save it. That animosity has remained in various forms throughout the city's history, particularly when it comes to important matters – none more so than baseball.

The Cubs play in a cute little ballpark on the North Side referred to as "the friendly confines" and named for a chewing gum manufacturer. For decades, the White Sox, long regarded as the city's working man's team, toiled on the South Side in a park named for a first-baseman called Comiskey. The park, at 35th and Shields, was built in 1910 and was the oldest in the major leagues until the White Sox built a new one across the street to open the 1991 season. The old stadium was knocked down shortly afterwards to create parking spaces. The new **Comiskey Park ❶** seats 40,000 spectators, four times more than the Cubs' Wrigley Field. It is easily reached via CTA, at the 35th Street station.

Bridge to City Hall

Since 1933, there has only been one mayor from the North Side. Richard J. Daley was almost canonized as

South Side

0   1 mile
0   1 km

Lake

Michigan

"Hizzoner da Mare" for his 21 years (1955 to 1976) in office. During the Daley era, Chicago saw the building of O'Hare Airport and the Dan Ryan Expressway, the vehicular spine of the South Side that was named for one of Daley's longtime political cronies.

Another South Sider, Harold Washington, who was elected in 1983 and died in office in 1987, enjoyed nearly Daley-like status in the black community when he became the city's first black mayor after an election scarred by race baiting.

Daley's son, Richard M. Daley, became mayor in 1989 and, like his father, continued to live in the old neighborhood – **Bridgeport** – until he bought a new home in the South Loop in 1993. While typical of the South Side's working-class roots, Bridgeport is not so typical politically. This small and otherwise insignificant neighborhood has produced five mayors, including three of the last six.

A favorite watering hole of Bridgeport and its movers and shakers of the 11th Ward is **Schaller's Pump**, 3714 S. Halsted Street. More than a century old, this tavern is nothing fancy but it's full of local color, right down to Frank Sinatra singing *Chicago* in style on the juke box.

Bridgeport, which is north of Pershing Road and outlined by the south branch of the Chicago River, was originally settled by German and Irish immigrants working on the Illinois and Michigan Canal. The I&M was a federal public works project designed to link Lake Michigan to the Mississippi River via local rivers connected to the canal. Bridgeport, named for the low bridge near Ashland Avenue that caused barges to unload and have their cargo portaged, became a boom town by the time the canal works were finished in 1848.

Later, Bridgeporters labored in the **Union Stock Yard**, as did the residents of neighboring Back of the Yards, named for its proximity to the stock yards. Here thousands of immigrants came to work, often in appalling conditions. Upton Sinclair's 1906 exposé *The Jungle* told of spoiled meats and miserable working conditions that caused a national uproar and brought about eventual reforms.

Map on page 218

Racial tensions

South Side working-class neighborhoods such as Bridgeport and Back of the Yards also figure in a problem that has plagued Chicago for decades: racial unrest. When strikes occurred in places such as the stock yards, blacks were often hired from southern states such as Alabama, Georgia and Mississippi to work as strike breakers. The two world wars also encouraged black migration to Chicago for jobs andthe economic competition led to frictionbetween the blacks and white immigrant workers. On July 27, 1919, a stone-throwing incident at the 29th Street beach led to the drowning of a black youth and the worst race riot in the city's history. It left 38 people dead and 537 injured. It is also part of a legacy of racism with which the city still struggles.

On March 21, 1997, three white Bridgeport teens beat a black teen who was riding his bike in the neighborhood so badly that he suffered brain damage. They were prosecuted for committing a hate crime, and one of them was sentenced to time in jail, while the other two got reduced sentences.

Like the stock yards, the once-mighty Chicago steel mills have faded away. Wisconsin Steel on 106th Street is a corrugated steel corpse: weeds and rust have replaced its 3,500 workers.

Historic Bronzeville

The area bordered by 31st Street on the north, 47th Street on the south, Martin Luther King Drive on the east, and South State Street on the west, is another South Side neighborhood of historical significance that the city is fighting to preserve: Historic Bronzeville. It was the final destination for many blacks in

BELOW: mural on Japanese-American Friendship Center.

TIP

You can be overwhelmed by the selection of places to eat in Chinatown, but the Sixty-Five Chinese Restaurant is the best to visit not only for its excellent food, but also for its convenience. It is located at the end of S. Wentworth Avenue, No. 2414, and it is the only restaurant on that crowded street with its own parking lot. Call 312-225 7060 for reservations.

BELOW: deep dish pizza is a specialty.

the Great Migration north between 1920 and 1950. It became a mecca of black culture in Chicago in a similar fashion to the role played by Harlem in New York City.

After it had been neglected for many years, the Richard M. Daley administration moved in the 1990s to develop it. King Drive was restored with a $10 million investment. The project included the installation of new park benches, 91 bronze plaques, and public artwork along King Drive, from McCormick Place to 35th Street, celebrating the area's black history. A new $65 million Chicago police headquarters was planned for 35th and State. Developers also moved in and started middle-class residential enclaves.

One such project was Bronzeville Point at 44th and King Drive, a development of 18 condos and town houses priced from $200,000. Notable buildings in the district are the **Robert W. Roloson Houses ②** at 3213–3219 S. Calumet, the only row homes that Frank Lloyd Wright built.

Chinatown

One of the South Side's most distinctly ethnic neighborhoods is Chinatown, a meandering gaggle of oriental architecture, restaurants and shops that was first settled by Chinese immigrants around 1912. Cermak Road and Wentworth Avenue is the main intersection of Chinatown. The neighborhood continues to serve as a Midwestern receiving area for immigrants from mainland China and Taiwan. Beneath the cheerful, crowded streets lined with many good restaurants, Chinatown sometimes seethes with crime and gang tensions. Even the On Leong building, considered the **Chinese City Hall,** has been raided for gambling in recent years by federal agents. Of course, this is not all that unusual for the

South Side – the home of Al Capone in his heyday. Indeed, not far from Chinatown is Capone's one-time headquarters at the old **Lexington Hotel** at Michigan Avenue and Cermak Road (2200 South). Capone had a suite on the corner, where he could keep an eye on the intersection below.

Map
on page
218

Mansion Row

In the mid 19th century the South Side was a place where worker and boss lived side by side. It was not unusual to see an early and perhaps sensory impaired meatpacker build his home right next to the slaughterhouse and its stench. By the late 1800s, however, the captains of Chicago industry had become a little more particular about their neighbors.

"Millionaires' Row" was **Prairie Avenue** between 16th and 22nd streets. It was the unofficial home roosting ground for the city's first entrepreneurs to make it big, including George Pullman of the Pullman railroad car, department store magnate Marshall Field, meatpacking mogul Phillip Armour and about 50 others who built mansions there. There is little here now to attest to the area's former pedigree, but the Prairie Avenue Historic District has preserved some of the old glory. Bertha Palmer, a major mover in Chicago society, helped bring status to the North Side when she convinced her husband to move away from Prairie Avenue.The elite of Prairie Avenue followed. With the millionaires moving north, the South Side's animosity toward the North Side grew.

By the late 1990s only 14 of the original millionaire mansions remained in the Prairie Avenue Historic District.Only about half of the 14 are being used for residential purposes. One of the grand survivors is Glessner House, at the corner of Prairie Avenue and 18th Street. It was designed by the famous architect

East meets West.

BELOW AND LEFT: welcome to Chinatown.

Henry Hobson Richardson for International Harvester Company founder John J. Glessner. It has been converted to the museum of the historic district, the **Glessner House Museum ❸**. A block away, and also managed by the Museum, is the city's oldest building, the **Clarke House ❹**, a Greek revival house originally built in 1836 about two blocks from where it stands now. Tours of both houses are available. A few blocks to the west is the **American Police Center & Museum ❺** (open Mon–Fri 9am–4.30pm; small entrance fee; tel: 312-431 0005). As its name suggests, this museum focuses on the history and working life of the police, and the exhibits include a disused electric chair.

A few miles south, just west of the University of Chicago, is the country's first black history museum, **DuSable Museum of African American History ❻** (open Mon–Sat 10am–5pm, Sun 12–5pm; Oct–April closed at 4pm; entrance free Thurs; tel: 773-947 0600), at 740 E. 56th Street. Founded in 1959, the museum has a permanent exhibit entitled *Up From Slavery* that describes the development of US slavery and includes documents and artifacts of slavery. The museum also has traveling exhibits in addition to memorabilia, sculptures, paintings and photos of and by African Americans.

Second city within the second city

The South Side has had a black population of varying sizes since the mid-1800s. That black population grew within the city as a separate Chicago, creating over the years a separate economy and a separate society. It was a kind of second city within the second city, a black metropolis.

The separateness of the city can best be seen through the lives of people such as Jesse Binga, a black man who came to Chicago with $5 in his pocket to look

BELOW: Buddy Guy, blues guitarist *extraordinaire*, hanging out outside the Checker Board.

POLITICAL CAREERS GO SOUTH

The South Side was the focus of much national political intrigue in the 1990s. The Illinois 2nd Congressional District, which includes much of the South Side, was represented successively by two Democratic congressmen, who found themselves leaving office for much the same reason – right under the dark cloud of sexual misconduct.

Rep. Gus Savage was an eccentric who represented the district for 12 years before he lost at the polls in 1992. A congressional investigation had found that Savage sexually assaulted a Peace Corps volunteer while on a trip to Africa.

The man who replaced Savage fared no better. Mel Reynolds, a university teacher and administrator, was forced to resign the seat in 1995 in the wake of allegations of sexual misconduct. Reynolds was eventually convicted on 12 felony counts, including criminal sexual assault and obstruction of justice, and sentenced to five years in prison.

A special election was held and the 2nd District voted for its third representative within five years. Reynolds' replacement was Jesse Jackson Jr., the son of the Rev. Jesse Jackson.

for opportunity at the 1893 Columbian Exposition. By the early 1900s he owned a bank and more than 1,000 ft (300 meters) of frontage on South State Street around 34th Street. He became a millionaire philanthropist, respected in the black community. But when he moved into a white neighborhood to fulfil the American dream of a spacious home, his house was repeatedly bombed. The Great Depression ransacked his fortune and his future. He was indicted for actions he took to save his bank and spent some time in jail. He died impoverished, working as a church janitor.

Map on page 218

Black spokesmen

Nonetheless, Jesse Binga was representative of a long line of black South Side millionaires who because of their race were often unknown to the white public. He was also one of a long line of South Siders who have offered strong and sometimes controversial leadership to the black community. Notable contemporary examples of spokesmen include Jesse Jackson and Louis Farrakhan, the leader of the Nation of Islam.

When Jackson resigned as national director of Operation Breadbasket, an aid group for the mainstream civil-rights movement, he was quoted as saying, "I need air. I've got to grow." With those words he founded People United to Save Humanity, commonly known to Chicagoans and throughout the nation as Operation PUSH.

PUSH was Jackson's launching pad. From the stage and pulpit of a converted temple at PUSH headquarters, 930 E. 50th Street, Jackson and just about every other major American black leader of the past quarter century has spoken to enthusiastic audiences. They are often accompanied by swaying, hand-clapping

South Side face in the crowd

BELOW:
Jesse Jackson.

choirs and peppery percussion sections. Everyone is welcome to visit and Saturday morning programs are perhaps the best time.

The Nation of Islam also has an institutional presence on the South Side that is worth checking out. The **Nation of Islam Headquarters Mosque** is located at 7351 S. Stony Island, just a five-minute drive to the southeast of the University of Chicago campus. The building is an impressive grey brick structure, with a domed roof crowned by a star and crescent.

Black leadership has been especially important on the South Side because of the racial divisions in a city called the most segregated in America. The South Side has often been portrayed as the base of the black political movement. It has been portrayed just as often as the poor side of town.

The projects

And indeed, driving south on the Dan Ryan Expressway past 35th Street, visitors see row after row of high-rises looming to the east – the Chicago Housing Authority developments, known locally as "the projects." This, the so-called **State Street Corridor**, is one of the poorest neighborhoods in the entire United States. These developments house some 37,000 residents, most of whom are black and 75 percent of whom are on welfare. It is a neighborhood of relentless poverty where drug abuse, violence and teenage pregnancy are commonplace. It is not a place to stop and sightsee.

In the 1990s the Clinton Administration brought change to the public housing situation in Chicago by assuming control of the Chicago Housing Authority and leading a plan that would make its properties more livable. The demolition of several of the public housing high rises was started and residents were

At one point the crime situation at and around the Robert Taylor Homes in the State Street Corridor was so bad that the US Postal Service refused to deliver mail there, and the authorities considered calling in the National Guard to protect children attending nearby schools.

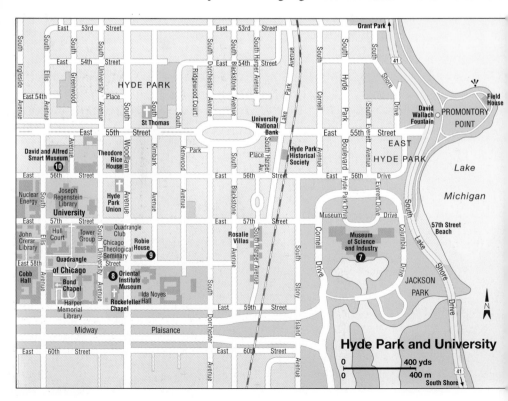

Hyde Park and University

relocated to mixed-income and private housing. Several of the State Street Corridor crime – infested high rises will soon be no more.

But only 50 blocks south is perhaps one of the largest black middle-class enclaves in the nation. **Chatham**, which runs east of the Dan Ryan around 87th Street, is a neighborhood of perfectly landscaped lawns and houses so neat and orderly they look as though they've been audited. Here, the black residents themselves joke that Chatham would seem like a typical middle-class white neighborhood – if the homeowners would stay indoors. Chatham is worth a visit for what many consider to be one of the finest soul food restaurants in America: Army and Lou's, at 422 E. 75th Street. The ribs, corn bread, and grits just don't get any better than here.

Beverly's hill

The nation's largest urban historic district, containing 3,000 buildings with national register status, is neighboring **Beverly**. Situated on a ridge 30 to 40 ft (9 to 12 meters) above the rest of the city, its residential architecture includes two homes designed by Frank Lloyd Wright and 17 houses designed by his student, Walter Burley Griffin, who designed Canberra, the capital of Australia.

To get a bit of local South Side flavor, stop in Top Notch Beefburger, 2116 W. 95th Street, for 1950s-style cheeseburgers and fries with chocolate shakes.

Pulled out

Farther south and east is another industrial ghost. The Pullman plant no longer manufactures luxury railroad cars in **Pullman**, a neighborhood once referred to as "the most perfect city in the world." That was over a century ago, when

Map on page 218

The South Side has produced some of the world's most talented musicians and singers, many of them spawned by the region's abundance of black churches. The list includes Lou Rawls, Minnie Ripperton, Chaka Khan, and Mahalia Jackson.

BELOW: Hotel Florence in Pullman.

Pullman had 8,000 residents, about a third of whom labored in the plants of George Pullman's Palace Car Company.

Pullman was a model industrial town, where the company owned everything. Workers were housed, according to their position, in tidy company homes on streets that were paved and landscaped by the company.

The village, located between 111th Street and 115th Street from Cottage Grove to Langley Avenue, is today a national landmark where even North Siders are known to visit, perhaps for an enjoyable brunch at the historic **Hotel Florence**, 11111 S. Forrestville. Some of the beauty of the buildings, fountains and reflecting ponds can still be seen, but restoration is a continuing battle. It's the kind of area that must be walked through, lingeringly, to be appreciated.

Despite the well laid plans of Pullman's corporate order, several years after the town was founded the workers began to feel squeezed. To them, it didn't seem fair that the company set rents and controlled prices at its local stores. In 1894, a precedent-setting strike brought violence and federal intervention to Pullman. Eventually, the Illinois Supreme Court ruled the company couldn't own the town. Employees were allowed to buy homes, but company support for the town disappeared. It was never the same. The last Pullman car was manufactured in 1981.

All in the numbers

South Siders then and now believe that their side of town is where "real people" live, the unpretentious folk who still rely on numbered streets – 95th Street is 95 blocks south of the Madison Street north-south dividing line in the Loop, for instance – instead of the regular descriptive named streets on the North Side.

BELOW:
Pullman homes.

The South Side also has machine shops, steel mills, can factories and, fittingly, the **Museum of Science and Industry** ❼, at 57th Street and Lake Shore Drive (open Mon–Fri 9.30am–4pm; weekends 9.30am–5.30pm; entrance free Thurs; tel: 773-684 1414). A $43.7 million improvement project was completed between 1997 and 1998 and gave the museum a new underground parking garage and more exhibition space. Most children (and grown-up children) love this museum for its clear explanations, practical demonstrations and hands-on exhibits of scientific principles and how they are applied to industrial uses and everyday life. The space center and Omnimax Theatre are also popular attractions.

Map on page 224

Fair tales

Another bit of South Side history was the World's Columbian Exposition of 1893, a giant fair that included: the first Ferris wheel, 250 ft (76 meters) in diameter with a capacity of 1,400 passengers, designed by George W. G. Ferris; "Little Egypt," a belly dancer who became a national sex icon of the Gay Nineties; the **Midway Plaisance**, a strip 1 mile long (1.5 km) and 300 ft (90 meters) wide that was lined with examples of the architecture of the world (now a wide grassway on 59th Street that runs through the University of Chicago); and grounds landscaped by Frederick Law Olmsted, who also designed New York City's Central Park.

Other legacies of the exposition include **Jackson Park**, the Museum of Science and Industry (originally the fair's Fine Arts building), and the name "Windy City," bestowed by the East Coast press because Chicago had been so loud and strident – also well-known South Side traits – in lobbying to

ABOVE AND BELOW:
Museum of Science and Industry.

Map on page 224

host the fair. In the end the event was a runaway roaring success, claiming 27 million admissions.

Just as the 1893 Columbian Exposition celebrated humankind's past, the next big fair in Chicago, the Century of Progress World's Fair of 1933, looked to the future. This expo, built amid man-made islands and lagoons along the South Side lakefront, used new building materials and modernistic designs to project a bold future despite the bleakness of the Great Depression. The 1933 fair unleashed another sex-bomb to titillate the American public – Sally Rand, the fan dancer who became famous for her glimpse-of-flesh routines.

The university

The cultural center of the South Side is the **University of Chicago** and the neighborhood known as **Hyde Park**. One local jewel is the **Oriental Institute Museum** ❽, a collection of antiquities at 1155 E. 58th Street (open Tues–Sat 10am–4pm, Sun 12–4pm; entrance free; tel: 773-702 9521). The institute has galleries representing many ancient societies, their art and artifacts: Egyptian, Assyrian, Mesopotamian, Persian and Palestinian. Each gallery is filled with hundreds of exhibits. The museum is due to reopen in 1999 after renovations.

Within walking distance from the Oriental Institute is the **Robie House** ❾ (several tours every day; entrance fee; tel: 773-702 8374), 5757 S. Woodlawn, a Prairie School architectural masterpiece designed by Frank Lloyd Wright in 1909. Along the majestic Midway Plaisance sits another South Side landmark, the **University of Chicago's Rockefeller Chapel**. Built in the mid-1920s, its modified Gothic design was intended "to remove the mind of the student from the busy mercantile condition of Chicago and surround him with the peculiar air of quiet dignity." The university today strives to maintain this theme of quiet dignity. Modeled after Oxford University in England, the gray stone buildings and the quadrangles they form can make for serene strolls with stops at some of the university's other sights, such as the **David and Alfred Smart Museum** ❿, at 5550 S. Greenwood Avenue, where exhibits feature quality art from ancient to contemporary (open Tues–Fri 10am–4pm, Sat and Sun 12–6pm; closed Mon; entrance free; tel: 773-702 0200). For fans of the very latest in art, there's the Renaissance Society on the fourth floor of the university's Cobb Hall at 5811 S. Ellis. This nearly 80-year-old museum has no permanent collection, but it is famous for helping to launch the careers of many contemporary artists.

The University of Chicago played a large role in the dawning of the atomic era. There, the first sustained and controlled production of atomic energy took place on December 2, 1942. A group of scientists, headed by Enrico Fermi, created the first nuclear reactor and, with it, the technology that resulted in the dropping of two atomic bombs on Japan in 1945 to hasten the end of World War II and, ultimately, usher in the four-decade-long Cold War. The Chicago experiments are commemorated by a **Henry Moore sculpture**, *Nuclear Energy*, on the site of old Stagg Field at 57th Street and Ellis Avenue. ❏

BELOW: cooling off at the university's Laredo Taft sculpture.

Urban Woodlands

Loosely ringing Chicago along much of its north, south and west borders is a green belt of natural lands, known as the forest preserves, set aside for conservation and recreation.

While other large cities have dedicated land to similar purposes, the Cook County Forest Preserves, comprising 66,746 acres of woodlands, recreation facilities and open space, is probably the oldest and largest forest preserve system in any US metropolitan area.

In addition to forests and fields, the preserves boast 15 golf courses and driving ranges, 33 fishing lakes and ponds, plus swimming pools, boat ramps, bicycle trails and picnic areas.

Unlike other cities, where forest land was set aside only after urban populations began moving away, in the 1950s, the concept of a forest preserve system for Chicago began last century. The goal was to establish areas where people could find relaxation in open space filled with natural flora and fauna. More than the mere acquisition of open tracts, the object was to preserve beautiful areas "for their own sake and... scientific value, which, if ever lost, cannot be restored for generations."

Run as a separate government agency, independent of both the city and the county, the Cook County Forest Preserve District is funded by taxes levied on all county property owners, and by small fees charged for use of its facilities. However, the Forest Preserve District board is made up of the same people who are elected to the County Board of Trustees. As a result, the district has long been a haven of patronage for the local Democratic party. In Chicago, even when you escape to nature, the political machine comes too.

Until the mid-1970s, the forest preserves were used mostly on Sundays for family outings, company picnics and the like. With so much of the metro- politan population having moved into the suburbs, however, the demand for picnic groves, bike and bridle paths is creating crowds for much of the week.

Overcrowding isn't the only problem caused by encroaching urbanization. Rural roads that had little impact on natural life within the preserves have been expanded into major highways; at the same time, housing and commercial developments have been built around forest preserve district holdings.

Fortunately, about 5 percent of the Cook County Forest Preserve District is set aside as part of the Illinois Nature Preserve system, which is even more conservation-oriented.

But the preserves aren't just used for daytime family fun. In the evening they are popular with couples, and are sometimes used to dump murder victims or deal drugs. Although the district has its own police force and civilization is never far away, it is best not to explore this area alone. ❑

RIGHT: beauty on the borders.

OAK PARK

Map
on page
237

Best known for its two famous sons, Frank Lloyd Wright and Ernest Hemingway, this Chicago suburb has other attractions, including a family-friendly conservatory and vibrant theater

O ak Park is a curious place – or perhaps two places. The inhabitants of this suburb 10 miles (16 km) due west of Chicago's Loop divide into two groups. One group includes all the normal citizens who get up, get dressed, go to work, clean the house, yell at the kids and run red lights when the street seems clear of police. The second, smaller group is a priestly class, the dead-serious Frank Lloyd Wright fans for whom Prairie School architecture ranks no lower than second or third in the history of great ideas.

Whether you are a Frank Lloyd Wright fan or not it is the popularity of him and other Oak Park notables such as Ernest Hemingway who keep the town a favorite day trip for visitors to Chicago all year round. Norman Mark, a Chicago broadcaster and a member of the latter group, reverently proclaimed, "To walk through Oak Park is to touch genius." He continues: "Oak Park reverberates with the ghost of Frank Lloyd Wright, an architectural genius who lived there, [and who] revolutionized residential building design…"

Which is true as far as it goes. Mark and other Wright advocates often fail to mention how dark and constricting his interior spaces may be as living quarters, how the flat roofs he gave to some Midwest houses implode under the weight of repeated snowfalls, or how ergonomically unsatisfactory some of his built-in chairs and tables appear on close acquaintance.

PRECEDING PAGES: a Wright-designed house in Oak Park. **LEFT:** fooling around in Oak Park. **BELOW:** Frank Lloyd Wright with a model apartment building, 1930.

Wright turns

Most visitors reach Oak Park via the suburban Metra commuter line or the El – the CTA Green Line – from downtown. Either way, get off at the Oak Park stop. The **Oak Park Visitor's Bureau ❶**, a few minutes' walk away at 158 N. Forest Avenue (tel: 708-848 1500), rents taped talks for self-guided tours, an ingenious idea for those who prefer a leisurely stroll to the frenetic pace often set by zealous tour leaders.

A quick count of shelves at the Visitor's Bureau reveals 26 books devoted exclusively to FLW, his designs and his philosophy, including a *Frank Lloyd Wright Home and Studio* coloring book for children. On sale are numerous postcards and posters, as well as mugs, T-shirts and shopping bags, clear indication that FLW has blossomed from mortal architect to immortal souvenir industry.

The reason for the adulation, of course, is the conspicuous near-absence of almost anything other than the Wright and the Queen Anne and Stick houses that make a walk through "historic" Oak Park irresistible for architecture buffs and an agreeable diversion for the rest of us.

But there are a few other things worthy of note in Oak Park, which has long been studied by sociologists who view the prestigious suburb as a classic

Oak Park's most revered man.

American suburb, not least for the way its more liberal-minded white residents encouraged middle-class blacks to become their neighbors in the 1950s and 1960s, countering the "white flight" that was furiously taking place in many other Chicago neighborhoods.

The **Children's Curiosity Corner** of the Oak Park Conservatory and Earth Shelter Classroom at 615 Garfield Street (open daily; entrance free, donation welcome; tel: 708-386 4700) keeps smaller youngsters happily occupied while dad and mom and the older siblings immerse themselves in exhibits that explore desert and tropical flora and the specialized biology of ferns. Collections of exotic plants, a waterfall and gardens of herbs combine with native Illinois prairie plants in this richly diverse part of Oak Park.

Cool diversions

Opposite the Visitor's Bureau, **Austin Garden** is equipped with benches and lots of shade trees which can be a godsend in the heat of July and August. A casual ice cream shop, a deli and a Starbuck's Coffee bar cluster nearby on Lake Street: Alonti Cafe features rustic Italian specialties including gourmet sandwiches on focaccia rolls, hot and cold pastas, soup and salads. After a delicious meal you can either move right next door for a coffee or stroll one block down Lake Street to Baskin-Robbins ice cream store.

Oak Park and contiguous River Forest share the **Village Players**, an air-conditioned and comfortable theater small enough to foster a sense of intimacy and engagement. As the view is good from anywhere in the house, tickets only a few dollars and productions usually light and contemporary (*A Funny Thing Happened on the Way to the Forum*, *Stepping Out*, an angst-free *Chorus Line*

BELOW:
a "bootleg" house.

WRIGHT AND WRONG

It could be said that Frank Lloyd Wright conducted his personal life as energetically as his professional, though the former earned him opprobrium. In 1911, he was widely condemned for leaving his wife and six children and moving with his mistress and her two children to Taliesin, Wisconsin.

In 1914, while he was working in Chicago, Wright received a telegram informing him there had been a fire at Taliesin. Upon arrival at Taliesin he learned the full, horrifying truth: a man who had been working in the Wright home had doused carpets in kerosene and set fire to them at the main door of the house.

As Mamah Cheney and her children, along with four other men who were in the house, desperately tried to escape the fire, they were butchered in cold blood with an axe by the man.

Wright looked for comfort to Miriam Noel, who had sent him a letter of sympathy when she learned the news of the tragedy. He married Noel in 1923, fathered a child to Olga Ivanovna just two years later, and divorced Noel in 1927. In 1928 he married again, and Olga Ivanovna became his third wife. She also turned out to be his last wife.

with tapdancing instead of high kicking), a walking tour can segue pleasantly into a light supper and show.

Oak Park has its share of special events in the summer, many devoted to the arts, or arts and crafts, or to historic buildings, or to literati such as Ernest Hemingway, who was born here, and Edgar Rice Burroughs, author of *Tarzan of the Apes*, who lived and worked in the suburb.

Art fairs punctuate the summer calendar, along with occasional special tours that take visitors into landmark homes, including some of Wright's, that are normally off-limits to the public. There is also a summer country fair as well as the **Kettlestrings Festival**, a jamboree named for settler who established Oak Park as a discrete urban entity back in 1839. Oak Park, famous for its literary talent, also hosts an art invitational in late July and the Heartland Poetry Festival in October.

The portion of Lake Street sandwiched between the Oak Park Metra station and Harlem Avenue has suffered some difficult times as a pedestrian mall. Now, open to cars and more accessible for shoppers, the area is once again filled with picturesque specialty shops as it was in its halcyon days.

Housing history

Still, Oak Park's main attraction for outsiders, apart from air refreshingly free of pollutants and a social fabric notably unrent by civic dissension, are the walking tours. An entire district, the area lying between Chicago Avenue and Randolph Street on the north and south and Linden and Marion streets east and west, has been given a listing in the *National Register of Historic Places*. Almost all of the houses are private homes, so the interiors have to be imagined from descriptions or viewed via photographs and line drawings that embellish books and pamphlets.

You can, however, tour the **Frank Lloyd Wright Home and Studio ❷**, 947 Chicago Avenue (tel: 708-848 1976), and the Unity Temple at 875 Lake Street. The former's initial structure, dating from 1889, did double duty as workshop and home until 1898, when Wright built a brick-and-shingle house next door to accommodate his expanding needs. All aspects of his architecture business, from conception to artistic design to drafted plans, were carried out here until 1909, the period to which the building – made over into a residence by Wright in 1911 – has been restored.

The 1889 home, the product of Wright's tradition-bound vision, is dominated by a bold pitched-roof second floor, an equilateral triangle pierced by diamond-pane casement windows set in a rectangular array. The studio features a squat octagonal library to go with a two-story drafting room and an inconspicuous side entrance, the latter consistent with Wright's belief, later developed and elaborated upon, that movement from an outer environment to an interior space should be an experienced transition, not an abrupt change. Furnishings designed by Wright fill the house, for which a one-hour tour is available.

The **Gingko Tree Bookstore** downstairs sells tour tickets, also available at the Visitor's Bureau, and any

Chicago-born Tarzan creator Edgar Rice Burroughs was expelled from school and failed at several jobs before he achieved success as an author. He wrote 22 of his books after moving to Oak Park in 1910.

BELOW: a Frank Lloyd Wright fan.

Map on page 237

TIP

If you use the train or El to go to Oak Park, make sure you are on the right side of the track before boarding for the return trip to Chicago. It would not be the first time someone has ended up hurtling off in the wrong direction.

BELOW: Wright's house for Mrs Thomas H. Gale.

number of books on architecture in general and Wright in particular. Mostly technical works or essays in secular hagiography, at least one volume deserves singling out for its amusing sidelights on Wright's prickly personality, *Letters to Clients* – which also includes letters from them. To a 1934 query about thresholds and keeping flies from getting into the house under the door, Wright replies, "Dear Nancy Willey: The screen doors can be cut on the slope and filled with leather flap. A half-inch clearance at the center and about half way back is all that will be needed. The rest will be in the clearance anyway. Let us have no thresholds. Amen. Frank Lloyd Wright."

A walk west on Chicago from Forest to Marion passes two **"bootleg" Wright houses**, at 1019 and 1027 Chicago. These are examples of architectural moonlighting for which Louis Sullivan, who had Wright under contract, fired his young associate in 1892. Nearly identical Queen Anne houses whose octagonal bays thrust out from a rectangular box, they suggest the simplification Wright's work was undergoing.

The following year saw the construction of the **Walter H. Gale House** a few doors down at 1031 Chicago, in which Wright moves from straight lines to curved forms within the Queen Anne format, yet introduces decorative complexity in the roof shingles and lead glass windows.

Triangles

Kenilworth Avenue unfolds a pastiche of styles in 14 houses, most built between 1880 and 1910, Queen Anne and Prairie School predominating. The overall effect is harmonious in spite of the numerous differences – notably from the Colonial Revival at 312 Kenilworth, sporting Ionian corner capitals and

centered doorway, to 417 Kenilworth, whose third floor is an intersection of steeply pitched isosceles triangles and deep dormer windows over a boxy second floor set on a central square rimmed by a colonnaded porch.

At 217 Home Avenue, the **Pleasant House**, a dramatic example of Prairie School architecture (1897-99) by George Washington Maher, looms at the end of a landscaped approach. The building retains its original furniture and fixtures, designed by the architect, as well as antique toys and memorabilia of Hemingway and Wright. The **Historical Society of Oak Park and River Forest** (open Thurs–Sun; tour fee; tel: 708-848 6755) is based in the building, and is open to the general public for touring a couple of afternoons a week.

Forest Avenue from Chicago past Pleasant contains several important buildings including four row houses circa 1888-89 (200-206 Forest) and the **Arthur Heurtley House** (318 Forest), built by Wright in 1902. Particularly noteworthy are the modified gable roof, like a Chinese coolie hat that caps the upper floor casement windows, and alternating light and dark horizontal bands of brick cut only by ground floor windows and a circular arched entrance behind an open porch. Although it wasn't much fancied by the public, the Heurtley House drew considerable praise from architects and remained one of Wright's personal favorites years later. Wright would later model the much-lauded Robie House in Hyde Park on this work.

The Moore House ❸, at 333 Forest Avenue, was Wright's first independent assignment in Oak Park after he left the offices of Adler and Sullivan. He was approached by a friend and neighbor, Nathan G. Moore, with a commission for a period home, in English Tudor style, which he completed in 1895. The design incorporated high gables, half-timbering in the upper story, medieval

ABOVE AND BELOW: Wright-designed houses.

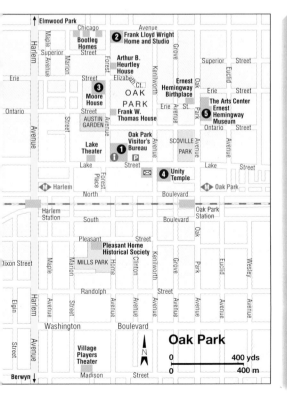

chimneys and diamond-pane casement windows. Following a fire that destroyed much of the house on Christmas Day, 1922, Wright was asked by Moore to redesign and rebuild it. One of the best examples of Wright's style in the 1894-1896 period, the Moore House is also one of the few homes open to the public with tours of the inside available during the summer months.

Open interior

The flattened S-curve of **Elizabeth Court** connecting Forest and Kenilworth makes an enjoyable departure from straight streets and avenues. Next to a rather overblown Queen Anne structure, the modest statement of the **Mrs Thomas Gale House** at 6 Elizabeth Court achieves a quiet dignity. Its open interior space permits passersby to look through the front ground floor windows to the green yard in the back. The **William G. Fricke House** at 540 Fair Oaks Avenue, at first glance similar, hedges the uncompromising horizontals with handsome vertical masses, and a varied, complex use of abrupt corners and multiple flat gable roofs almost suggest the flaring rooflines of pagoda architecture.

The Wright church

The construction of Wright's 1905 magnum opus, **Unity Temple ❹**, began in 1906 and wound to a close three years later. A scarcity of money in the church coffers enabled Wright to get the commission and dictated, in part, his use of poured concrete, which was cheap but relatively untested. The construction has stood the test well, though visitors are cautioned not to stand under the overhanging eaves, which 80 years of weathering have rendered crumbly.

From the street, Unity Temple presents a set of cubic masses whose jutting

Oak Parkers are divided in their attitude towards tourists. Many residents — some no doubt seeing dollar signs — welcome the gawkers, while others are less than thrilled by the spectacle of Wright fans traipsing through their neighborhood.

BELOW: Unity Temple interior.

horizontal slabs and fret-ornamented vertical blocks only in part overcome an essential stolidity and heaviness. A skylight and windows send natural light flooding over the soft earth tones of the church. The muted colors of the sanctuary's interior, plus hanging lamps, heating ducts in quasi-sculptured columns and ribbons of wood trim, help to move the eye rhythmically from space to space.

Map on page 237

Hemingway museum

Oak Park proudly claims Ernest Hemingway, author of books such as *A Farewell to Arms, The Sun Also Rises* and *Men Without Women,* as one of its sons. At Oak Park Visitor's Bureau you can see letters written to Hemingway, who was born in 1899, while serving in World War I or you can visit his home at 339 N. Oak Park Avenue where the Nobel Prize-winning author did his first writing while a student at Oak Park River Forest High School. Dyed-in-the-wool Hemingway fans will want to visit the **Ernest Hemingway Museum ❺** at 200 N. Oak Park Avenue (open Thurs, Fri and Sun 1-5pm. Sat 10am-5pm; entrance fee; tel: 708-848 2222;). The museum features rare photos of Hemingway, his childhood diary, letters, and early writings. The exhibits and videos cover the first 20 years of the writer's life, highlighting four themes: family life, the role the outdoors played in his development, his Oak Park education, and his experiences in World War I.

He published his first work at 14, learned to fish and hunt with his father and studied cello at the insistence of his musician mother. In 1917, after graduating from high school, he became a reporter for the *Kansas Star* and by 1918 was driving an ambulance on the Italian front in World War I. Between adventures in Spain and Africa Hemingway returned to Oak Park throughout his life. ❏

TIP

The entrance fee to the Hemingway Museum will also gain you admission to the nearby Hemingway's Birthplace at 339 N. Oak Park Avenue.

BELOW:
Wright's Moore house design.

DAY TRIPS

Smell the roses or just enjoy solitude at the Chicago Botanic Garden, take a hike around sparkling Lake Geneva, or treat the kids to Brookfield Zoo or the Great America amusement park

Map on page 244

Wisconsin

Chicago

Illinois   Indiana

A lifelong New Yorker on his first trip to the Midwest had several meetings that took him to small towns outside Chicago. He returned home with the idea of some day moving to one of those towns himself. "I just couldn't believe the relaxed lifestyles, and the way people were so nice to each other," he said in amazement. "Sure, they were the type that said 'Have a nice day' to everyone. But you know what? They really meant it. They were friendly and helpful, especially to strangers."

Many travelers, particularly those from abroad whose image of America has been shaped by films, television programs, books and magazines focusing on the big US cities, are pleasantly surprised by their forays beyond the well-beaten concrete paths of the major urban centers. Chicagoans themselves are devoted to what they call day trips, and joining them for a day away from the city is a fine way to rub shoulders. The Loop shows how Chicagoans work; a day trip shows how they play.

Chicago Botanic Garden

Any Chicagoan's list of favorite day trips is likely to include the **Chicago Botanic Garden ❶** (open daily 8am–sunset; entrance free, but parking fee; tel: 847-835 5440). Even the most frenetic commodities trader is certain to be calmed by the 300 peaceful acres of landscaped hills, lakes, wooded areas and many, many gardens.

Romantics may choose the spacious **Rose Garden**, which exhibits some 5,000 rosebushes representing 100 varieties, including All American Rose Selections. Depending on the season, there are rose-growing demonstrations and gardening tips. For those who seek solitude, there is the **Japanese Garden**, set on three serene islands. Gardeners with mobility difficulties will be interested in the ideas demonstrated in the wheelchair accessible **Buehler Enabling Garden**.

For the strollers interested in Illinois, there's the **Naturalistic Garden** exhibiting native plants and landscaping, presented in woodland and bird gardens illustrating how the Prairie State used to look.

Children will enjoy the **Natural Trail**, a scenic one-mile path that winds through the oak-hickory forest. There are wild flowers in the spring, brilliant foliage in the fall and frozen beauty in the winter.

From May through September, musicians come from all over the world to play the **Theodore C. Butz Memorial Carillon**. During the concerts, visitors spread blankets on the lawn south of the greenhouses and enjoy a rare treat. A carillon is a musical instrument made up of at least two octaves of cast-bronze

PRECEDING PAGES: suburban church. **LEFT:** Grant Wood's *American Gothic*. **BELOW:** beads and braids.

Day Trips

0 _____ 10 miles
0 _____ 10 km

bells. The carillonneur plays the bells with his or her hands and feet from a console. The Butz carillon is one of only about 150 true carillons – those played without electrical assistance or amplification – in North America.

When hunger strikes, the Food for Thought cafe is open all year round for breakfast and lunch. There are also two other restaurants available in the summer months, at weekends only. You are also welcome to bring your own picnic.

Those who prefer to sit back and enjoy than explore under their own steam can take the **tram tour**. The 45-minute narrated tour encompasses most of the Botanic Garden. The tram operates all year round; in the winter months, it's enclosed and heated for your comfort. There are also bicycle paths throughout the area.

Despite its name, the Chicago Botanic Garden is in fact located 25 miles (40 km) north of the city in **Glencoe**, a half-mile east of the Edens Expressway on Lake-Cook Road.

Winter woes.

Evanston

The first town north of Chicago's city limits is **Evanston**, the city's most cosmopolitan suburb. It has a racially diverse population, a famous university, superior restaurants, unique shops, a tradition of progressive politics, big-city sophistication and small-town warmth. It's an all-round good town, especially now that you can buy a beer there.

Evanston is the national headquarters of the Women's Christian Temperance Union, the folks who gave America Prohibition, the national alcohol ban that perhaps inadvertently allowed the gangsters to flourish. Until only a few years ago, it was illegal to sell packaged alcohol in Evanston and, even now, the town has no taverns.

BELOW: Chicago Botanic Garden.

Local legend has it that, thanks to Evanston's teetotalers, the ice-cream sundae was invented here. Seltzer water was banned on Sundays in the 1880s, so when the local druggists were obliged to remove it from their ice-cream sodas, they enterprisingly called what was left – ice-cream with syrup – a "sundae."

Evanston is also special because of **Northwestern University**, its cultural and economic anchor. Founded by Chicago Methodists in 1855, the university has grown from 10 students in one three-story building to almost 11,000 students and more than 160 buildings. Its football team, the Wildcats, went to the Rose Bowl in 1996 and the Citrus Bowl in 1997, and its academics are superior. In this part of the country, only the University of Chicago has a better reputation and Northwestern surpasses its downtown rival in several areas.

Evanston is a walker's town, with miles of stately mansions along its lakefront. One of the finest is open for public viewing, the 28-room **Charles Gates Dawes House**, at 225 Greenwood Avenue. Dawes was America's vice president from 1925 to 1929 under President Calvin Coolidge. The **Evanston Historical Society**, which has offices in the mansion, offers a list of other landmark homes that are also worth viewing. A more recent addition to Evanston's cultural scene is the **Mitchell Museum of the**

American Indian at 2600 Central Park Avenue (open Tues–Fri 10am–6pm, Sat and Sun 11am–4pm; entrance fee; tel: 847-475 1030).

For a store with a difference, check out Dave's Down To Earth Rock Shop, at 704 Main Street, which sells rocks, precious and otherwise.

North Shore

If you think you would enjoy a relaxing 30-mile (48-km) or so drive that will reveal to you how the other half live, and you can take the culture shock, head north through Evanston for the suburbs on the lake that make up an exclusive area known as North Shore. The trip will first take you past the grand homes and landscaped gardens of **Wilmette**. Look out for the **Baha'i Temple ❷** at Linden and Sheridan in Wilmette, just over the Evanston town line (open October–May 10am–5pm, May–October 10am–10pm; tours available; tel: 847-869 9039; entrance free). This 1953 architectural masterpiece by Louis Bourgeois, with its lacy walls and delicate bell-like shape, is on the National Register of Historic Places. Drivers who unexpectedly come across this magnificent white building on a moonlit night as they turn the corner of **Sheridan Road** will be amazed by its sheer splendor. Beyond Wilmette, a leisurely drive with real bends in the road and 15mph (24 kmph) speed limits, will take you through **Winnetka**, **Glencoe**, **Highland Park** and, most exclusive of all, **Lake Forest**.

Garfield Park Conservatory

BELOW: North Shore locals rollerblading.

Located at 300 N. Central Park Ave the **Garfield Park Conservatory ❸** (open daily 9am–5pm; entrance free; tel: 312-746 5100) was built in 1907 and is one of the nation's largest gardens under glass. The Conservatory features a series

of connected greenhouses that are home to a first-rate collection of plants and flowers. One of the most stunning displays is the **Palm House** which was designed as "an idealized tropical landscape where graceful palms interspersed with a variety of other tropicals soar up to a vaulted ceiling." Look for the very rare Double Coconut Palm, grown from the largest seed in the world, and thought to be the largest of its kind in any conservatory in the country. The Palm House is also graced with a white marble statue by the American sculptor **Laredo Taft**.

Map on page 244

Other notable areas of interest are the **Show House**, where special floral displays are shown and the **Aroid House**, displaying tropical plants. Be sure to see the **Sunken Fernery** where a waterfall cascades down over rock walls into a pool and where two more Taft sculptures are on display. Particularly delightful is the **Sensory Garden**, a seasonal outdoor garden featuring fragrant plants that is a real treat for the senses.

The Garfield Park Conservatory is only 10 minutes west of downtown Chicago by car. Or you can take the Green Line El west to Kedzie and then walk some four blocks to the Conservatory.

A respected resident of Brookfield Zoo.

Indiana Dunes

The Indiana Dunes are highly popular with hill-deprived locals and the beach draws sun-seekers like a magnet in the summer. If, however, you can happily live with the flatness of Illinois during your visit, the drive is probably not worth the effort. There are plenty of great beaches in the city.

BELOW:
Baha'i Temple.

Pullman

Visit George Pullman's "model town" 14 miles (22 km) south of Chicago, just west of Lake Calumet and east of the Illinois Central Railroad tracks.

Construction of America's first planned industrial town began in 1880, when George Pullman, manufacturer of Pullman sleeping cars, began building homes near his factory for his workers and their families. Pullman believed his "practical philanthropy" would guarantee large profits with fewer problems from his workers. In the end 11,000 workers and families lived behind Pullman's facade.

Although the town of **Pullman ❹** was declared a National Landmark in 1971, it is really a monument to the architect and town planner Solon Beman. Among the notable buildings are the workers' block houses, officers' row houses for the company officials, the club building, school, casino, arcade, theater, bank and police station.

Brookfield Zoo

Only 16 miles (26 km) west of the Magnificent Mile is **Brookfield Zoo ❺**, one of the most respected in the United States (open daily 10am–4.30pm; May–Sept 9.30am–5.30pm; entrance fee almost half price Tues and Thurs April–Sept, and free on those days during the remainder of the year; tel: 708-485 0263). More than 2,000 animals reside on 200 acres. Habitats include the **Small Mammal House** with more than

375 bats and the **Lion House**, one of the original buildings unveiled to the public when the zoo opened in 1934.

A middle-aged Londoner still regales his children with stories of his first visit as a boy to Chicago and the big zoo in the suburbs. Particularly vivid are his tales of the giant Kodiak bears, standing on their hind legs to a height of 9 ft (3 meters) and roaring.

Several teenagers were tossing slices of bread across the ravine setting off the bears' "natural habitat" enclosure. The boy opened his brown paper bag and handed one of the teenagers a peanut butter sandwich that promptly went sailing towards a Kodiak. The bear stretched its massive neck, snagged the sandwich in its sharp teeth and swallowed the boy's lunch in one gulp. "It was worth missing a meal to see that," the man still says today.

Among the most popular exhibits are the **Seven Seas Panorama** and Tropic World. Dolphins perform daily at the Seven Seas complex, a 2,000-seat indoor "dolphinarium" that features tropical plants and interconnected pools holding more than 1 million gallons (3.8 million liters) of salt water.

Outside the arena, strollers can explore the naturalistic rocky shores created to resemble the Pacific Northwest. There, seals and sea lions provide more aquatic entertainment.

Although it's always pleasurable, winter may be the best time to take in **Tropic World** because of the warm indoor temperatures. It is located in a huge building, the size of one-and-a-half football fields. Within are three separate exhibits, each representing rain forests in Asia, South America or Africa, complete with rocks, cliffs and waterfalls. Tropic World was completed in the summer of 1984 at a cost of $11 million and strives for a total environment. Here

BELOW:
Brookfield Zoo seal.

more than 100 mammals and three dozen birds interact with one another – and with the visitors. Zoological purists may argue that it is not perfectly authentic because there aren't any mosquitoes, but few visitors complain.

The **Fragile Kingdom** exhibit represents three very different exhibits all sharing one characteristic: fragility. Again, the idea behind the two-acre setting of desert, rain forest and rocky grottos is to create realistic exhibits. These, in turn, aim to help viewers appreciate the African and Asian environments and the animals that inhabit these delicate ecosystems, depending on their surroundings and on one another for survival. Here are the black-backed jackal, the Burmese python and the Siberian tiger, among many other residents.

The size of the Brookfield Zoo is apparent in some of the background statistics. For example, zoo veterinarians see more than 1,000 patients a year and still make house calls – or rather, cage and cave calls. More than 20,400 bales of hay are used each year – which, if placed end to end, would stretch almost 12 miles (19 km). Brookfield visitors consume half a million hamburgers and hot dogs and sip 850,000 soft drinks a year.

The gift shops sell more than 50,000 stuffed toy animals annually for those who want a cuddly memory of the wilds. Brookfield Zoo is located at **1st Avenue** and **31st Street** in west suburban Brookfield. By car, take either Interstate 55 or Interstate 290 and watch for exit signs for the zoo. By train, take the **Burlington/Metra** to the Zoo Stop at Hollywood Station.

The Morton Arboretum

The **Morton Arboretum ➏**, off Highway 53 near Interstate 88, is a 1,700-acre (690-hectare) garden of trees, a haven for nature-lovers. The arboretum

A road well traveled.

BELOW: day tripper.

(open daily 7am–5pm, central standard time; 7am–7pm daylight savings time; entrance half price Wed; tel: 630-719 2400) specializes in the display and study of shrubs and vines as well as trees, and more than 30,000 plants are exhibited, representing 3,600 different types of plants from around the world,

Although it may not seem natural for nature to be maintained, if developers had their way every inch of valuable Chicago suburban land would be developed with homes and stores. So, we have specially maintained fields of daffodils, winding, marked and mapped paths, and visitors' centers complete with restaurant and gift shop. During the summer there is an open air tram you can ride in for a tour of the arboretum.

St Charles and Geneva

St Charles, located on the eastern border of Northern Illinois on the Fox River, is a wonderful place to take a day trip. Full of old homes and farm houses, the town offers country charm near the city. Upriver rides are available on one of the two double-decker paddlewheelers, the St Charles Belle and the Fox River Queen. Both are docked in **Pottawattomie Park** and sail from May to mid-October. Cruises last one hour.

Also in Potawatomie Park are picnic areas and an 18-hole miniature golf course complete with waterfalls, ponds and gardens. If you happen to be in the area in mid-October you'll catch the **St Charles Scarecrow Festival**. At this festival you'll see handcrafted scarecrows and have the opportunity to make one yourself.

Just south of St. Charles is **Geneva**. The easiest entrance to this town from the east or west is Highway 38. If you're taking interstate 88, exit north at the

BELOW:
ice fishermen.

Farnsworth-Kirk exit and proceed north to Highway 38, or if you're coming from the city the Metra West line commuter train conveniently makes its last stop at Geneva. Downtown Geneva is full of historical homes, most of which have been converted to specialty shops selling art, pottery, jewelry, wine, cheese, crafts and toys.

The major attraction to Geneva, however, is the Kane County Cougars, the state's most popular minor-league baseball team. This team plays at **Phillip B. Elfstrom Stadium** off Highway 38. Weekend tickets for the stadium's 5,800 seats sell out early in the season. But, don't worry, there are plenty of lawn seats available and the beer, soda and hot dog vendors can reach you wherever you are sitting.

Six Flags Great America

Among the memories of those Chicago residents over 30 is Riverview Park, a long-time amusement center at Western and Belmont avenues in the heart of the city. In place of those heart-stopping, creaking old wooden roller coasters, which cranked up for the last time in 1967, stands a shopping mall. But nine years after Riverview closed, **Six Flags Great America** ❼ arrived (open May–Sept 10am–9pm; tel: 847-249 1776; entrance fee). It seems there is no shortage of challenges for the adventurous: here's the official description for the **Iron Wolf**, the nation's tallest and fastest looping, stand-up roller coaster, launched in 1990: "Riders who accept the standing challenge will travel down a 90-ft (27-meter) drop reaching speeds up to 55 miles (88 km) per hour entering a hair-raising 360-degree vertical loop, towering 80 ft (24 meters) into the sky. Dashing from the loop, riders spiral through intertwining hairpin curves, culminating in a

Only in emergencies.

Below:
rural Illinois barn.

spine-tingling corkscrew-type single loop that takes riders nearly parallel to the ground." The Demon does an 82-ft (25-meter) vertical drop, a double corkscrew and several vertical loops. The Tidal Wave accelerates to high speeds, then hits a 76-ft-(23-meter) tall vertical loop, forward and then backward.

There are also rides that are only slightly more sedate, such as the Rue Le Dodge bumper cars, or the White Water Rampage rubber boats – great for cooling off in hot weather. For the little ones, there is **Bugs Bunny Land** and the grand double-deck carousel with over 100 gaily-colored animals.

The park is divided into regional theme areas such as **Hometown Square**, **Yankee Harbor** and **Orleans Place**. The colors of the various attractions are vibrant against the bright blue sky, and people watchers will have a great time. For more structured, non-riding entertainment, Great America features the **Pictorium Theater**, one of the world's largest screens, showing fast-paced action movies of rushing rapids or men in flight. Several theaters around the park offer singing and dancing cartoon characters, high diving acts and Broadway-style reviews.

To get the most out of Great America, a few pointers may prove helpful. Avoid Saturdays and Sundays if at all possible. Get there early – when school's in session, hundreds of children seem to be on field trips. Pick up a map and note the rides and attractions that are most appealing. The park is circular in design, so go in one direction instead of back and forth. Even on what seem to be mild days, bring sun block and a light jacket as the weather can change quickly.

Finally, pack a lunch or pick up some food on the way and leave it in the car for a picnic in the parking lot. The park – and the parking lot – have many food stands, but the prices are high and the quality is probably not as good as

TIP

Beware of congestion on the highways. If you're planning a day trip be sure to leave early in the morning.

BELOW:
thrills at Six Flags Great America.

THE TALE OF A MODEL TOWN

While Pullman may have had good intentions his "model town" ended a failure. Pullman, who claimed he built his town to increase efficiency and prosperity among his workers, took advantage of his control over not only wages but also rent, utility prices and insurance. In 1885, he cut wages in different parts of the assembly line at different times creating tension among his workers. Anybody who dared strike was fired.

In 1893, a financial panic hit the country and thousands of workers lost their jobs. A workers' union was formed and in 1894 the workers finally went on a strike. Trains were stopped from the east coast to the west and finally Governor Altgeld ordered the use of 14,000 federal troops against the strikers.

Although the workers lost this strike it brought national attention to the problems at Pullman. Pullman was accused of charging his workers exorbitant rents relative to the wages he paid them, manipulating water, gas and fire insurance prices and housing 50 to 60 people in homes where there was only one tap of running water and one washroom. In 1907, the "model town" of Pullman was sold to its inhabitants by an order of the Supreme Court of the State of Illinois.

whatever you might bring. However, Great America does offer one taste treat, for those who don't mind waiting in lines: the **Funnel Cake Foundry**, located in the County Fair area. Fried dough is funneled into a circle and covered with chocolate, strawberry, cherry, hot caramel or – the favorite – powdered sugar.

Six Flags Great America is located in **Gurnee**, halfway between Chicago and Milwaukee, just off Interstate 94 at Route 132 (Grand Avenue). Pets are not allowed at Six Flags, but the park has a boarding facility for a nominal fee. Strollers and wheelchairs are also available on a first-come, first-serve basis for a nominal fee. Cameras can be borrowed with a security deposit.

Milwaukee

It's another city and another state, but it's worth a trip of a couple hours into another world: **Milwaukee**, Wisconsin. If driving, take Interstate 94 and just head north. Around **Lincolnshire**, there's an exit sign for Half Way Road. Downtown to downtown, the journey is only about 90 miles (144 km). There's also the train. Amtrak schedules several trains back and forth each day.

Milwaukee is a compact city of 640,000 people. Short walks and cab rides open up a city of old-world charm, uncrowded streets, and great German food and beer. For a glimpse of the past, stop off at the **Milwaukee Public Museum** (800 W. Wells St; open daily; entrance fee; tel: 414-278 2702). Outside the museum, check out Third Street, between State Street and Highland Avenue, for the **Old World** section of town with its vivid 19th-century architecture.

Across the street from Usinger's Sausage store sits **Mader's**, a Milwaukee classic for more than 90 years. Visited by presidents and presidential candidates, Mader's ranks as one of the most celebrated German restaurants in North

Map on page 244

A small slice of Chicago life.

BELOW: the Milwaukee horticulture domes.

Map on page 244

America and has won scores of dining awards. Complete dinners are no longer 20 cents with tip, as they were in 1902, but they remain high in quality and are good value for money. There are several brewery tours in Milwaukee, but if you'd rather hoist a stein, Mader's has a large selection.

Another good place to eat is **Karl Ratzsch's Old World Restaurant**, which provides even more hearty German fare, as well as continental cuisine. From here, head west on Mason to **Water Street**. At 779 N. Front Street, an alley west of Water, between Mason and Wells, there's a tiny office marked "International Exports Limited."

Go into the office, follow the instructions and a bookcase will slide open to reveal a secret passage that takes you to the Safe House, a nightclub shrine to Agent 007, spies and espionage. Each area of this unusual bar has a different decor, such as the Mata Hari booth and the Checkpoint Charlie room.

Sports fans can check out the action with the Milwaukee Brewers (baseball) and the Green Bay Packers (football) at **County Stadium**. The Milwaukee Bucks (basketball) and the Milwaukee Admirals (ice hockey) are at the **Milwaukee Exposition, Convention Center and Arena**. Locals tend to call it "the Mecca."

The **Performing Arts Center** showcases theater, ballet and several other cultural events. For outdoor activities, **Summerfest** in early July is an event to highlight on the calendar: an 11-day outdoor party on the lakeshore with a selection of favorite Wisconsin foods, such as roast corn on the cob and grilled bratwursts, and an impressive lineup of well-known entertainers at its jazz, rock, country and main stages.

BELOW:
farmyard art.
RIGHT:
retired farmer.

The **Mitchell Park Horticultural Conservatory** features three massive glass domes, each seven stories high. Inside are tropic, arid and seasonal displays, great for taking pictures. The **Milwaukee County Zoo** rates among the finest zoological parks in the world with some 4,500 animals on exhibit. The **Annunciation Greek Orthodox Church** was the last major building to come off Frank Lloyd Wright's drawing board, and is the scene of an annual July Greekfest.

Lake Geneva

One section of Wisconsin, northwest of Chicago on the Illinois-Wisconsin state line, is a walker's dream come true. A gorgeous 26-mile (42-km) footpath completely circles the glistening waters of **Lake Geneva**.

Many hikers choose the sweet-smelling springtime to follow the old trail, tramped out by the original Indian inhabitants; others opt for the season of winter snows to crunch, wrapped and booted, along the icy, but still walkable path.

The trail occasionally cuts through private property, though the courts have ruled that common law over generations has made the path a public right of way. Legally, however, entrance to the footpath itself must come through public property.

Experienced hikers in the area suggest using Big Foot Beach Park, Lake Geneva Library Park, Williams Bay and Fontana Beaches, all of which make good entry points. ❏

INSIGHT GUIDES

Travel Tips

Insight Guides portray destinations in depth, providing the complete picture and the top photography

Insight Pocket Guides focus on the best choices for places to see and things to do and include large fold-out maps

Insight Compact Guides' portability makes them the perfect books to carry with you for on-the-spot reference

Three types of guide for all types of travel

INSIGHT GUIDES Different people need different kinds of information. Some want *background information* to help them prepare for the trip. Others seek *personal recommendations* from someone who knows the destination well. And others look for *compactly presented data* for on-the-spot reference. With three carefully designed series, Insight Guides offer readers the perfect choice. Insight Guides will turn your visit into an experience.

The world's largest collection of visual travel guides

CONTENTS

Getting Acquainted

The Place

Situation 41.50°N, 87.37°W, on the same latitude as Rome and Tashkent. Located in the northeast corner of Illinois in the section of the United States referred to as the Midwest, Chicago is situated on the Great Lakes, at the southwest tip of Lake Michigan, which makes up the city's entire eastern border.
Population Almost 3 million in the city itself. Of approximately 11.5 million people in Illinois, 7.5 million live in the Chicago area.
Area 228.5 sq miles (592 sq km).
Language English.
Religion Chicago has the biggest Catholic archdiocese in the country. But there are houses of worship for over 100 denominations in the city.
Time Zone Chicago is in the Central Time Zone, which is 1 hour behind New York, 2 hours ahead of California, 6 hours behind GMT and 7 hours behind France.
Currency US dollar (US $), divided into 100 cents.
Electricity The standard for the US is 110 volts DC. Electrical plugs have two flat pins plus an occasional round one.
Weights & Measures Imperial.
International Dialing Code 1 (for the US), followed by the relevant area code, e.g. downtown Chicago is 312, the rest of the city, 773..

The People

Chicagoans are often friendly, but their forwardness sometimes puts off visitors. Courtesy is appreciated, but so is getting to the point. Good service is expected and visitors should not hesitate to ask for assistance, even if it is for some-

thing out of the ordinary. Unusual requests may deserve a tip – even if declined, Chicagoans won't take offense that it has been offered.
The population breaks down as follows: whites 38 percent, African-Americans 39 percent, Hispanics 20 percent, Asians and others 4 percent. Hispanics represent the fastest-growing ethnic group.

Climate

Chicago is a great place to experience all four seasons. It can be very hot and humid in summer, but it's usually slightly cooler near the lake (as mentioned in almost every weather forecast) because of cooling breezes coming off Lake Michigan. Winter in Chicago can mean very low temperatures, often with snow and biting wind. Spring brings its share of rain, but the temperatures are usually moderate, as in the autumn.
Dramatic temperature changes, sometimes within minutes, mean you can experience all the seasons at once – temperatures of 70°F+ (15°C) followed later by snow is not unheard of.

Government

Chicago is governed by a city council, headed by the mayor. The city is divided into 50 wards, based on the population, each with about 60,000 residents. Each ward is

Time Zones

On the first Sunday of April the clock is moved ahead an hour for daylight savings time, and on the last Sunday in October it's moved back an hour to return to standard time.
When it's noon in Chicago (Standard Time) it is:
● 8am in Hawaii
● 10am in California
● 1pm in New York and Montreal
● 6pm in London
● 10pm in Moscow
● 2am (the next day) in Singapore and Hong Kong

Temperatures

Average daily Fahrenheit high temperatures in Chicago:

Month	Temperature
January	29°F (-2°C)
February	34°F (1°C)
March	44°F (7°C)
April	59°F (15°C)
May	70°F (21°C)
June	79°F (26°C)
July	85°F (29°C)
August	82°F (28°C)
September	75°F (24°C)
October	64°F (18°C)
November	48°F (9°C)
December	35°F (2°C)

represented by an elected alder-man, who is part of the council.
In theory, this is a "strong council, weak mayor" system. In reality, the mayor of Chicago wields a great deal of power.
The entire city of Chicago is located in Cook County, which is governed by the Cook County Board, made up of 17 members: 10 from Chicago, and 7 from the suburbs.
Both Chicago and Cook County have "home rule," which allows them to decide many local issues, such as taxation, without approval from the State legislature in Springfield, the capital of Illinois.

The Economy

While agriculture is the main source of income in southern Illinois, Chicago's economy is based on big business.
The Loop is regarded as the business and commercial district. LaSalle Street is the financial district, the "Wall Street" of the Midwest, and the home of the commodities exchanges that influence world production and prices of agricultural and other products.
Besides white-collar industries such as insurance, accounting, publishing and state-government administration, Chicago is also one of America's retail capitals which is

demonstrated vividly along wealthy shopping streets such as Michigan Avenue's "Magnificent Mile."

As in most large cities, there is a wide gap between the richest and poorest. The overall standard of living is quite high.

Public Holidays

Many government agencies, local banks and businesses close during these holidays:

Jan 1: New Year's Day
3rd Mon in Jan: Martin Luther King's Birthday
Feb 12: Abraham Lincoln's Birthday
3rd Mon in Feb: Presidents' Day
Last Mon in May: Memorial Day
July 4: Independence Day
1st Mon in Sep: Labor Day
2nd Mon in Oct: Columbus Day
1st Tues in Nov: Election Day
Nov 11: Veterans' Day
4th Thurs in Nov: Thanks-giving
Dec 25: Christmas

Vital Statistics

Chicago is home to:
● 46 museums
● more than 200 theaters
● almost 200 art galleries
● around 7000 restaurants
● 29 miles (46 km) of lakefront
● 15 miles (24 km) of bathing beaches
● 18 miles (29 km) of lakefront bicycle paths

Planning the Trip

Visas & Passports

To enter the United States, travelers must have a passport that's valid for at least six months longer than their stay. Before leaving their own countries, foreign visitors should check with the nearest US Embassy or Consulate whether or not they require a visa..

While most visitors clear immigration without incident, the US Immigration and Naturalization Service (INS) has no hesitation in sending anyone without the correct paperwork straight back home.

Certain countries operate a reciprocal visa waiver program with the US, which means visitors from these countries can enter and stay for up to 90 days without a visa. Those are Andorra, Argentina, Australia, Austria, Belgium, Brunei, Denmark, Finland, France, Germany, Iceland, Italy, Japan, Liechtenstein, Luxembourg, Monaco, the Netherlands, New Zealand, Norway, San Marino, Slovenia, Spain, Sweden, Switzerland and the UK. A round-trip ticket is required, and you may need to provide proof of solvency, such as a healthy bank statement.

Customs

After collecting baggage, visitors need to present customs documents which are usually passed out on planes but can be picked up at the customs desks as a last resort.

Narcotics and many foods cannot be brought in. Other items may be banned depending on the traveler's origin. Pets are okay, though you must have proof that their

inoculations are current. Visitors' personal possessions are not normally liable for duty provided they intend to take them out of the country with them, though the value of gifts is restricted to $100. There are limits on tobacco, alcohol and certain foreign products: Cuban cigars are banned because of a US trade embargo. Check with a travel agent or US consulate beforehand.

What to Wear

It's pretty much "anything goes" as far as clothing is concerned. For daytime sightseeing and casual meals, shorts and a T-shirt in summer or jeans and a sweatshirt in winter are fine. Pack a pair of comfortable walking shoes. Dressier clothes are recommended for some evening activities. For the more upscale establishments, men should wear jackets and ties, women dresses or smart pants.

In summer, bring a bathing suit to enjoy the beaches along Lake Michigan, and be prepared for hot, humid weather. Because it's cooler in the evening, take a light jacket. In winter, a warm coat, hat, gloves, scarf, and, in case of snow or slush, a pair of sturdy, waterproof boots are all essential.

Tax

There's no escape from tax in Chicago unless you intend to spend all your time reading newspapers and magazines, two of the few items that are tax-free.

Sales tax is 8.75 percent, which includes food apart from some items that are taxed at 2 percent. Alcohol has additional levies, depending on what you buy. Hotel

Health & Insurance

As there is no national health service in the US, and some hospitals or clinics will not provide treatment without assurances of payment, it is essential to buy sufficient private medical insurance in advance.

tax is 14.9 percent, and car rental an outrageous 18 percent. Another good reason not to rent a car in Chicago. It all adds up, and you'll need to budget accordingly.

Money Matters

Bureaux de change are relatively rare in America. For obtaining US dollars at O'Hare Airport, there is a foreign currency exchange in Terminal 5, the international terminal, that is open from 9am–8pm daily and exchanges about 40 of the major currencies. Tel: 773-686 7965.

Another source for exchanging currency is American Express, which has a number of offices in Chicago, including one at 625 N. Michigan Avenue, tel: 312-435 2570. Some large banks, such as American National Bank and Trust, 1 N. LaSalle, tel: 312-661 5000, also have currency exchange windows. Take your passport if cashing travelers checks. (Many shops will accept payment directly by travellers' checks.)

But your best bet is to come armed with enough dollars to get you by for a day or two, and a bank card that you can use in one of the hundreds of cash machines (ATMs). Check with your bank or credit card company before you go to make sure your card is compatible with machines in the US. As you will likely be charged a fee each time you use an ATM, consider how much you should take out each time to minimize your costs.

Don't be misled by the "currency exchanges" that you see: these are aimed mostly at people without bank accounts, not tourists with fistfuls of unusable French francs or Italian lire.

Maps

Rand McNally has good maps of Chicago (444 N. Michigan Avenue, tel: 312-321 1751 and 150 S. Wacker Drive, tel: 312-332 2009). Most bookstores offer a variety. The CTA publishes a transit map that can also serve as a good guide to the streets in the city. Obtain by mail from CTA (Chicago Transit Authority), Merchandise Mart, Chicago, Illinois 60654. It's also theoretically available in hotels, visitor centers and El stations.

Getting There

BY AIR

Airports

Chicago is the home of the world's busiest airport in terms of the number of daily flights handled:
O'Hare International Airport (tel: 773-686 2200), 18 miles (29 km) from downtown, handles international and domestic flights.

Midway Airport (tel: 773-838 0600) handles domestic flights only, and is located 7 miles (11 km) from downtown. See *Getting Around* for information on how to travel from the airports into town.

Services

All the major airlines serve Chicago. British Airways, United and American offer non-stop direct Chicago–London flights. London-based visitors should check out the Travel section of the classified ads at the back of *Time Out*, where bargains can often be found.

Departures

Confirm flight numbers, times, terminal and check-in time beforehand, and make seat reservations if possible. Confirm any special meals you may have requested. Most airlines require international travelers to check in two hours before departure. Late check-in can mean losing your seat.

Airline Numbers

- **United 1-800-241 6522**
- **American 1-800-433 7300**
- **British Airways 1-800-247 9297**
- **Continental 1-800-523 3273**
- **Delta 1-800-325 1999**
- **Northwest 1-800-447 4747**
- **Southwest 1-800-435 9792**
- **TWA 1-800-221 2000**
- **US Airways 1-800-428 4322**

Plan Ahead

Chicago is generally an informal town, but it's also the kind of place where people go out a lot. That means reservations are recommended – sometimes well in advance – for the most popular theaters, restaurants and special events with limited seating. If your plans change, restaurants appreciate a call that lets them know.

BY RAIL

Chicago is serviced by **Amtrak**, a passenger line offering nationwide service, tel: 1-800-872 7245. Amtrak comes in to Chicago's Union Station at Jackson and Canal streets, tel: 312-558 1075.

BY BUS

Greyhound has nationwide service to its main terminal at 630 W. Harrison Street, west of the Loop. It also has a station at the 95th Street and Dan Ryan Expressway CTA station on the South Side. Call 1-800-231 2222 for fares and schedule information.

BY CAR

The major east–west route across northern Illinois is Interstate 80, which passes near Chicago from Indiana to the east or Iowa to the west. Coming from the north, the main interstates are 90 and 94, which merge about 10 miles (16 km) north of downtown to form the Kennedy Expressway (I-90/94), a direct route into downtown. I-57 runs across the state from the south, and connects with the Dan Ryan Expressway (I-90/94) for the downtown area.

Practical Tips

Business Hours

Businesses and government offices in Chicago are generally open from 9am–5pm Monday to Friday, but many people start work earlier. Because many commute from the suburbs the rush hour – a misnomer if ever there was one – tends to be 6-9am and 4-7pm when traffic often comes to a virtual standstill. Banking hours are generally 8.30 or 9am–5pm. Some banks have longer hours; some are open a half-day on Saturday.

Tipping

The actual amount of a tip should depend on satisfaction with the service received. Use the following as a guide:
Waiter/Waitress: 15–20 percent
Bartender: 10–15 percent
Hotel Doorman: $1–$3 for carrying bags; 50¢–$1 for calling tax.
Hotel Porter/Bellman: $1–$3 per bag; $1–$2 for opening room
Room-Service Waiter: 15 percent.
Hotel Chambermaid: $1–$2 per night
Taxi Driver: 15 percent

Electricity

The standard for the US is 110 volts DC. Electrical plugs have two flat pins plus an occasional round one. Unless they already have built-in dual voltage, appliances on a different system may need a transformer/converter (to deal with the voltage difference) as well as an adaptor (to connect them to the electrical outlet). Note that it's much easier to find these before you leave, in your home country.

Pricier hotels supply hair driers and irons in the room – check whether yours does before you pack – and others will usually have some tucked away. Call up housekeeping and ask if they can provide what you need.

Postal Services

Full-service post offices are, frankly, thin on the ground. You will find one in the Loop, by Calder's *Flamingo* sculpture at Dearborn and Adams, and in the James R Thompson Center. Avoid the lunchtime period (11.30am –1pm or so) and rush hour.

Opening Times

Most post offices are open from 8.30am–5pm from Monday to Friday, and 8.30am–1pm on Saturday. The post office at 540 N. Dearborn also opens 9am–2pm Sunday. Check the phone book for the nearest one.

Post Offices

The main post office is open 24 hours a day but is inconveniently located at 433 W. Harrison, tel: 312-654 3895, and only worth the trek if you need its services out of normal hours.

Full service post offices are listed in the "US Government Office" pages at the front of the Ameritech Chicago *White Pages* directory. You can also find a useful area code and time zone map for the whole country in the White Pages, which can save you calling the operator and having to pay for the information. The *Yellow Pages* directory has a useful section at the front with the zip code for every number of every street in Chicago.

Mail Boxes Etc is a chain of postal, communications and business service centers, which specialize in packing and shipping. The following are in the Loop or downtown area: 47 W. Polk, tel: 312-427 7839; off Michigan Avenue at 207 E. Ohio, tel: 312-644 6245; and a little further north at 60 E. Chestnut, tel: 312-787 7277. There are other branches throughout the city.

Useful Numbers

- call **411** to find out local phone numbers or area codes.
- to find out US long distance numbers, call **1** then the appropriate area code, then **555 1212**.

Area Codes
- Downtown Chicago: 312
- Rest of the city: 773.
- Suburban area codes: 708, 630, 847 and 815.

Phone Calls

Public telephones are located everywhere, both on the street and in major buildings.

Local calls usually cost 35c – coins only are accepted, which you insert before dialing. For long-distance calls, it's better to buy a prepaid phonecard, which you use by punching in a series of numbers.

Dialing within the US

When calling within the same area code, dial only the seven-digit phone number; when calling another area code, you have to dial 1 plus the three-digit area code followed by the seven-digit phone number. Calls between the two Chicago area codes are charged as local calls. (If you are unsure about the city area code, simply dial with or without it and a recording will advise you if you need to dial something different.)

The number 800 indicates a toll-free (no charge) call, and as with long-distance numbers, should be preceded by 1 when dialing.

Dialing Overseas

Most overseas cities can be dialed direct. Start by dialing 011 to exit the US, and follow with the code for the country you want to reach, then the city code and number. So, for example, to phone London, England, you would dial 011 + 44 + 171 (omitting the usual '0') + the seven-digit city number. If you require assistance, dial 0.

Faxes & E-mail

Most hotels and many copy or printing shops, and other businesses such as Mail Boxes Etc (*see page 261*) and Kinko's, have facilities that visitors can use for a fee to send or receive faxes. Faxes can also be sent through most hotels, and telegrams can be sent through Western Union.

Check e-mail or access the Web at Screenz, tel: 773-348 9300 or 773-244 1633, 2717 N. Clark.

Medical Services

Hospitals
Rush-Presbyterian–St Luke's Hospital
1753 W. Congress Parkway
Tel: 312-942 5000.
Cook County Hospital
1835 W. Harrison
Tel: 312-633 6000.
Northwestern Memorial,
Superior Street and Fairbanks Court
Tel: 312-908 2000.
Michael Reese,
31st and Lake Shore Drive
Tel: 312-791 2000.

Dentists
For **dental** care, the Chicago Dental Society emergency service can help 24 hours a day: Monday to Friday 9am–5pm, tel: 312-836 7300; all other hours, tel: 630-978 5745.

Poisoning
Poison control is handled at Rush-Presbyterian – St Luke's, tel: 312-942 5969. Can also be called toll free on 1-800-942 5969.

Pharmacies
Those with long opening hours are:
Walgreen
757 N. Michigan Avenue
Tel: 312-664 8686;
Walgreen
1200 N. Dearborn
Tel: 312-943 0973;
Cosmopolitan Drugs
754 N. Clark Street
Tel: 312-787 2152.

Emergency Calls

- In an **emergency**, dial **911**. It's free – just pick up and dial.
- For a non-emergency, call the Medical Referral Service, tel: 312-670 2550.

Visitor Information

Information on Chicago is readily available from:

Chicago Office of Tourism,
Chicago Cultural Center,
78 E. Randolph, Chicago, IL 60602.
Tel: 312-744 2400.
Illinois Bureau of Tourism,
100 W. Randolph, Suite 3-400,
Chicago, IL 60601.
Tel: 312-814 4732 or
1-800-223 0121.
Visitor Information Center,
Pumping Station, 811 N. Michigan Avenue, Chicago, IL 60611.
Walk-in facility only.
Mayor's Office of Special Events,
121 N. LaSalle Street, Chicago, IL 60602.
Tel: 312-744 3315; and a 24-hour hotline, tel: 312-744 3370.

Chicago Convention and Tourism Bureau,
McCormick Place on the Lake,
2301 S. Lake Shore Drive, Chicago, IL 60616.
Tel: 312-567 8500.
Groups and conferences only.

Security & Crime

As in any metro area, care has to be taken. Gangsters no longer roam the streets of Chicago with their Tommy guns, but there are still security risks, especially in some of the lower income neighborhoods, or in the less populated downtown areas late at night.

Visitors who stick to the main hotel, shopping and tourist areas have little cause for concern. The more adventurous who set off to explore Chicago's neighborhoods should first seek the advice of locals. Most areas are safe and friendly but a few, particularly in the public housing areas of the West Side and South Side, are not. Joggers should stick to daytime routes in well-populated areas.

Hotel rooms and cars should be locked when not in use, of course, and don't leave valuables in hotel rooms. Use the hotel safe instead.

As in other big cities everywhere, pickpockets are drawn to large crowds, such as those at festivals, concerts and sporting events. Don't carry large amounts of cash or credit cards. Wallets should be carried in inside pockets, and women should keep a hand on their purses. Similarly, purses should not be hung off the backs of chairs in restaurants. For theft or other minor

Traveling for the Physically Challenged

Chicago tries to make itself accessible to the physically challenged. Almost all the museums and many restaurants have wheelchair access.
● **The Mayor's Office for People with Disabilities**, tel: 312-744 6673 (Voice), or tel: 312-744 4964 (TTY only) offers information and referral. The city's 24-hour

hotline, tel: 312-744 5000, includes information for the physically challenged.
● **American United Taxicabs**, tel: 773-248 7600, can arrange door-to-door transportation for those with limited mobility, including the wheelchair-bound.
● **Access Living**, although aimed primarily at Chicago residents, can

provide information on travel for visitors too. Contact them at 310 S. Peoria, Chicago, IL 60607, tel: 312-226 5900.
● **Wheelchair Getaways of Illinois**, Inc, PO Box 338, Wilmette, tel: 1-800-637 2597, leases vans specially converted for wheelchair users.

crimes about which you can do little apart from make a report, dial 312-746 6000. For life-threatening incidents call emergency services on **911** (free call).

Consulates

Australia: 150E. 42nd Street, 34th floor, New York, NY 10017-5612, tel: - 212-351 6500. The Chicago consulate is closed; this is the nearest one to Chicago. :
Canada: 2 Prudential Plaza, Suite 2400, 180 N. Stetson Avenue, tel: 312-616 1860.
France: 737 N. Michigan Avenue, tel: 312-787 5359.
Germany: 676 N. Michigan Avenue, tel: 312-580 1199.
Ireland: 400 N. Michigan Avenue, tel: 312-337 1868.
Israel: 111 E. Wacker Drive, tel: 312-565 3300.
Italy: 500 N. Michigan Avenue, tel: 312-467 1550.
Japan: 737 N. Michigan Avenue, tel: 312-280 0400.
New Zealand: 6250 N. River Road, Suite 9000, Rosemont, tel: 847-384 5400.
United Kingdom: 400 N. Michigan Avenue, tel: 312-346 1810.

Media

Newspapers
There are two major daily newspapers in Chicago, the *Chicago Tribune* and the *Chicago Sun-Times*. Both are morning papers and are available in hotels, newspaper boxes on the street, newsstands, bookstores, convenience stores and supermarkets. The papers carry local, national and (limited) international news. They also have weekend sections (check Friday editions) with up-to-the-minute information on entertainment events in Chicago.
Other papers to look out for:
● The *Chicago Defender* – a daily paper with emphasis on the black community.
● The *Reader* – a liberal free weekly, available on Thursday primarily on the north side.
● *Crain's Chicago Business* – a

weekly paper for Chicago's business news and other issues.
● *Streetwise* – a paper sold by, and benefiting, the homeless. It can be bought from ID-displaying vendors all over the city.
● *Chicago* – a monthly magazine that contains a good guide to restaurants and events in addition to its feature articles.

Television
The main channels available on all television sets are:

Channel 2	WBBM	CBS
Channel 5	WMAQ	NBC
Channel 7	WLS	ABC
Channel 9	WGN	Independent
Channel 11	WTTW	PBS
Channel 32	WFLD	Fox

In hotels that offer cable (and most of them do), a listing will be provided showing what programing is available on each channel. Here are some specialty channels:
● Sports: ESPN, ESPN 2, FSCH
● Comedy: COM
● News: CNN, TMC
● Movies: HBO, SHO, TNT, MAX
● Family fare: DIS
● Children's: NICK
● Music Videos: VH-1, MTV
● Weather: TWC

Radio
Radios pick up two frequencies, AM and FM. The most popular stations include:
AM

670 WMAQ	News
720 WGN	Variety, Talk
780 WBBM	News
890 WLS	Talk
1000 WMVP	Sports

FM

93.1 WXRT	Progressive Rock
93.9 WLIT	Light Favorites
94.7 WXCD	Classic Rock
95.5 WNUA	Smooth Jazz
96.3 WBBM	Top 40
97.9 WLUP	Rock
98.7 WFMT	Classical, Fine Arts
99.5 WUSN	Country
100.3 WNND	Adult Contemporary
101.9 WTMX	Adult Contemporary
103.5 WRCX	Rock
104.3 WJMK	Oldies
105.9 WCKG	Talk, Rock
107.5 WGCI	Urban Contemporary

Newsstands

A large selection of local, national and international papers and periodicals can be obtained from the following stores:
Barnes and Noble, 1130 N State, tel: 312-280 8155
Borders, 830 N. Michigan Avenue, tel: 312-573 0564
Borders, 2817 N. Clark, tel: 773-935 3909
Tower Records, 2301 N. Clark, tel: 773-477 5994

Gay Chicago

Gays are very much a part of every day life in Chicago, The hub of the city's gay community is Lakeview East or, as it's often nicknamed by locals, Boys' Town. Halsted, Broadway and Clark Streets between Diversey and Addison Streets is the approximate area for many shops owned and supported by gays (*see also page 70*).
The City of Chicago has a gay liaison officer who can be contacted on 312-744 7911.
Gay and Lesbian Pride Week is celebrated each year in late June, and culminates with a popular gay and lesbian pride parade that the whole city turns out to watch.
There are also many places, organizations and publications that specialize in gay life:

Gay Publications
Windy City Times,
325 W. Huron,
tel: 312-397 0020.
Outlines,
1115 W. Belmont,
tel: 773-871 7610.
Gay Chicago Magazine,
3121 N. Broadway,
tel: 773-327 7271.

Gay Community Service
Horizons Community Services, Inc. 961 W. Montana, has a gay and lesbian helpline, tel: 773-472 6469, offering confidential counseling and referrals.
Howard Brown Memorial Clinic. 945 W. George Street, tel: 773-871

5777, provides confidential diagnosis and treatment.

Gay Business

Chicago Area Gay and Lesbian Chamber of Commerce, Box #805, 3712 N. Broadway, 60613, tel: 1-888-452 4262.

Gay Politics

Central Illinois Gay & Lesbian Task Force, tel: 217-544 1765.

Gay Choruses

Windy City Performing Arts, tel: 312-404 9242.

Gay Library

Gerber-Hart Library, 1127 W. Granville Ave, tel: 773-381 8030. This is Chicago's premier gay and lesbian library and resource center, and one of the largest in the US. The collection consists of nearly 13,000 books and periodicals.

Gay Disabled Resources

The following resources can offer support to the gay physically challenged:
Rainbow Bridge, PO Box 90-367, Chicago 60690-0367, tel: 312-494 2654.
The Mayor's Office for People with Disabilities, TTY/TDD 312-744 4964, voice 312-744 9586.
Access Living Independent Center, TDD 312-226 1687, voice 312-229 5900.

Doing Business

If you are interested in doing business in Chicago, or starting up a business, here are a couple of sources of information:
Illinois Department of Commerce and Community Affairs, International Business Division, tel: 312-814 7164.
Chicagoland Chamber of Commerce, tel: 312-494 6700.

Translating Services

Some hotels can provide translators, or have a multilingual concierge. Or try:
Advance Language, 58 W. Erie, tel: 312-654 9900.

Berlitz Translation Services, 875 N. Michigan Avenue, tel: 312-943 5178.
International Language and Communications Center, Inc., 79 W. Monroe Street, tel: 312-236 3366.

Complaints

For help with a problem, or to file a complaint, some contacts are:
Better Business Bureau, tel: 312-832 0500. 10am–2.30pm.
City of Chicago Consumer Information and Complaints, tel: 312-744 9400.
Governor's Office of Consumer Affairs, tel: 1-800-814 2754.
  If the complaint is serious enough to require legal assistance, the **Illinois Lawyer Referral Service** (tel: 217-525 5297) will make referrals to lawyers who are registered with the service.

Religious Services

The following are churches and synagogues in the downtown and Near North area. For more, look in *Yellow Pages* under Churches:
Annunciation Greek Orthodox Cathedral
1017 N. LaSalle Street
Tel: 312-664 5485.
Assumption Church Servite Fathers (Roman Catholic)
323 W. Illinois Street
Tel: 312-644 0036.
Cathedral Church of St James
(Episcopal)
65 E. Huron Street
Tel: 312-787 7360.
Central Church of Chicago
(Non-denominational)
18 S. Michigan Avenue, 9th Floor
Tel: 312-332 4840.
Central Synagogue of the Southside Hebrew Congregation
(Conservative)
150 E. Huron Street
Tel: 312-787 0450.
Chicago Loop Synagogue
(Traditional)
16 S. Clark Street
Tel: 312-346 7370.
Chicago Temple
(First United Methodist Church)

Restrooms

Chicago is a public restroom-challenged city. There's never a shortage of portable toilets at open-air events but, unless you're actually in a museum or restaurant, finding a restroom can be a challenge. Your best policy is to take advantage whenever the opportunity arises. All the malls on Michigan have restrooms, as do department stores Marshall Field's and Carson's. Borders and Barnes & Noble bookstores have them (although Borders in Lakeview make customers ask for the key). McDonald's is a good bet. When you're desperate, find the nearest bar and ask politely.

77 W. Washington Street
Tel: 312-236 4548.
Church of the Ascension
(Episcopal)
1133 N. LaSalle Street
Tel: 312-664 1271.
Congregation Kol Ami (Reform)
845 N. Michigan Avenue
Tel: 312-664 4775.
First St Paul's Evangelical Lutheran Church
1301 N. LaSalle Street
Tel: 312-642 7172.
Fourth Presbyterian Church
126 E. Chestnut Street
Tel: 312-787 4570.
Grace Episcopal Church
637 S. Dearborn Street
Tel: 312-922 1426.
Holy Name Cathedral
(Roman Catholic)
735 N. State Street
Tel: 312-787 8040.
Lake Shore Drive Synagogue
(Traditional)
70 E. Elm Street
Tel: 312-337 6811.
Lubavitch Chabad of the Loop
(Orthodox)
401 S. LaSalle Street, Suite 9-770
Tel: 312-427 7770.
Second Presbyterian Church
1936 S. Michigan Avenue
Tel: 312-225 4951.
St Peter's Church (Roman Catholic)
110 W. Madison Street
Tel: 312-372 5111.

Weights & Measures

The United States, unlike most of the world, uses the imperial system for measurements including gasoline which is sold by the gallon. Although the metric system is slowly working its way into usage, it's still not widespread. Mainly Fahrenheit is used for temperatures. Nutritional information on food packaging is metric, however.

Some basic conversions:

1 ounce = 28.5 grams
1 pound (16 ounces) = 453 grams
1 pint = 0.568 liter
1 quart = 1.137 liters
1 gallon = 4.5 liters
1 inch = 2.54 centimeters
1 foot (12 inches) = 0.3048 meters (30.48 centimeters)
1 yard (3 feet) = 0.9144 meters
1 mile (1,760 yards) = 1.609 kilometers
1 gram = 0.035 ounce
1 kilogram = 2.205 pounds
1 millimeter = 0.039 inch
1 centimeter = 0.393 inch
1 meter = 3.28 feet
1 kilometer = 0.62 mile
1 liter = 1.056 quarts

Converting °F and °C

To convert Fahrenheit to Centigrade temperatures, deduct 32, multiply by 5, then divide by 9. To convert Centigrade to Fahrenheit, multiply by 9, divide by 5, and add 32.

Centigrade	Fahrenheit
0	32 (Freezing)
15	59
20	68
25	77
30	86
37	99
100	212 (Boiling)

Getting Around

Public Transportation

From the Airport

O'Hare International Airport, served by most American and international air carriers, is about half an hour to an hour's drive from downtown depending on traffic, along the Kennedy Expressway (Interstates 90 and 94). Allow at least an hour for travel time. O'Hare has an international terminal (Terminal 5) and three domestic terminals (Terminals 1, 2 and 3); there is no Terminal 4 any more. There are information booths on the upper level of each terminal and outside the "Meeter-Greeter" area of the international terminal. There is a foreign currency exchange in the international terminal.

Continental Air Transport, tel: 312-454 7800, provides a bus service between the airport baggage claim area and about 35 downtown hotels. Many hotels provide a shuttle service, so inquire when making reservations. Taxis are on the lower level of each terminal; a ride downtown will cost between $25 and $30. A shared ride program is available for a flat rate of $15; maximum four. Limousine service or car rentals can be arranged in advance or at the booths near baggage claim.

If you don't have a lot of luggage, you could use the El (which stands for elevated as opposed to subway). It's the cheapest way to get downtown and the surest way to avoid traffic. The trains run frequently and the journey takes about 45 minutes. If you're arriving at Terminal 5, head for Terminal 2 on the airport rail shuttle; it's much easier to find the El from there.

At 5700 S. Cicero Avenue, **Midway Airport** is a smaller, less crowded alternative to O'Hare for domestic flights, has one terminal, divided into three concourses. Continental Air Transport (tel: 312-454 7800) provides a bus service between the airport and about a dozen downtown hotels.

Taxis, which are in front of the main terminal, charge between $18 and $22 to go downtown. A shared ride program is available for a flat rate of $10 per person; maximum four. Limos and car rentals are near baggage claim. Some hotels provide a shuttle service. If you're traveling light, you can take the El downtown from Midway.

Porter Services

Porter services are available in most airports and stations, as well as in most hotels. The fee is usually up to the traveler, but reckon on $1–3 a bag, depending on distance and difficulty involved.

In addition, most airports and transportation centers have self-push baggage carts, sometimes free and sometimes for a rental fee ranging from 25 cents to $1.

Left Luggage

Most airports, train and bus terminals have left-luggage rooms or coin-operated lockers. Most hotels also have a left-luggage room for visitors who check out but who have a few precious hours to spare before leaving.

Buses

Bus stops are marked with signs which indicate the bus routes they serve. Buses run about every 15 minutes during the day, more often during rush hour, and less at night.

Trains

An easy way of getting around the city is by the rapid transit trains, either subway or elevated, (El).

The RTA provides commuter trains to the suburbs and exurbs via the Metra lines that leave the city from four central stations. These are:

Travel Information

The Chicago Transit Authority (CTA) and Regional Transport Authority (RTA) provide travel information from 5am–1am every day. Tel: 312-836 7000.

● **Richard B. Ogilvie Transportation Center**, a.k.a **Northwestern Station**, 500 W. Madison, tel: 312-836 7000.
● **Union Station**, 210 S. Canal, tel: 312-655 2385 (Amtrak services also).
● **Randolph Street Station**, at Randolph and Michigan, tel: 312-836 7000.
● **LaSalle Street Station**; 414 S. LaSalle, tel: 312-836 7000.

Tickets and Passes

If you're paying by cash for the buses, you have to have the right amount: $1.50 per ride. An extra 30 cents will buy you a transfer, which you can use twice in two hours, as long as you're taking a different route each time from that of the first bus/El.

More convenient is a regular CTA pass, which you can buy at El stations for any amount between $3 and $100, and which has no time limit. You can keep adding value to it as you use it. Or obtain a 1-, 2-, 3- or 5-day visitor pass, ranging from $5-$18 – timeless until you start to use it – from hotels, Hot Tix booths, Navy Pier, visitor centers, and attractions such as the Adler Planetarium and the Field Museum. Visitor passes are also available from the Shop at the Cultural Center, 77 E. Randolph, tel: 312-744 6630.

Maps

A good transit system map can be requested free from CTA (Chicago Transit Authority), Merchandise Mart, Chicago, IL 60654. In theory, you can obtain the map from hotels, visitor centers and El stations.

Taxis

Taxis in Chicago are metered. Fares begin at $1.60 and each additional

mile is $1.40. There's a 50-cent charge for each additional passenger between the ages of 12 and 65. A 15 percent tip is standard for the driver.

Here are three cab services (see *Yellow Pages* under Taxicabs for many more):
● **Yellow Cab Co**, tel: 312-829 4222.
● **Checker Taxi Co**, tel: 312-243 2537.
● **Flash Cab Co**, tel: 773-561 1444.

Driving

Visitors concentrating on the downtown area are wise to avoid using a car. Between public transportation and a little walking, the usual tourist areas are all accessible. Taxis are plentiful.

Car Rental

If you do decide to drive, here is a small sample of rental agencies (more in *Yellow Pages* of the phone book under Automobile Rentals). Reservations are advised:
● **Alamo**, tel: 1-800-327 9633.
● **Budget**, tel: 1-800-527 0700.
● **Hertz**, tel: 1-800-654 3131.
● **Avis**, tel: 1-800-331 1212.
● **Dollar**, tel: 1-800-800 4000.
● **Enterprise**, tel: 1-800-325 8007.

Parking

While navigating is easy, parking is not, unless you want to spend a lot of time and money in parking garages. There are quite a few parking lots, including underground parking at Grant Park, but these can be expensive. On-street parking can be frustratingly difficult to find.

While meters abound, available ones are like gold dust. It's not unusual to have to drive around the same block for 30 minutes, waiting for someone to leave. Many Chicagoans who use street parking leave their cars in the same place all week in order not to lose their spot. To add to the fun, the number of meters is reduced further when an area is used as a movie location (which, in Chicago, is often).

It is not worth parking illegally, by

Driving Dos & Don'ts

The following is worth knowing if you are driving:
● Front seat passengers must wear a seat belt.
● Don't drink and drive – apart from the fact that it's dangerous, you run the risk of a night in jail.
● You can turn right on red at many junctions – when you can't, warning signs are clearly posted.
● Gas is considerably cheaper outside the city.

the way, as the chances of getting a parking ticket or finding that your car has been towed away are high. Parking police and tow personnel lurk around every corner, waiting for the moment you leave.

If you do have a car, which you park illegally on a public street, and it disappears, call the Chicago Police Department, tel: 312-744 6000. If it has been towed, you can check with them where to collect it. You will need at least $110, in cash, to get your car back. Check the ransom amount when you call the car pound.

City Layout

The numbering system in Chicago makes it easy to find your way around. The city is laid out in a grid pattern. The corner of State and Madison Streets (downtown) is the center point. Any address N., S., E., or W., is north, south, east, or west of that point. Each block is equal to 100 address numbers, and eight blocks equals a mile, so 800 N. State Street is a point eight blocks – one mile – north of Madison. Keep in mind that Lake Michigan is to the east. (*See page 260 for information on obtaining maps.*)

The lakefront in Chicago has been developed for public use. Starting from the lake, the first area of land is the parkland, consisting of beaches, recreational lands, gardens and some of the popular museums. Heading west away from the lake, the next area is downtown, with its stores, businesses and hotels. Here are the skyscrapers and interesting buildings that make up Chicago's famous skyline.

To the north, west, and south of the downtown are residential areas. Chicago is a city of diverse neighborhoods: Beverly, Bridgeport, Hyde Park, Lincoln Park, Rogers Park and so on – each a part of the same city, yet with its own name and identity, and often its own ethnic flavor.

Surrounding Chicago in an ever-widening band are the suburbs, primarily residential areas. Each suburb may use its own numbering system for addresses, but many follow the city pattern.

Walking & Cycling

Chicago is a great walking town for those who are fit, but like most American cities it is much more spread out than most European cities. Visitors who aren't used to extensive walking shouldn't overdo it on foot.

Little known to visitors – and many residents – is the downtown underground pedway (walkway) system, linking over 40 blocks in the Loop. Look out for pedway entrance points; there is one at the Cultural Center, where you can also pick up a pedway map.

Besides using bicycles for cruising along the lakefront, some visitors find that if they are able to brave the traffic, cycling is an efficient, cheap way to see a lot of the city quickly. If you are confident enough to ride in the city, you can rent bicycles from:
● **Bike Chicago**, Navy Pier, tel: 312-944 2337; 1-800 915 2453.
● **Bike Stop**, 1034 W. Belmont, tel: 773-868 6800.

Hitchhiking

Besides being dangerous, hitchhiking is strictly illegal in and around Chicago – as it is in most of the United States. The practice is regarded as too risky by both drivers and travelers, particularly in urban areas.

Tours

Bus Tours
Double Decker Bus Tours
Tel: 312-922 8919.
Narrated tours of Chicago landmarks by Chicago Motor Coach Co, departing every 20-25 minutes from Sears Tower, Water Tower, Art Institute, Navy Pier and several other stops.
American Sightseeing & Gray Line
Tel: 312-251 3100.
Operate tours that take in a wide area of Chicago. Very useful for giving you an overview of the city.

Chicago Architectural Tours
224 S. Michigan Avenue
Tel: 312-922 3432.
Walking, bus, boat and bike tours of Chicago's world-famous architecture; also exhibitions, lectures, books, gifts and memorabilia dedicated to design in the city.
Chicago Supernatural Tours
Tel: 708-499 0300.
Five-hour ghost tours. Reservations essential.
Untouchable Tours
Tel: 773-881 1195.
Visit Prohibition-era gangster sites. Most days, from 610 N. Clark Street. Call ahead for schedule. Reservations are strongly recommended.

Horse & Carriage
J.C. Cutters
Michigan and Chicago Avenues
Tel: 312-664 6014.
The Noble Horse
A block west of Michigan Avenue at the Water Tower
Tel: 312-266 7878.

Multilingual Tours
Chicago Europe Language Center
180 N. LaSalle Street, Suite 2510
Tel: 312-276 6683.
On The Scene Tours
505 N. LaSalle Street
Tel: 312-661 1440.

Boat Tours

Note that many of the boat tour companies operate during the warmer months only.
Chicago Architecture Foundation River Cruise, tel: 312-902 1500. This is probably the best cruise for informative content. It leaves from the southwest corner of Michigan Avenue and the river for a 90-minute tour. Very popular, so reserve ahead.
Chicago From The Lake, North Pier Terminal, 509 E. Illinois Street, tel: 312-527 1977. Architectural tour of 90 minutes. Reservations required.

Mercury, tel: 312-332 1353. Chicago's Skyline Cruiseline, departs from the south side of Chicago River at Michigan Avenue.
Shoreline Sightseeing, tel: 312-222 9328. Cruises lasting 30 minutes from Navy Pier and the Shedd Aquarium all day and evening. They also operate water taxis between Navy Pier and Sears Tower and Navy Pier and the Shedd Aquarium.
Spirit of Chicago, tel: 312-836 7899, south side of Navy Pier. Lunch, brunch, dinner, and moonlight cruises with

entertainment. All year round.
Odyssey, tel: 630-990 0800, Navy Pier. Lunch, brunch, dinner, and moonlight cruises with entertainment.
Wendella Sightseeing Boats, tel: 312-337 1446, north side of Chicago River at Michigan Avenue. One to two-hour cruises.
Tall Ship Windy, tel: 312-595 5555. Impressive to watch as it docks at Navy Pier. 90-minute cruises.
Ugly Duck Cruises, tel: 312-396 2220, Navy Pier. Specialize in tours for large groups.

Where to Stay

Chicago can be fairly expensive for accommodations (and impossible during big conventions), but there is also a wide variety of hotels and motels in different price ranges. Seasonal bargains and packages with both overseas and domestic flights are often available, along with "weekender" rates offered by hotels that cater to expense-account business travelers during the week.

Tourists trying to save money may find the best bargains a few blocks away from downtown, but still within an easy bus or taxi ride.

In this section, hotels are divided into four categories: Deluxe, Expensive, Moderate and Budget. Prices can vary widely so it's worth calling hotels in the price category above your budget first as you may be pleasantly surprised.

In any case, never accept the first room price you are offered without asking about any special deals they may be offering.

Deluxe

The Drake Hotel
140 E. Walton Place, 60611.
Tel: 312-787 2200 or toll free
1-800-553 7253.
Fax: 312-787 1431.
Lavish lobby, worth a visit even if you're not staying here. Shopping arcade and three restaurants including the Cape Cod Room.
Four Seasons Hotel
120 E. Delaware Place, 60611.
Tel: 312-280 8800 or toll free
1-800-332 3442.
Fax: 312-280 7585.

Located above Bloomingdale's. Indoor pool and health center.
The Ritz-Carlton Chicago
160 E. Pearson Street, 60611.
Tel: 312-266 1000 or toll free
1-800-621 6906.
Fax: 312-266 1194.
Located above Water Tower Place. Grand lobby. Won best Midwest Chef award in 1998. Recent "multi-million dollar" refurbishment.

Expensive

Ambassador West
1300 N. State Parkway, 60610.
Tel: 312-787 3700 or toll free
1-800-300 9378.
Fax: 312-640 2967.
Good choice for a special occasion, especially if there's a promotion.
Chicago Hilton and Towers
720 S. Michigan Avenue, 60605.
Tel: 312-922 4400 or toll free
1-800-445 8667.
Fax: 312-663 6528.
Sumptuous. Some of the rooms have two bathrooms.
DoubleTree Guest Suites Hotel
Tel: 312-664 1100, or toll free
1-800-222 8733.
Fax: 312-664 8267.
Gym, indoor pool, and two rooms to each suite.
Embassy Suites
600 N. State, 60611.
Tel: 312-943 3800.
Fax: 312-943 5979.
Complimentary full breakfast available daily. Indoor pool.
Executive Plaza, A Clarion Hotel
71 E. Wacker Drive, 60601.
Tel: 312-346 7100 or toll free
1-800-621 4005.
Fax: 312-346 1721.
Great views of the river.
Fairmont
200 N. Columbus Drive, 60601.
Tel: 312-565 0381 or toll free
1-800-527 4727.
Fax: 312-861 3656.
Located at the Illinois Center. Complete business services. Afternoon tea served.
Hotel Inter-Continental
505 N. Michigan Avenue, 60611.
Tel: 312-944 4100 or toll free
1-800-628 2112.
Fax: 312-321 8877.
Exquisite swimming pool. Try to

stay in the old, restored section of hotel, not the modern addition.
The Knickerbocker
163 E. Walton Place, 60611.
Tel: 312-751 8100 or toll free
1-800-621 8140.
Fax: 312-751 9663.
Has had a mega-bucks renovation. Impressive lobby.
Midland
172 W. Adams Street, 60603.
Tel: 312-332 1200 or toll free
1-800-621 2360.
Fax: 312-332 5909.
European-style hotel in the Financial District.

Omni Ambassador East
1301 N. State Street, 60610.
Tel: 312-787 7200 or toll free
1-800-843 6664.
Fax: 312-787 4760.
Old-fashioned elegance. Home of the Pump Room.
Omni Chicago Hotel
676 N. Michigan.
Tel: 312-944 6664 or toll free
1-800-843 6664.
Fax: 312-266 3015.
Guests who need to toil in their rooms will appreciate the work area.
The Palmer House Hilton
17 E. Monroe Street, 60603.
Tel: 312-726 7500 or toll free
1-800-445 8667.
Fax: 312-917 1779.
A 1920s Loop hotel with magnificent murals on lobby ceiling.
Radisson Hotel and Suites
160 E. Huron, 60611.
Tel: 312-787 2900 or toll free
1-800-333 3333.

Fax: 312-787 4069.
Spacious rooms, all on high floors.
Outdoor rooftop pool. Renovated in
the mid-1990s.

Renaissance Chicago Hotel
1 W. Wacker, 60611.
Tel: 312-372 7200.
Fax: 1-800-468 3571.
Large rooms, geared to business
travelers' needs.

Sheraton Chicago Hotel & Towers
301 E. North Water Street, 60611.
Tel: 312-464 1000 or toll free
1-800-325 3535.
Fax: 312-329 6929.
Great views from all the rooms.

Summerfield Suites
166 E. Superior Street, 60611.
Tel: 312-787 6000.
Fax: 312-787 6133.
All suites, in a good location. Full
complimentary breakfast buffet.

Airport Hotels

No choice but to check into one
of the chains around O'Hare?
Hotel Sofitel has a nice touch –
a bakery, from which tasty
croissants emerge.
5550 N. River Road, Rosemont.
Tel: 847-678 4488.
Fax: 847-678 9756.

Holiday Inn O'Hare International
may be the ideal place if you
have a bunch of bored kids to
cope with – Holidome, whirlpool,
arcade games, all are here.
5440 N. River Road, Rosemont.
Tel: 847-671 6350 or toll free
1-800-465 4329.
Fax: 847-671 5406.

Sutton Place Hotel
21 E. Bellevue Place, 60611.
Tel: 312-266 2100 or toll free
1-800-606 8188.
Fax: 312-266 2141.
Penthouse suites available. Jazz
pianist. 24-hour room service.

Swissôtel Chicago
323 E. Wacker Drive, 60601.
Tel: 312-565 0565 or toll free
1-800-654 7263.
Fax: 312-565 0540.
At Illinois Center. Aims for quiet
European ambience. Health spa
with indoor lap pool.

Price Guide

Prices here are per double room.
- **Deluxe** $250 and over
- **Expensive** $150–$250
- **Moderate** $100–$150
- **Budget**   Under $100

Tremont
100 E. Chestnut Street, 60611.
Tel: 312-751 1900 or toll free
1-800-621 8133.
Fax: 312-751 9253.
Rooms have VCRs, CD-players and
fax machines. Good casual dining.

The Westin River North
320 N. Dearborn, 60610.
Tel: 312-744 1900 or toll free
1-800-228 3000.
Fax: 312-527 2650.
Formerly the Hotel Nikko. Good
views, health club.

Whitehall
105 E. Delaware Place, 60611.
Tel: 312-944 6300 or toll free
1-800-323 7500.
Fax: 312-573 6250.
A 1920s hotel that was
completely refurbished in the mid-
1990s.

Moderate

Best Western Inn of Chicago
162 E. Ohio, 60611.
Tel: 312-787 3100 or toll free
1-800-557 2378.
Fax: 312-573 3180.
Excellent location, good price.

Best Western River North Hotel
125 W. Ohio, 60611.
Tel: 312-467 0800 or toll free
1-800-727 0800.
Fax: 312-467 1665.
Right in the heart of gallery land.
Year-round rooftop pool.

Hotel Chains

These are the telephone numbers
for some hotel groups represented
in Chicago:
Best Western 1-800-528 1234
Clarion 1-800-252 7466
Comfort Inn 1-800-228 5150
Courtyard by Marriott 1-800-321
2211
Days Inn 1-888-576 3297

Blackstone
636 S. Michigan Avenue, 60605.
Tel: 312-427 4300 or toll free
1-800-622 6330.
Fax: 312-427 4736.
Plenty of gangster history and
ambience of bygone days.

**Courtyard by Marriott Chicago
Downtown**
30 E. Hubbard, 60611.
Tel: 312-329 2500 or toll free
1-800-321 2211.
Fax: 312-329 0293.
Guests can have meals at Shaw's
Crab House or Tucci Milan put on
their room account.

Gold Coast Group
Tel: toll free 1-800-621 8506.
Small hotels in renovated older
buildings. The group includes the
following four hotels:

Claridge Hotel
1244 N. Dearborn Street, 60610.
Tel: 312-787 4980 or toll free
1-800-245 1258.
Fax: 312-787 4069.
Attractively renovated hotel.

The Delaware Towers
25 E. Delaware Place, 60611.
Tel: 312-944 4245.
Fax: 312-943 7319.

The Elms
18 E. Elm Street, 60611.
Tel: 312-787 4740.
Fax: 312-642 8448.

The Talbott
20 E. Delaware Place, 60611.
Tel: 312-944 4970.
Fax: 312-944 7241.

Hampton Inn and Suites
11 W. Illinois, 60611.
Tel: 312-832 0330.
Fax: 312-832 0333.
Local calls are free in this new-ish
River North hotel. Some of the
suites have full kitchens.

DoubleTree 1-800-222 8733
Embassy Suites 1-800-362 2779
Hilton 1-800-445 8667
Holiday Inn 1-800-465 4329
Hyatt 1-800-233 1234
Motel 6 312-787 3580
Omni 1-800-843 6664
Ramada 1-800-228 2828
Westin 1-800-937 8461

Bed and Breakfast

Rather than a European-style inn that includes breakfast as part of the payment, a B&B in Chicago is more likely to be a privately owned apartment. **Bed and Breakfast Chicago** is a clearing-house of available bed and breakfast facilities in the Chicago area. Reservations must be made. Contact Bed & Breakfast Chicago, PO Box 14088, Chicago, IL 60614.
Tel: 773-248 0005.
Fax: 773-248 7090.

Holiday Inn Chicago City Centre
300 E. Ohio Street, 60611.
Tel: 312-787 6100 or toll free
1-800-465 4329.
Fax: 312-787 6259.
No surprises, but there is a decent sports complex next door, free to guests.
Hyatt on Printer's Row
500 S. Dearborn.
Tel: 312-986 1234 or toll-free
1-800-233 1234.

Fax: 312-939 2468.
If you don't mind the seeming remoteness of the South Loop, this is good value, especially at weekends.
Lenox Suites
616 N. Rush Street, 60611.
Tel: 312-337 1000 or toll free
1-800-445 3669.
Fax: 312-337 7217.
European-style hotel, in the heart of the downtown.
Motel 6
162 E. Ontario, 60611.
Tel: 312-787 3580 or toll free
1-800-621 8055.
Fax: 312-787 1699.
Public areas are a notch above the usual Motel 6, though no surprises with the rooms.
Neighbourhood Inns of Chicago
A group of three quaint, moderately priced hotels in the Lakeview/Wrigleyville area. Guests are delighted with their price, location and character:
City Suites Hotel
933 W. Belmont Avenue, 60657.
Tel: 773-404 3400, or toll free
1-800-248 9108.
Fax: 773-404 3405.

Looking For Something A Little Different?

Bored with bland hotel rooms? This trio of relatively recent arrivals, all unabashedly offbeat (and all in the expensive category) may suit you.
Hotel Allegro
171 W. Randolph, 60601.
Tel: 312-236 0123 or toll free
1-800-643 1500.
Fax: 312-236 3440.
"Like no other hotel in Chicago," says the Allegro management. And they are probably right. An "award-winning designer" was commissioned..., with the result that the rooms are daringly decked out in hot colors which they admit may not be to everyone's taste. In-room fax and 2-line speakerphone supplied. Suites have terry robes, VCR and Jacuzzi, and there's an on-site fitness center.
Hotel Monaco
225 N. Wabash, 60601.

Tel: 312-960 8500 or toll free
1-800-397 7661.
Fax: 312-960 1883.
Near State Street shopping, another boldly designed newcomer – "unique artifacts are surrounded by chocolate browns, pistachio greens and lipstick reds". Pets are welcome and a "complimentary named goldfish is available for every guest" (which we hope isn't offered to Kitty). Evening wine service by the fireplace.
House of Blues Hotel
333 N. Dearborn, 60610.
Tel: 312-245 0333.
Fax: 312-923 2442.
Now blues fans have their own place to stay. In the Marina City complex, alongside the House of Blues music venue, the hotel plans to open Buddy Guy's Legends No 2. Guests have a 36-lane bowling center and health and fitness club at their disposal.

Price Guide

Prices here are per double room.
- **Deluxe** $250 and over
- **Expensive** $150–$250
- **Moderate** $100–$150
- **Budget**   Under $100

Surf Hotel
555 W. Surf Street, 60657.
Tel: 773-528 8400, or toll free
1-800-787 3108.
Fax: 773-528 8483.
Park Brompton Inn
528 W. Brompton, 60657.
Tel: 773-404 3499, or toll free
1-800-727 5108.
Fax: 773-404 3495.
The Raphael
201 E. Delaware Place, 60611.
Tel: 312-943 5000 or toll free
1-800-821 5343.
Fax: 312-943 9483.
Good-size rooms, some with sitting-rooms.
The Seneca
200 E. Chestnut, 60611.
Tel: 312-787 8900.
Fax: 312-988 4438.
Comfortable, without all the frills of a big hotel, and in a good location.

Budget
Cass Hotel
640 N. Wabash, 60611.
Tel: 312-787 4030.
1-800-227 7850.
Nothing special, but great location.
Hotel Wacker
111 W. Huron, 60610.
Tel: 312-787 1386.
Clean, and in good location.
Ohio House Motel
600 N. LaSalle, 60610.
Tel: 312-943 6000.
Fax: 312-943 6063.
No frills, but it's convenient.

Hostels
Arlington House
616 Arlington Place
Tel: 773-929 5380
Spartan but clean, and in a great location.
Chicago International Hostel, 6318 N. Winthrop Ave, tel: 773-262 1011. Well away from the downtown area.

Where to Eat

Restaurant Listings

The following restaurants, grouped in alphabetical order by style of food, are recommended. Note that not every Chicago restaurant opens every day of the week – Monday is a particular favorite day for closing – so it's best to check ahead of time.

American
Mr Beef
666 N. Orleans Street
Tel: 312-337 8500.
Offers the best beef sandwich in Chicago. Very casual, with celebrity photos on the wall. **$**
Billy Goat Tavern
430 N. Michigan Avenue
Tel: 312-222 1525.
Lower level Michigan Avenue. Hangout for the city's press corps. Cheeseburgers are the thing here. **$**
Blackhawk Lodge
41 E. Superior Street
Tel: 312-280 4080.
Generous helpings of contemporary American cooking. **$$$**
Boston Blackie's
164 E. Grand
Tel: 312-938 8700.
Tasty burgers and sandwiches. **$$**
Cheesecake Factory
875 N. Michigan Avenue (in the Hancock Center)
Tel: 312-337 1101.
Wildly popular eatery, with a vast choice of cheesecakes. **$$**
Demon Dogs
944 W. Fullerton Avenue
Tel: 773-281 2001.
Best hot dog stand in the city. Among the best fries. **$**
Ed Debevic's
640 N. Wells Street
Tel: 312-664 1707.
A campy, upbeat 1950s diner known for its homestyle food and sassy service. **$$**
Entre Nous
200 N. Columbus Drive
(Fairmont Hotel)
Tel: 312-565 8000.
An intimate restaurant with "classique" cuisine. **$$$$$**
The Fireplace Inn
1448 N. Wells Street
Tel: 312-664 5264.
Ski lodge atmosphere. Barbecued ribs, steaks, seafood, sandwiches. Outdoor dining available. **$$$**

Price Guide

Prices are for the cost of a three-course meal and coffee for one, without tax or tip.
$$$$$ $40 and over
$$$$ $30–40
$$$ $20–30
$$ $10–20
$ under $10

Gold Coast Dogs
418 N. State Street
Tel: 312-527 1222.
159 N. Wabash
Tel: 312-917 1677.
Chicago hot dogs, also burgers and sandwiches. **$**
Hard Rock Café
63 W. Ontario Street
Tel: 312-943 2252.
Mick Jagger's guitar, George Harrison's Beatles suit, Michael Jackson's platinum records and yes, even food, especially hamburgers. **$$**
Harry Caray's Restaurant
33 W. Kinzie Street
Tel: 312-828 0966, 773-465 9269.
Baseball memorabilia decorate the walls, while steaks and chops dominate the menu. **$$$**
Houston's Restaurant
612 N. Rush Street
Tel: 312-649 1121.
Something for everyone here; fish, ribs, soups, steaks, etc, served in a convenient location. **$$$**
Michael Jordan's Restaurant
500 N. LaSalle Street
Tel: 312-644 3865.
Basketball star Michael Jordan opened this restaurant, featuring his favorite foods with a bit of sport thrown in; a multi-media lounge decorated with memorabilia. **$$$**
Planet Hollywood
633 N. Wells
Tel: 312-266 7827.
Restaurant and entertainment complex owned and frequented by celebrities. **$$**
Printer's Row
550 S. Dearborn Street
Tel: 312-461 0780.
New American. Highly acclaimed South Loop restaurant. **$$$$**
The Pump Room
1301 N. State Parkway
Tel: 312-266 0360.
A Chicago institution and the place to celebrate that special occasion. Known since the 1930s for its "Booth One," which is reserved for celebrities. **$$$$$**
Rock & Roll McDonald's
600 N. Clark Street
Tel: 312-664 7940.
Eat a Big Mac in a pop-music motif. **$**
Signature Room at the 95th
875 N. Michigan Avenue
Tel: 312-787 9596.
Enjoy elegant dining and a great view of the city from the 95th floor of the John Hancock Center. **$$$$$**
Inexpensive buffet lunch. **$$**

Doggie Bags

Helpings are often large, and will feed someone with a normal appetite twice; family restaurants expect diners to take what they can't eat in a doggie bag and will happily offer to "wrap" for you.

Barbecued Ribs
Army's and Lou's
422 E. 75th Street,
Tel: 773-483 3100.
Many consider this to be one of the finest soul food restaurants in America. Friendly service; open for breakfast, lunch and dinner. **$$**
Chicago Chop House
60 W. Ontario
Tel: 312-787 7100.
Excellent steaks served in intimate three-story restaurant; equally enjoyable seafood dishes are also available for non-carnivores. **$$$$**

Tipping

The standard tip for restaurant waitstaff is 15 percent, 20 percent if you are particularly pleased with the service, or 10 percent if you are not thrilled by it. If it's plain bad, then don't tip at all (but you've probably complained to the management by this time anyway).

As tax on restaurant meals is just over 10 per cent, a simple trick for calculating the tip is to multiply the tax by one and a half times for 15 percent, or double it for 20 per cent.

Miller's Pub
134 S. Wabash
Tel: 312-263 4988.
Popular spot for sports fans and theatergoers. Casual atmosphere. Possible celebrity sightings. **$$$**
Twin Anchors Restaurant and Tavern
1655 N. Sedgwick Street
Tel: 312-266 1616.
Among the best ribs in Chicago. Great burgers too. Pleasant neighborhood watering hole. **$$$**

Cajun
Heaven on Seven
Garland Building, 111 N. Wabash
Tel: 312-263 6443 and,
600 N. Michigan (2nd level)
Tel: 312-280 7774.
Redfish
400 N. State
Tel: 312-467 1600.
Fun decor, and Louisiana cooking.

Chinese
Mandar-Inn Restaurant
2249 S. Wentworth Avenue
Tel: 312-842 4014.
Good service. **$$**
65 Seafood Restaurant
336 N. Michigan
Tel: 312-372 0306 and 2414 S. .
Serving sizes are generous in this small, basic eatery frequented at lunchtime by Loop office workers. **$**
Also at Wentworth Avenue
Tel: 312-225 7060 **$**
Three Happiness Restaurant
209 W. Cermak Road

Tel: 312-842 1964.
This is a tiny storefront with limited seating. Serves very good Cantonese and Szechwan food. **$$**

Delicatessen
The Bagel Restaurant
3107 N. Broadway
Tel: 773-477 0300.
North Side. Traditional deli, serves bulging sandwiches and award-winning soups. **$$**
Manny's Coffee Shop & Deli
1141 S. Jefferson Street
Tel: 312-939 2855.
Dine in or carry out, a complete breakfast menu, plus sandwiches, homemade soups and salads. The specialty is corned beef. **$$**

Ethiopian
Mama Desta's
3216 N. Clark Street
Tel: 773-935 7561.
Diners eat with their hands, using delicious injera bread to scoop the food. Bring several friends. **$$**

French
Ambria
2300 N. Lincoln Park West
Tel: 773-472 5959.
Serving Chef Gabino Sotelino's French- and Spanish-influenced cuisine. **$$$$$**
Bistro 110
110 E. Pearson Street
Tel: 312-266 3110.
Hospitable and comfortable, specialties include roasted garlic, angel-hair pasta, oven-roasted chicken and crème brulée for dessert. Extensive French-American wine list. **$$$**
Café Bernard
2100 N. Halsted Street
Tel: 773-871 2100.
Country French cuisine. Located in the heart of Lincoln Park. **$$$**
Charlie Trotter's
816 W. Armitage
Tel: 773-248 6228.
Contemporary multi-cultural cuisine. **$$$$$**
The Dining Room
160 E. Pearson Street (Ritz-Carlton)
Tel: 312-573 5223.
Beautiful setting, daily specials; foie gras salad is a specialty. **$$$$$**

Everest Room
440 S. LaSalle Street
Tel: 312-663 8920.
One of the top restaurants in the country, with a view to match. **$$$$$**
Le Français
269 S. Milwaukee Avenue, Wheeling
Tel: 847-541 7470.
Although not located in Chicago, this suburban restaurant is world famous. Contemporary French cuisine in a provincial atmosphere. **$$$$$**
Mon Ami Gabi
2300 N. Lincoln Park West
Tel: 773-348 8886.
Lively, authentic Parisian bistro overlooking Lincoln Park. You can dine on the patio in warm weather. **$$$$$**
Yvette Wintergarden
311 S. Wacker Drive
Tel: 312-408 1242.
Art deco Loop bistro located in a tropical atrium. Serves light French-American cuisine. **$$$$**

Price Guide

Prices are for the cost of a three-course meal and coffee for one, without tax or tip.
$$$$$ $40 and over
$$$$ $30–40
$$$ $20–30
$$ $10–20
$ under $10

German
The Berghoff Restaurant
17 W. Adams Street
Tel: 312-427 3170.
Wide selection of meat, poultry and fish items. German fare among the best in the city. They make their own beer and root beer. **$$**
Golden Ox
1578 Clybourn Avenue
Tel: 312-664 0780.
"Old World" atmosphere, strolling musicians, good German food and a good beer garden. Re-opening late 1999 after remodeling. **$$$**
Zum Deutschen Eck
2924 N. Southport Avenue
Tel: 773-525 8121.
A cozy German restaurant featuring classics such as Schnitzel Dijon

and sauerbraten. Live
entertainment. **$$$**

Greek
Greek Islands
200 S. Halsted Street
Tel: 312-782 9855.
Festive, with room to dance. An
exposed steam table showcases
many of the house offerings. **$$$**
Papagus
620 N. State Street
Tel: 312-642 8450.
Features regional Greek cuisine and
a variety of *mezedhes*. **$$$**
The Parthenon
314 S. Halsted Street
Tel: 312-726 2407.
Big and bustling. Saganaki, lamb,
Greek sausage, suckling pig. **$$$**

Indian
Bukhara Restaurant & Bar
2 E. Ontario Street
Tel: 312-943 0188.
Authentic cuisine from the
Northwest Territory of India.

Tandoori dishes. Glass-walled
kitchen to view the chefs'
preparations. **$$$**
Gaylord India
678 N. Clark Street
Tel: 312-664 1700.
Traditional tandoori specialties. **$$$**
Jaipur Palace
440 N. Wabash Avenue
Tel: 312-595 0911.
Roomy and elegant. Sidewalk tables
in summer. **$$$**
Klay Oven Restaurant
414 N. Orleans Street
Tel: 312-527 3999.
Traditional tandoori and Karhai
dishes. **$$$**

Italian
Bice Ristorante
158 E. Ontario Street
Tel: 312-664 1474.
Northern Italian cuisine. Homemade
pastas. Signature carpaccio,
risottos, mussels, *vongole*, and veal
Milanese style. Elegant dining room
or outdoor garden. **$$$$**
Carlucci Restaurant
2901 N. Sheffield Avenue
Tel: 773-281 1220.
Regional Italian cuisine. Patio
seating in summer. **$$$$**
Centro
710 N. Wells Street
Tel: 312-988 7775.
A serious place for pasta, prime
steaks, chops and broiled seafood
in the art district. **$$$**
Coco Pazzo
300 W. Hubbard
Tel: 312-836 0900.
Elegant loft space. **$$$$**
Como Inn Restaurant
546 N. Milwaukee Avenue
Tel: 312-421 5222.
Serving Chicago since 1924. Free
parking. **$$$**
Gennaro's Restaurant
1352 W. Taylor Street
Tel: 312-243 1035.
Family business specializing in
gnocchi, ravioli, stuffed eggplant,
fried calamari and homemade
pasta. **$$$**
Gene & Georgetti
500 N. Franklin Street
Tel: 312-527 3718.
For over 50 years this restaurant
has offered delicious Italian

Seafood Restaurants
Cape Cod Room $$$$$
140 E. Walton Place (Drake Hotel)
Tel: 312-787 2200.
A famous dining spot whose
specialties include the
Bookbinder red snapper soup.
Catch 35 $$$$
35 W. Wacker
Tel: 312-346 3500. More than
30 fresh seafood specialties.
Oyster bar and display kitchen.
Live entertainment.
Nick's Fishmarket $$$$$
51 S. Clark Street
Tel: 312-621 0200.
Sophisticated atmosphere, good
service and wide range of fresh
fish and seafood.
**Shaw's Crab House and Shaw's
Blue Crab Lounge $$$$**
21 E. Hubbard Street
Tel: 312-527 2722.
Some of the freshest seafood in
the city can be enjoyed here.

specialties, steaks and other
dishes. **$$$$**
Italian Village
71 W. Monroe Street
Tel: 312-332 7005.
Three restaurants featuring Italian
American dishes. **$$$$**
Lino's
222 W. Ontario Street
Tel: 312-266 0616.
Casual but elegant dining in a club-
like setting featuring Northern
Italian cuisine. **$$$**
Maggiano's Little Italy
516 N. Clark
Tel: 312-644 7700.
A classic recreation of a New York
City pre-war "Little Italy" dinner
house. Family-style dining available.
$$$
Rico's Restaurant
626 S. Racine Avenue
Tel: 312-421 7262.
Located in "Little Italy", with home
cooking specialties. **$$$**
The Rosebud Café
1500 W. Taylor Street
Tel: 312-942 1117 and,
55 E. Superior
Tel: 312-266 6444.
A "Little Italy" institution. **$$$**

Scoozi
410 W. Huron Street
Tel: 312-943 5900.
The neoclassic atmosphere of a 15th-century artist's studio recreated in the River North gallery district. Italian countryside cuisine. **$$$**

Spiaggia
980 N. Michigan Avenue
Tel: 312-280 2754.
Main dining room on the 2nd floor offers a view of Lake Michigan; northern Italian cuisine, including homemade pastas and brick-oven pizza. **$$$$$**

Café Spiaggia
Next door to Spiaggia above.
Tel: 312-280 2764.
A casual European-style café with some of the same items as Spiaggia and an extensive antipasto bar. **$$$$**

Stefani's
1418 W. Fullerton Parkway
Tel: 773-348 0111.
Northern Italian cuisine. Host restaurant for politicians of note from Italy. **$$$**

Trattoria No. 10
10 N. Dearborn Street
Tel: 312-984 1718.
Charming and warm, featuring a variety of Italian dishes. **$$$$**

Coffee Bars

Coffee addicts need never fear being unable to get a caffeine fix in Chicago. Coffee bars abound, and Starbucks bars in particular have spread like a rash throughout the yuppier areas.

Here are three pleasant places that haven't yet been swallowed up by Starbucks, where you can relax with a cup of coffee, and a decent snack too.

The 3rd Coast
1260 N. Dearborn
Tel: 312-649 0730.

Bittersweet
1114 W. Belmont
Tel: 773-929 1100.
Heavenly pastries.

Tempo
1 E. Chestnut
Tel: 312-943 4373.
Open 24 hours a day.

Tuscany
1014 W. Taylor Street
Tel: 312-829 1990.
Little Italy restaurant. Open kitchen, woodburning oven and grill reminiscent of a Tuscan eatery. **$$$$**

Price Guide

Prices are for the cost of a three-course meal and coffee for one, without tax or tip.
$$$$$ $40 and over
$$$$ $30–40
$$$ $20–30
$$ $10–20
$ under $10

Japanese
Hatsuhana
160 E. Ontario Street
Tel: 312-280 8808.
A large sushi bar, with many varieties of ocean fish flown in daily. **$$$$**

Ron of Japan
230 E. Ontario
Tel: 312-644 6500.
Japanese steakhouse. The flashing knives-style showmanship doesn't get in the way of the food, which is described by one Japanese expatriate as "very authentic." **$$$**

Sai Cafe
2010 N. Sheffield,
Tel: 773-472 8080.
Very popular with Lincoln Park yuppies. **$$**

Tsunami
1160 N. Dearborn
Tel: 312-642 9911.
Posh Gold Coast yuppie hangout. **$$$$**

Korean
Woo Lae Oak
30 W. Hubbard
Tel: 312-645 0051.
Authentic Korean cuisine. **$$$**

Mexican
Frontera Grill
445 N. Clark Street
Tel: 312-661 1434.
Wonderful Mexican cooking in a Southwestern setting. Menu changes weekly and represents several regions. Reservations for large groups only. **$$$**

Topolobampo
Address/phone number as above.
Under the same owner as the Frontera Grill, though the food is even more refined, and the setting more formal. Reservation essential. **$$$$**

El Jardin
3335 N. Clark Street
Tel: 773-528 6775.
Mexican cuisine, two outdoor gardens, Sunday brunch. **$$**

Su Casa
49 E. Ontario Street
Tel: 312-943 4041.
In an 18th-century hacienda setting. Specialties include chicken fajitas and red snapper. **$$$**

Middle Eastern
Cousin's
2833 N. Broadway
Tel: 773-880 0063 and,
5203 N. Clark Street
Tel: 773-334 4553.
Cousin's has been described as one of the best non-vegetarian restaurants in Chicago for vegetarians. Extensive and imaginative menu. **$$**

Sayat Nova
157 E. Ohio Street
Tel: 312-644 9159.
Romantic restaurant with a reputation for good food. Authentic Armenian-Middle Eastern dishes include *mezedhes*, kebabs and vegetarian specialties. **$$$**

Uncle Tannous
2626 N. Halsted
Tel: 773-929 1333.
Welcoming, cozy atmosphere. **$$$**

Pizza
Bacino's
75 E. Wacker Drive
Tel: 312-263 0070.
One of the best pizza joints around. Spinach pizza is a specialty. **$$**

California Pizza Kitchen
414 N. Orleans
Tel: 312-222 9030 and,
Water Tower Place, 7th level
Tel: 312-787 7300.
Delicious wood-fired pizzas (26 varieties). Also pastas, salads, soup. Children's menu available. **$$**

Edwardo's
1212 N. Dearborn Street

Tel: 312-337 4490 or,
521 S. Dearborn Street
Tel: 312-939 3366.
Chicago-style stuffed pizza. Dining in, carry out or delivery. **$$**
Father and Son Pizza and Italian Restaurant
645 W. North Avenue,
Tel: 312-654 2550.
Family-run business with gourmet bakery. Home delivery available. **$$**
Gino's East
160 E. Superior Street
Tel: 312-943 1124.
There's often a wait to get in. **$$**
Pizzeria Uno
29 E. Ohio Street
Tel: 312-321 1000.
Where the Chicago-style pizza was born. **$$**
Pizzeria Due
619 N. Wabash Avenue
Tel: 312-943 2400.
Chicago-style, deep-dish pizza was created at Pizzeria Uno in 1943. Pizzeria Due opened in 1955 to handle the overflow. A must-try for pizza lovers. **$$**

Polish
Orbit
2948-54 N. Milwaukee Avenue
Tel: 773-276 1355.
A popular and boisterous restaurant in the Jackowo (Polish downtown area), known for *pirogi* (savory dumplings). **$$**

Late-night Eating

For the general populus, Chicago is an early-to-bed, early-to-rise city. Consequently, out-of-towners may be surprised by how early some of the restaurants close. Europeans in particular will be open-mouthed to see restaurants packed with diners at 5.30 to 6.30pm. Conversely, it's not unusual to see the doors close, with staff eager to get home, around 10.30pm. So if you don't feel like being thrown out at this hour, call ahead and find out how late your chosen restaurant serves. For some, the policy is to stay open "till the last diner leaves."

Dining Al Fresco

A refreshing development over recent years has been the proliferation of sidewalk tables outside restaurants during the summer. The following restaurants have outdoor eating areas – always specify this is what you want when you reserve:
Cafe BaBaReeba!
2024 N. Halsted,
tel: 773-935 5000.
Paella fans will love this Spanish eatery. Tasty appetizers include baked goat's cheese and marinated octopus. **$$$**
Joy's Noodles
3257 Broadway,
tel: 773-327 8330.
Good food, generous helpings and friendly service are all on the menu here. Plus you can BYOB. No reservations. Just turn up and ask for a patio table. **$$**

Russian
Russian Teatime
63 E. Adams
Tel: 312-360 0000.
Wide and interesting menu. Very popular Loop restaurant; reservations essential. **$$$**

Spanish
Café Iberico
737 N. LaSalle
Tel: 312-573 1510.
A downtown favorite – there's always a line. **$$**
Emilio's Tapas
444 W. Fullerton Parkway
Tel: 773-327 5100.
Good service, agreeable bar where it seems you can always get a seat. Don't leave without trying their garlic potato appetizer. Heaven. **$$$**

Steak
Chicago Chop House
60 W. Ontario Street
Tel: 312-787 7100.
Meat and potato place. Specialties include prime rib and aged, broiled steak. Piano bar nightly. **$$$$**
Eli's The Place for Steak
215 E. Chicago Avenue
Tel: 312-642 1393.

Prime aged steaks are the specialty. As famous for its cheesecake as for its steaks and excellent service. **$$$$**
Gibson's Bar & Steakhouse
1028 N. Rush Street
Tel: 312-266 8999.
1940s style, with supersized steaks. Piano bar with the late night food. **$$$$$**
Kinzie Street Chop House
400 N. Wells Street
Tel: 312-822 0191.
Clubby and sophisticated, featuring local art. Serves prime dry-aged steaks, chops, seafood and pasta dishes. **$$$**
Lawry's the Prime Rib
100 E. Ontario Street
Tel: 312-787 5000.
Roast prime rib carved tableside from a rolling cart, in one of four thicknesses. Huge salad bowls, spun on a bed of ice. **$$$$**
Morton's of Chicago
1050 N. State Street
Tel: 312-266 4820.
Clubby atmosphere. "Menu" consists of a selection of prime cuts on a platter. Strictly for the meat-eating fraternity. **$$$$$**
Palm Restaurant
323 E. Wacker Drive
Tel: 312-616 1000.
Specializing in steak and lobster since 1926. **$$$$$**
Ruth's Chris Steak House
431 N. Dearborn
Tel: 312-321 2725.

Pubs

Duke of Perth $$
2913 N. Clark
Tel: 773-477 1741.
At least 80 types of Scotch are available in this rarity, a Scottish pub. Good fish and chips – turn up on Friday evenings for "all you can eat" deal.
Red Lion Tavern $$
2446 N. Lincoln Avenue
Tel: 773-348 2695.
A refreshing change for sports-haters – you're unlikely to find ballgames on TV in this English pub. Fish and chips and steak and kidney pie are on the menu.

American prime steaks, lamb veal, pork chops. Fresh fish and select Creole dishes. **$$$$**

The Saloon
200 E. Chestnut
Tel: 312-280 5454.
Comfortable, club-like setting. Its specialties include prime dry-aged steaks, chops, prime rib and seafood. **$$$$**

Swedish
Ann Sather
929 W. Belmont
Tel: 773-348 2378.
There's always a line for breakfast. The cinnamon rolls are a favorite. **$$**

Price Guide

Prices are for the cost of a three-course meal and coffee for one, without tax or tip.
$$$$$ $40 and over
$$$$ $30–40
$$$ $20–30
$$ $10–20
$ under $10

Thai
Star of Siam
11 E. Illinois
Tel: 312-670 0100.
Handy for Michigan Avenue. **$$**
Thai Classic
3332 N. Clark Street
Tel: 773-404 2000.
Spicy Thai fish, along with sate and other standards. **$$**

Vietnamese
Le Colonial
937 N. Rush
Tel: 312-255 0088.
Lush, plush setting. The shrimp on sugar cane (appetizer) is a delight. **$$$$**
Pasteur
5525 N. Broadway
Tel: 773-878 1061.
A critically- acclaimed café situated in New Chinatown. **$$**

Culture

Theater

Theater is enjoying a resurgence in Chicago, with plans well under way for several new – or renovated historic – venues.

Tickets and Information
The League of Chicago Theatres offers half-price tickets for the same day, or on Friday for weekend shows, for many theaters, through its Hot Tix booths. Hot Tix also sells full-price advance tickets. (*For Hot Tix locations see page 87.*)

For information on the shows themselves, pick up a free *Reader*, which will save you around $3 calling 1-900 225 2225 at $1 a minute for the same information, or buy a Friday newspaper. Hot Tix imposes a service charge, as do some theaters for telephone or even box-office service. Tickets are generally available at the box office, sometimes by mail, and through Ticketmaster, tel: 312-559 1212 for payment by credit card. You can also call 1-888-225 8844 to pay by credit card, but that will cost you $1 a minute, which somewhat defeats the object of buying Hot Tix.

Downtown
Arie Crown Theater
2301 S. Lake Shore Drive
Tel: 312-791 6000.
In McCormick Place, primarily road companies of Broadway shows. The place to see *The Nutcracker* at Christmas.
Auditorium Theater
50 E. Congress Parkway
Tel: 312-922 2110.
Great acoustics.
Chicago Theatre
175 N. State
Tel: 312-902 1500.

Ford Center for the Performing Arts, Oriental Theatre
24 W. Randolph
Tel: 312-902 1400.
Goodman Theater
200 S. Columbus Drive
Tel: 312-443 3800.
Specializes in contemporary work with many well-known actors.
Shubert Theatre
22 W. Monroe Street
Tel: 312-977 1700.

Off Loop
About Face Theatre
Jane Addams Center Hull House, 3212 N. Broadway
Tel: 773-549 7943.
Steppenwolf Theater
1650 N. Halsted Street
Tel: 312-335 1888.
National reputation for method acting. Alumni include John Malkovich.
Theatre on the Lake
Fullerton Park-way and the Lakefront.
Tel: 312-742 7994
Strictly community theater performing well-known Broadway shows at 8pm Tuesday through Saturday during the summer.
Victory Gardens Theater
2257 N. Lincoln Avenue
Tel: 773-871 3000.
Serious plays. Very professional.

Suburban
Drury Lane/Oakbrook Terrace
Roosevelt and Butterfield, Oakbrook Terrace
Tel: 630-530 8300.
Dinner theatre. Mainly musicals.
Marriott Lincolnshire Theatre
Route 21 and Milwaukee Avenue, Lincolnshire
Tel: 847-634 0200.
Pheasant Run Theatre
4051 E. Main Street, St Charles
Tel: 630-584 6342. Dinner theatre. Musicals.
Village Players
1010 W. Madison, Oak Park
Tel: 708-222 0369.
Shared by the suburbs of Oak Park and River Forest, a small theater with locals taking roles in many of the famous Broadway shows.

Cinema

For additional theaters to those in the list below, or to find out what's currently playing, check the *Reader*, which has a very user-friendly guide, *Showtime*, within the Movie section.

Some of the cinemas listed below, including Water Tower, McClurg Court, Pipers Alley, 600 N. Michigan, Fine Arts and the Music Box are wheelchair accessible; those providing sound systems for the hearing impaired include the Esquire, McClurg Court, 600 N. Michigan and Water Tower and some of the Pipers Alley cinemas.

Water Tower
845 N. Michigan Avenue
Tel: 312-649 5790.

McClurg Court
330 E. Ohio Street
Tel: 312-642 0723.

Biograph
2433 N. Lincoln Avenue
Tel: 773-348 4123.
Where Dillinger was gunned down by the FBI.

Esquire
58 E. Oak Street
Tel: 312-280 0101.

900 N. Michigan
Tel: 312-787 1988.

Pipers Alley Theatre
1608 N. Wells
Tel: 312-642 7500.

600 N. Michigan
(entrance on Rush)
Tel: 312-255 9340.

Three Penny
2424 N. Lincoln
Tel: 773-935 5744.

Village
1548 N. Clark
Tel: 312-642 2403.

Fine Arts Theatre
418 S. Michigan Avenue
Tel: 312-939 3700.
A good selection of foreign and domestic independent films.

Music Box Theatre
3733 N. Southport Avenue
Tel: 773-871 6604.
Beautiful old-fashioned movie house with premieres, previews and classic old American and foreign films.

Concerts

Classical

It's hard to get downtown tickets for the Chicago Symphony Orchestra as they've all usually gone to subscribers, but you could try your luck just before the performance – there may be a cancellation available, or someone who can't make it trying to sell their ticket.
Chicago Symphony Orchestra, Orchestra Hall (September–May), 220 S. Michigan Avenue, tel: 312-294 3000. In summer, at Ravinia, Highland Park, tel: 847-266 5100.
Grant Park Symphony Orchestra, Free concerts through the Chicago Park District at Petrillo Music Shell, Grant Park, tel: 312-742 7638.

Popular Music

World Music Theatre
19,100 Ridgeland Avenue, Tinley Park
Tel: 708-614 1616.
Nice suburban location. Public transportation not available.

Park West
322 W. Armitage Avenue
Tel: 773-929 5959.

Poplar Creek Music Theatre
4777 W. Higgins Road, Hoffman Estates
Tel: 312-559 1212.
Outdoor concerts.

Ravinia
Highland Park
Tel: 847-266 5100.
Features varied music acts (eg. jazz, classical, R&B, dance) during the summer months that can be heard and seen from the pavilion or from the huge grassy picnic area.

Rosemont Horizon
6920 N. Mannheim Road, Rosemont
Tel: 312-559 1212.

Ballet

Ballet Chicago
185 N. Wabash Avenue
Tel: 312-251 8838.
School at same address, tel: 312-251 8833.
Hubbard Street Dance Co.
218 S. Wabash Avenue
Tel: 312-663 9095.

Opera

Opera goers should note that tickets for the Lyric are particularly hard to get. As with the Chicago Symphony Orchestra, many tickets are distributed in advance to subscribers, but you may be able to get a cancellation on the day.
Lyric Opera of Chicago, 20 N. Wacker Drive, tel: 312-332 2244 (season September–March).
Chicago Opera Theatre, 2501 N. Keeler, tel: 773-292 7578.
The Light Opera Works, 927 Noyes, Evanston, tel: 847-869 6300. (June–December). Specializes in Gilbert and Sullivan.

Art Galleries

River North has the greatest concentration of galleries in Chicago – as a matter of fact the largest concentration outside of Manhattan. The majority are located within a block or two of Superior and Franklin Streets, an area sometimes referred to as SuHu (for Superior and Huron), in a play on New York's SoHo art district.

There are galleries galore scattered around the city, however. You'll find them in Wicker Park and Bucktown and they are also beginning to appear in the South and West Loop. Look in the weekly listings newspaper, the *Reader*, or in *Chicago Gallery News*, which you can pick up in most galleries.

In River North, most galleries are open weekdays and Saturdays 10am or 11am–5pm. Some open earlier, some stay open later, but if you plan on these hours you'll be playing it safe. Friday night is opening night for new exhibits, with complimentary wine available in the galleries to anyone who cares to wander in. The artists themselves are often present.

In similar vein, the Museum of Contemporary Art offers live entertainment and a cash bar on the first Friday of every month and the Art Institute does likewise on the third Thursday of the month.

Annual Events

Chicago's annual events tend to have a very different atmosphere from the city's festivals (*listed in the box below*). The latter often have an ethnic flavor and generally involve a broader range of activities, including entertainment, music, food and stalls.

January/February
Chinese New Year Parade
Wentworth Avenue and Cermak Road
Tel: 312-225 6198

February
Chicago Auto Show
McCormick Place
Tel: 312-791 7000.
Azalea and Camellia Show
Lincoln Park Conservatory
Tel: 312-742 7736.
Garfield Park Conservatory
Tel: 773-638 1766.
Sportsmen's Show of Chicago
Tel: 847-914 0630.

Spring Dog Show
Tel: 773-237 5100.

March
Magnificent Mile Crystal Carnival/Shopper's Weekend
Tel: 312-744 3315.
Chicago Cubs Convention
Tel: 773-404 2827.
Medinah Shrine Circus
Medinah Temple, 600 N. Wabash Ave.
Tel: 312-266 5050.
Ice Capades
Rosemont Horizon, Rosemont
Tel: 847-635 6601.
St Patrick's Day
Parade starts at Dearborn Street
and Wacker Drive
Tel: 312-421 1010, 312-942 9188.
In Feb/Mar, before the Parade.
South Side Irish Parade
103rd Street and Western Avenue.
The weekend before St Patrick's Day.
Chicago Flower & Garden Show
Tel: 312-595 7437.

April
Spring and Easter Flower Show,
Lincoln Park Conservatory
Tel: 312-742 7736.
Chicago Cubs Baseball Season,
Wrigley Field
Tel: 773-404 2827.
Chicago White Sox Season,
Comiskey Park
Tel: 312-674 1000.

May
Buckingham Fountain Re-opens
Grant Park
Tel: 312-742 7529.
Polish Constitution Day Parade
Tel: 312-744 3315.
Chicago Bike Week
Tel: 312-744 3315.

June
Old Town Art Fair
1900 N. Lincoln Avenue
Tel: 312-337 1938.
Ravinia
Highland Park opens for a summer full of outdoor concerts

Festivals

MARCH
Chicago Chevy Vette Fest,
tel: 708-563 4300.

APRIL
Chicago Latino Film Festival,
various locations.

MAY
Mayor Daley's Kids & Kites Fest,
tel: 312-744 3315.
Cinco de Mayo, tel: 312-744 3315.
Chicago Neighborhood Summer Festivals, tel: 312-744 3370.

JUNE
Celebrate on State Street Festival, tel: 312-782 9160.
International Theater Festival of Chicago, various theaters.
Chicago Blues Festival, Petrillo Music Shell, Grant Park, tel: 312-744 3315.
Chicago Gospel Festival, Petrillo Music Shell, Grant Park, tel: 312-744 3315.
Chicago Country Music Festival, tel: 312-744 3315.

Taste of Chicago, Grant Park, tel: 312-744 3315. Continues into July.

JULY
Fourth of July, fireworks on the lake-front and in almost every Chicago neighborhood.
Taste of Lincoln Avenue, food fair between Fullerton and Wrightwood Avenues, tel: 773-472 9046.
Old St Patrick's World's Largest Block Party, Adams and Des Plaines streets, tel: 312-648 1021.
Annual Mayor's Cup Youth Soccer Fest, tel: 312-744 3315.
Chinatown Summer Festival, tel: 773-868 3010.

AUGUST
Viva! Chicago Latin Music Festival, Grant Park, tel: 312-744 3315.

SEPTEMBER
Chicago Jazz Festival, Petrillo Music Shell, Grant Park,

tel: 312-744 3315.

OCTOBER
Chicago International Film Festival, international films shown at various theaters, tel: 312-425 9400/hotline: 312-332 3456.
History Mystery Bicycle Tour and Festival, 2153 West 112th Street and Longwood Drive, tel: 773-233 3100. A puzzle-solving bicycle tour, followed by food, music and games.
Chicago Park District Halloween Festivities, tel: 312-742 7529.
Octoberfest, Navy Pier.

NOVEMBER
Magnificent Mile Lights Festival, tel: 312-642 3570.

DECEMBER
Magnificent Mile Lights Festival, continues, tel: 312-642 3570.
In the Spirit, annual festival celebrating Christmas, Hanukkah and Kwanzaa at Chicago Cultural Center, tel: 312-346 3278.

Tel: 847-266 5100.
Grant Park Concerts
Petrillo Music Shell, Grant Park.
Free concerts by the Grant Park
Symphony Orchestra.
Gay & Lesbian Pride Parade
Tel: 773-348 8243.
57th Street Art Fair
Tel: 773-493 3247.

July
**Old St Patrick's World's Largest
Block Party**
Adams and Des Plaines Streets
Tel: 312-648 1021.
Chicago to Mackinac Yacht Races
Sailing from Monroe Street Harbor
Tel: 312-861 7777.
Annual Race to the Taste
Tel: 312-744 3315.
Venetian Night Boat Parade,
Monroe Harbor
Tel: 312-744 3315.
Newberry Library Book Fair.

August
Bud Billiken Parade
35th Street and South King Drive
Tel: 312-225 2400.
Chicago International Sky Nights,
Lakefront
Tel: 312-744 3315.
Air and Water Show
North Avenue Beach
Tel: 312-744 3370.

September
Chicago Bears
Season-opening games, Soldier
Field
Tel: 847-615 2327.
Lyric Opera
Season-opening concerts, Civic
Center for Performing Arts
Tel: 312-332 2244.
Around the Coyote
Art/performance exhibition, various
locations
Tel: 773-342 6777.
Chicago Symphony Orchestra
Season-opening concerts,
Orchestra Hall
Tel: 312-294 3000.
Mexican Independence Day Parade
Tel: 312-744 3315.

October
Columbus Day Parade
Dearborn Street and Wacker Drive

Tel: 312-828 0010.
Halloween Pumpkin Plaza
Tel: 312-744 3370.
Chicago Marathon
Tel: 1-888-243 3344.

November
**Lighting of the City's Christmas
Tree**
Daley Center Plaza
Tel: 312-744 3315.
Christmas Parade
Michigan Avenue from Balbo to
Wacker Drives
Tel: 773-935 8747.
Chriskindlmarket
Tel: 312-744 3315.

December
A Christmas Carol
Goodman Theater
Tel: 312-443 3800.
The Nutcracker
Arie Crown Theater
Tel: 312-791 6000.
Caroling to the Animals
Lincoln Park Zoo
Tel: 312-742 2000.
Christmas Around the World
Museum of Science and Industry
Tel: 773-684 1414.
Christmas trees as they're
decorated in various countries.
Christmas Flower Show
Lincoln Park Conservatory
Tel: 312-742 7736.
New Year's Eve River Walk
Tel: 312-744 3315.

Children

Chicago is a great place to bring
kids. Many hotels let children stay
in their parents' room for a small
charge or for free; ask when making
reservations. Many restaurants can
provide a special children's menu –
usually for children under 12, with
smaller portions and lower prices.
Pick up a copy of *Chicago Parents*,
a free monthly magazine usually
available in libraries or children's
bookstores, which lists events of
interest to children and their
families. Copies or annual
subscriptions are available from:
Wednesday Journal, Inc., 141 S.
Oak Park Avenue, Oak Park, IL
60302, tel: 708-386 5555.
 Below are listed a variety of
places especially geared towards
entertaining the children:
**Art Institute's Kraft Education
Center**
South Michigan Avenue at Adams
Street
Tel: 312-443 3600.
The Center offers an assortment of
absorbing activities for children of
all ages. There are workshops,
tours and demonstrations, including
such things as puppet making and
calligraphy. Some games send
children throughout the museum in
search of clues. Open daily: Mon,
Wed–Fri 10.30am–4.30pm, Tues
10.30am–8pm, Sat 10am–5pm,
Sun 12 noon–5pm. Entrance free
Tues.
Brookfield Zoo
1st Avenue and 3lst Street in west
suburban Brookfield.
Tel: 708-485 0263.
Open daily 10am–4.30pm;
May–Sept 9.30am–5.30pm;
entrance fee almost half price Tues

and Thurs April–Sept, and free on those days during the remainder of the year. *For more information on the zoo, see page 247.*

Chicago Children's Museum,
Navy Pier
Tel: 312-527 1000.
A godsend for parents; the museum has activities for children of all ages, such as the Climbing Schooner, the Inventing Lab, and the "television studio," plus a host of other activities. Open Tues–Sun 10am–5pm, and Mon during summer; entrance free Thurs 5pm–8pm.

Chicago Fire Academy
558 W. De Koven Street
Tel: 312-747 7239.
Located on the site where the Chicago Fire of 1871 is believed to have started. One-hour guided tours of the facilities for training firefighters are offered. Open Mon–Fri. Visits by appointment only. Admission free.

DisneyQuest
A five-story, indoor interactive theme park recently opened at the corner of Rush and Ohio. Here the idea is that fun-lovers of all ages can embark on all sorts of daring adventures, aided and abetted by virtual reality.

It's a Bug's World

By the time you read this the Field Museum (*see below for details*) should have launched its $10million **Underground Adventure** – the first of its kind in the world – where visitors will be "shrunk" to a hundredth of their size before setting off to explore the world of suddenly gigantic bugs, plants and fungi in the undergrowth.

Field Museum of Natural History
Roosevelt Road and Lake Shore Drive
Tel: 312-922 9410.
There are many exhibits for children, like the giant dinosaurs and Egyptian mummies. Workshops are offered on weekends. The Place of Wonder is specifically for kids.

ESPN Zone opened recently at the corner of Wabash and Ohio. Billed as a "three-dimensional ESPN experience, combining interactive games and live broadcasting with great American grill food in the ultimate sports-viewing environment."

Kohls Children's Museum
165 Green Bay Road, Wilmette
Tel: 847-256 6056.
"A place to pretend, invent, touch explore, discover, learn" is the museum's aim. A hands-on museum geared toward children aged 1–9. Exhibits rotate throughout the year, plus there are story times and puppet shows. The learning store offers a variety of creative toys. Open: Mon–Sat 9am–5pm and Sunday noon–5pm.

The Lambs
Interstate 94 and Route 176,
Libertyville
Tel: 847-362 4636.
A community for the developmentally disabled, there's a restaurant, bakery, ice cream parlor, country store, farmyard, petting zoo, miniature golf, picnic area and special events. Open daily 9am–5pm, except major holidays.

Lifeline Theatre
6912 N. Glenwood Avenue
Tel: 773-761 4477.
Geared toward 5–12 year olds.

Lincoln Park Zoo
2200 N. Cannon Drive
Tel: 312-742 2000.
A free zoo right in the city. Children will enjoy everything, especially the Pritzker Children's Zoo, where they can pet some of the animals, and the Farm in the Zoo. Very popular are the underwater viewing window in the Polar Bear Pool and the Great Ape House.

South Pond, south of the zoo, next to Café Brauer. Rent a paddleboat, May–Sept.

Museum of Science and Industry
57th Street at Lake Shore Drive
Tel: 773-684 1414.
Education disguised as fun at its best. Favorites include Colleen Moore's Fairy Castle, Hatching Chicks and a giant train set. Younger children wll especially enjoy the Curiosity Place.

Puppet Parlor
1922 W. Montrose Avenue
Tel: 773-774 2919.
Weekend performances, including children's classics.

Santa's Village
Routes 25 and 72, Dundee
Tel: 847-426 6751.
Amusement rides, especially for younger children, shows that the whole family can enjoy, a water park and picnic groves are among the attractions. But best of all, Santa is always there. Open: May–Sept, Mon–Fri 10am–6pm, Sat and Sun 11am–7pm.

Shedd Aquarium
1200 S. Lake Shore Drive
Tel: 312-939 2426.
The world's largest fishbowl. A favorite spot is the Coral Reef at feeding time as the turtles, sharks and other fish are fed by hand.

Six Flags Great America
I-94 at Route 132 East, Gurnee
Tel: 847-249 1776.
The largest amusement park around, open May–Oct, call for hours. Plenty of rides and shows for one admission fee. It's fairly expensive so plan on spending the whole day. For some thrill-seekers, the roller coasters alone make the trip worthwhile. *For more information see page 251.*

United Skates of America
4836 N. Clark Street
Tel: 773-271 5668 ext 12.
Two roller skating floors, game room, state of the art sound and light system. Food available; and a bar for the adults. Open daily unless they've booked a private party, so call ahead first.

Nightlife

There is plenty of nightlife in Chicago. Most hotels have one or more lounges, many of which are popular spots. The local listings magazines have descriptions. Cover charge varies.

Coq D'Or
Drake Hotel, 140 E. Walton
Tel: 312-787 2200.
Pianist Buddy Charles has played here for over half a century. Catch him Tuesday–Sunday.

Liquid
1997 N. Clybourn
Tel: 773-528 3400.
Popular swing venue.

Lounge Ax
2438 N. Lincoln Avenue
Tel: 773-525 6620.
Indie rock club, dark and crowded.

Excalibur
632 N. Dearborn Street
Tel: 312-266 1944.
Another popular spot; long lines.

Schuba's Tavern
3159 N. Southport
Tel: 773-525 2508.
Great music, tiny club.

Toulouse Cognac Bar
2140 N. Lincoln Avenue
Tel: 773-665 9071.

Zebra Lounge
1220 N. State
Tel: 312-642 5140.
Black and white décor, of course. The audience usually sings along with the piano.

Cabaret & Comedy

All Jokes Aside
1000 S. Wabash
Tel: 312-922 0577.
Stand up comedy club featuring African American and Latino performers.

Comedy Sportz
3209 N. Halsted
Tel: 773-549 8080.

Funny Firm
318 W. Grand Street
Tel: 312-321 9500.
River North location. Up and coming local talent and national standup comedians.

ImprovOlympic
3541 N. Clark Street
Tel: 773-880 0199. Cozy venue, free on Wednesdays.

Second City
1616 N. Wells Street
Tel: 312-337 3992.
Improvisation. This famous spot was a springboard for Jim and John Belushi, Bill Murray, Dan Aykroyd and John Candy, to name a few.

Second City ETC.
1608 N. Wells
Tel: 312-642 8189.
Sister to Second City.

Zanies
1548 N. Wells Street
Tel: 312-337 4027.
First full-time comedy club in Chicago. Local and national talent.

Blues Clubs

As the home of Chicago blues, the guitar-driven music form that evolved from the downhome Mississippi Delta folk music and then had so much influence on modern rock, the city still has a number of clubs and bars devoted almost exclusively to the form, and often featuring many of the legendary bluesmen. They include:

Blue Chicago on Clark
536 N. Clark Street
Tel: 312-661 0100.
1940s-style bar.

Blues
2519 N. Halsted Street
Tel: 773-528 1012.

Blue Chicago
736 N. State Street
Tel: 312-642 6261.

Kingston Mines
2548 N. Halsted Street
Tel: 773-477 4646.

Buddy Guy's Legends
754 S. Wabash Avenue (owned by guitar great, Buddy Guy.)
Tel: 312-427 0333.

House of Blues
329 N. Dearborn
Tel: 312-923 2000.
Part-owned by Blues Brother Dan Aykroyd. Not exclusively blues – could be gospel or salsa, for instance, depending on when you go. By the time you read this, if all goes according to plan, the House of Blues Hotel (*see Hotels section, page 270*) will include a second Buddy Guy's Legends.

New Checkerboard Lounge
423 E. 43rd Street
Tel: 773-624 3240.
Considered a rough area. Home of the Blues Hall of Fame. (Also called Checkerboard Lounge as it's not so new any more)

Discos

CroBar Nightclub
1543 N. Kingsbury Court
Tel: 312-413 7000.
Multilevel, and the biggest dance floor in Chicago.

Drink
702 W. Fulton Street
Tel: 312-733 7800.
Eat, drink and dance the night away. Specialty drinks served in buckets…and baby bottles.

56west
56 W. Illinois Street
Tel: 312-527 5600.
Aims straight for the smart set.

The Hangge-Uppe
14 W. Elm Street
Tel: 312-337 0561.
Another multilevel nightclub, on the Gold Coast, with four bars and two dance floors.

Jazz Clubs

Andy's
11 E. Hubbard Street
Tel: 312-642 6805.
A Chicago institution in the heart of downtown.

Backroom
1007 N. Rush
Tel: 312-751 2433.
It's so small you may have to view the performers by a mirror, but at least you'll get to know your neighbor quickly.

Cotton Club
1710 S. Michigan Avenue
Tel: 312-341 9787.
Features dance club.
Green Dolphin Street
2200 N. Ashland
Tel: 773-395 0066.
This site was once home to beat-up old cars. Now it's a trendy supper club.
Green Mill
4802 N. Broadway
Tel: 773-878 5552.
A legendary jazz club once owned and frequented by gangsters. Now there's good music every night except Monday.
Jazz Showcase
59 W. Grand
Tel: 312-670 2473.
Chicago institution. Big names, comfortable venue.
Lush Life
226 E. Ontario
Tel: 312-649 5874.
Mostly mainstream jazz here.
New Apartment Lounge
504 E. 75th Street
Tel: 773-483 7728.
Friendly venue. Von Freeman is a regular performer here.
Pop's for Champagne
2934 N. Sheffield
Tel: 773-472 1000.
Nightly live jazz in champagne bar. Sunday brunch.

Bars

Bar, tavern, saloon, pub – in Chicago, all these terms mean a place to get an alcoholic beverage. At most bars, mixed drinks and bottled beer are available, as well as the beers "on tap" or "draft." Beer can often be bought by the pitcher. Soft drinks are always available and sometimes coffee. Soft drinks and mixed drinks will typically be served with generous amounts of ice, unless otherwise requested.

Some bars allow customers to run a tab; the waitress or bartender keeps track and presents the bill upon departure. Don't forget the tip for the waitress (15–20 percent) or bartender (10–15 percent).

The neighborhood bar is usually a simple, friendly place, often with a regular crowd, where it might be easy to strike up a conversation. Hotel bars or lounges have traditionally been quiet and elegant, sometimes with piano music. But some newer ones offer more variety, such as bands or comedy.

Many Chicago bars are open late, until 1am or 2am, and some places that feature entertainment are allowed to remain open until 5am. Downtown bars are often open by midday, although neighborhood taverns may open for breakfast.

Neighborhood Bars
Déjà Vu,
2624 N. Lincoln
Tel: 773-871 0205.
Friendly atmosphere, open till 5am at weekends.
Goose Island Brewing Co.
1800 N. Clybourn Avenue
Tel: 312-915 0071.
Serves home-brewed beer.
John Barleycorn
658 W. Belden
Tel: 773-348 8899.
Popular Lincoln Park bar. Beer garden at the back.
Sheffield's Wine and Beer Garden
3258 N. Sheffield Avenue
Tel: 773-281 4989.
An easy-going corner bar, with many brands of beer and a summer beer garden.

Singles Bars
The Rush Street area has traditionally been considered the place for singles bars, catering to the under-40 crowd, and a good number of tourists. This is the place to find wet T-shirt contest aficionados – you have been warned. Among the most popular bars are:
Bootleggers
13 W. Division
Tel: 312-266 0944.
Butch McGuire's
20 W. Division Street
Tel: 312-337 9080.

Sports Bars

Theme bars have become very popular, and in Chicago the theme is sports.

In fact, Chicago claims to have invented the American sports bar, though most places now calling themselves such are not the old shot-and-a-beer neighborhood joints, but rather trendy spots popular among both men and women – including some who aren't necessarily interested in the latest scores.

Some are owned by sports figures, some are near sports stadiums, others have a sports theme and frequently a big screen TV for watching games.

Among Chicago's best–known sports bars are:
Cubby Bear
1059 W. Addison Street
Tel: 773-327 1662.
Across from Wrigley Field, a popular spot for Cubs games. Three big TV screens and 15 smaller monitors.
Gamekeepers Tavern and Grill
1971 N. Lincoln Avenue
Tel: 773-549 0400.
Young professionals.
Harry Caray's
33 W. Kinzie Street
Tel: 773-465 9269
This bar and dining room, owned by the late Cubs announcer, is decorated with baseball photos and memorabilia.
Ranalli's Sports Bar and Grill
1925 N. Lincoln Avenue
Tel: 312-642 4700.
Satellite sports TV on a large screen as well as 10 smaller screens. This Old Town bar is a popular gathering-place for famous American athletes, fans and sports personalities.
Sluggers
3540 N. Clark Street
Tel: 773-248 0055.
Located across from Wrigley Field, this place is packed after Cubs games. Try the batting cages for baseball practice.

Mother's
26 W. Division Street
Tel: 312-642 7251.

Gay Bars
There are many bars in the Lakeview
East area. Some are strictly gay or
lesbian, others welcome all.
Legacy 21
3042 W. Irving Park Road
Tel: 773-588 9405.
Open since 1961, formerly the "21
Club."
Berlin
954 W. Belmont
Tel: 773-348 4975.
Primarily gay but caters to – and
attracts – everyone.
Buddies' Restaurant & Bar
3301 N. Clark
Tel: 773-477 4066.
Full service bar and restaurant.
Girlbar
2625 N. Halsted
Tel: 773- 871 4210.
Two-level women's dance club, with
pool tables and two outside decks.
Girlbar is Boybar every Wednesday.
Roscoe's Tavern
3354 N. Halsted
Tel: 773-281 3355.
Cocktails, music, videos, dancing,
pool tables, and live entertainment.

Riverboat Casinos

All the casinos are within an hour's
drive of Chicago. Special buses are
often available from downtown
locations. Although the boats rarely
move from their spot, "departure
times" for boarding are still
imposed.
Grand Victoria Casino
Elgin
Tel: 847-888 1000.
Empress Casino
Joliet
Tel: 888-436 7737.
Harrah's Casino
Joliet
Tel: 800-427 7247.
Hollywood Casino
Aurora
Tel: 800-888 7777.
Trump Casino
Gary, Indiana
Tel: 888-218 7867.

Shopping

Where to Shop

Downtown has a number of smart
vertical shopping malls, in
particular along N. Michigan
Avenue. It also has several of
America's best department stores
and a myriad boutiques, fashion
shops and discount houses. For
those with access to a car there's
no shortage of manufacturers'
outlets in the suburbs. Most stores
and shops open at 9 or 10am and
stay open until at least 6pm; many
often remain open until 8 or 9pm.
Here's a taster:

Downtown
State Street has two major
department stores: Carson Pirie
Scott, at State and Madison
Streets, tel: 312-641 7000, and
Marshall Field's, at 111 N. State
Street, tel: 312-781 1000. Open
daily.
Magnificent Mile
Michigan Avenue from Chicago River
to Oak Street (*see page 165*).
This is *the* glamorous shopping
area including Tiffany, Cartier, Saks
Fifth Avenue, and Bloomingdale's.
Nike Town Chicago
669 N. Michigan Avenue
Tel: 312-642 6363.
Nike shoes, clothes, hats, posters
and displays. A one-of-a-kind sport
store.
Chicago Place Mall
700 N. Michigan Avenue
Tel: 312-642 4811.
Fifty specialty shops including Saks
Fifth Avenue and Williams-Sonoma.
Eighth floor food court in a tropical
garden. European gourmet
supermarket.
Water Tower Place
835 N. Michigan Avenue
Tel: 312-440 3165.

Sales Tax

The sales tax in Chicago is 8.75
percent, and it is added to the
listed cost of almost everything,
including books, food and
clothing. Unlike many European
countries, where the value-added
tax can be deducted when
purchases are being exported,
there are no provisions for
reimbursement of the sales tax.

An atrium shopping mall with
Marshall Field's, Lord & Taylor and
seven floors of specialty shops.
900 North Michigan Shops
900 N. Michigan Avenue
Tel: 312-915 3916.
This is home to the Chicago branch
of Bloomingdale's, plus dozens of
boutiques.
Oak Street's outstanding specialty
shops emphasize diversity and
quality. A fun place to window shop.

Suburban
Gurnee Mills Outlet Mall, I-94 and
Route 132, Gurnee
Tel: 1-800-937 7467.
Over 200 stores and outlets
offering savings on top-name
brands.
Northbrook Court
Tel: 847-498 1770
An upscale mall with 144 shops in
suburban Northbrook.
Old Orchard
Tel: 312-915 0017
A large, well-designed mall in
suburban Skokie.
Woodfield Mall
Tel: 847-330 1537
In suburban Schaumburg,
Woodfield has 235 shops and
stores and is said to be the second
largest mall in the United States.
Buses run regularly to Woodfield
from downtown.

Antiques
The antique district is on the North
Side in Lakeview and there are a
number of stores and malls on W.
Kinzie as well:
Belmont Antique Malls
2132 W. Belmont
Tel: 773-549 9270 and,

2227 W. Belmont
Tel: 773-871 3915.
Chicago Antique Centre
3045 N. Lincoln Avenue
Tel: 773-929 0200.
Jay Robert's Antique Warehouse
149 W. Kinzie
Tel: 312-222 0167.
Lincoln Antique Mall
3141 N. Lincoln Avenue
Tel: 773-244 1440.
Wrigleyville Antique Mall
3336 N. Clark Street
Tel: 773-868 0285.

Architectural Salvage
Architectural Artifacts
4325 N. Ravenswood
Tel: 773-348 0622.
Salvage One
1524 S. Sangamon
Tel: 312-733 0098.

Books
Barbara's Bookstore
Navy Pier
Tel: 312-222 0890 and,
1350 Wells Street
Tel: 312-642 5044.
Barnes & Noble
1130 N. State
Tel: 312-280 8155 and,
659 W. Diversey Parkway
Tel: 773-871 9004.
Borders
830 N. Michigan Avenue
Tel: 312-573 0564 and,
2817 N. Clark
Tel: 773-935 3909.
Crown Books
105 S. Wabash
Tel: 312-782 7667 and,
144 S. Clark
Tel: 312-857 0613.
Unabridged Books
3251 Broadway
Tel: 773-883 9119.

Open-Air and Farmers' Markets
Find them from June through
October throughout the city. Call
312-744 9187 for a schedule.

Souvenirs
All the major attractions and
museums including the Museum of
Science & Industry, the Shedd
Aquarium and Lincoln Park Zoo
have gift stores that are worth

checking out. You should also try:
Accent Chicago
835 N. Michigan Avenue (Water
Tower, 7th floor)
Tel: 312-944 1354.
Complete Chicago themed gift
store.
Chicago Tribune Gift Store
435 N. Michigan Avenue
Tel: 312-222 3080.
Unique gifts.
Fannie May Candies
38 N. Clark
Tel: 312-236 0608 and,
343 N. Michigan Avenue
Tel: 312-726 8409, and several
other branches.
Chocolate-lover's paradise. Buy
boxes of Pixies – a Pixie is a huge
flat toffee- and chocolate-covered
pecan – and you can't go wrong.
The Art Institute Store
111 S. Michigan Avenue
Tel: 312-443 3533, and,
level 5 of the 900 N. Michigan mall
Tel: 312-482 8275
A stylish range of products from
prints of the works on exhibit to
jewellery, books, bottle openers and
dishes.

Toys
Toys R Us,
10 S. State Street
Tel: 312-857 0667.
FAO Schwartz
840 N. Michigan
Tel: 312-587 5000.
Toyscape
2911 N. Broadway
Tel: 773-665 7400.
A great place for adults to browse in
as well as kids.

Clothing Sizes

The table below provides a
comparison of US, Continental
and British clothing sizes. It is
always best to try on any article
before buying it, however, since
sizes can vary.

Women's Clothes

US	CONTINENTAL	UK
8	40/36N	10/32
10	42/38N	12/34
12	44/40N	14/36
14	46/42N	16/38
16	48/44N	18/40

Women's Shoes

US	CONTINENTAL	UK
4½	36	3
5½	37	4
6½	38	5
7½	39	6
8½	40	7
9½	41	8
10½	42	9

Men's Suits

US	CONTINENTAL	UK
34	44	34
–	46	36
38	48	38
–	50	40
42	52	42
–	54	44
46	56	46

Men's Shirts

US	CONTINENTAL	UK
14	36	14
14½	37	14½
15	38	15
15½	39	15½
16	40	16
16½	41	16½
17	42	17

Men's Shoes

US	CONTINENTAL	UK
6½	–	6
7½	40	7
8½	41	8
9½	42	9
10½	43	10
11½	44	11

Sport

Baseball
Two major league teams make their homes in Chicago, playing from early April through early October.

Chicago Cubs play in the National League. Their home park is **Wrigley Field**, the oldest park in the major leagues. Located at Clark and Addison Streets (1060 W. Addison Street), Wrigley can be reached by the Howard (Red Line) "El" train. Spend an afternoon or an evening (possible since the highly controversial installation of lights in 1988) amid the ivy-covered walls. For tickets, tel: 312-831 2827; for information, tel: 773-404 2827.

The Chicago White Sox play in the American League. They can be seen at **Comiskey Park**, just off the Dan Ryan Expressway at 35th and Shields Streets. The park can be reached on the Dan Ryan "El" Line. To get tickets, tel: 312-831 1769; for any other information, tel: 312-674 1000.

Basketball
The Chicago Bulls entertain their fans at **United Center**, 1901 W. Madison Street, which can be reached on the Madison Street Bus No. 20, tel: 312-455 4000.

Football
The Chicago Bears play at **Soldier Field**, at 12th Street and the lakefront, tel: 847-615 2327.

Ice Hockey
The Chicago Blackhawks play in the **United Center**, 1901 W. Madison Street, tel: 312-455 7000.

The **Chicago Park District**, tel: 312-742 7529, has a wide range of affordable (and in many cases, free) recreation, sports and cultural activities for all ages. It also offers theater, acting and dance classes.

Bicycling
A 20-mile path runs along the lakefront. Bicycle rentals are available at:
Bike Chicago
Navy Pier
Tel: 312-944 2337; 1-800-915 2453.
Bike Stop
1034 W. Belmont
Tel: 773-868 6800.

Canoeing
Friends of the Chicago River
Tel: 312-939 0490
Organizes a wide range of canoe trips in the city.

Fishing
In addition to fishing in Lake Michigan and the Chicago River, you can also cast your rod and reel in designated harbors and lagoons. Smelt fishing season begins April 1. For information on fishing, including where to get the necessary license, and fishing spots call the **Chicago Park District** or the city's **Fishing Hotline**, tel: 312-744 3370.

Golf
The Chicago Park District has a number of nine-hole courses, 18-hole and miniature golf courses as well as driving ranges, as follows:

The Chicago area has a number of tracks where horse racing, both thoroughbred and harness, can be enjoyed.
Hawthorne Racetrack
3501 S. Laramie Avenue, Cicero
Tel: 708-780 3700.
Maywood Park Racetrack
8600 W. North Avenue, Maywood
Tel: 773-626 4816.
Sportsman's Park Racetrack

Jackson Park Golf Course and Driving Range; Robert A. Black Golf Course, at Warren Park; Columbus Park Golf Course; Diversey Driving Range and Miniature Golf at Lincoln Park; Marquette Park Golf Course; South Shore Cultural Center Golf Course; Sydney R. Marowitz Golf Course; and Washington Park Miniature Golf.

Ice Skating
Outdoor skating is available when the weather is suitably cold at **Skate on State**, on State between Randolph and Washington, tel: 312-744 3315. From Thanksgiving through March 1, the Chicago Park District operates a dozen outdoor ice rinks, several of which convert to in-line skating rinks during the summer months. They also have an indoor ice rink. For further details, tel: 312-747 5283.

Jogging
The path along the lakefront is shared by bicyclists and joggers. Avoid jogging in deserted areas after dark. For additional information, contact the **Chicago Area Runners Association**, tel: 312-666 9836.

Sailing
Sailing lessons are available for adults and youth through the Rainbow Fleet at Montrose Harbor, Burnham Harbor and South Shore Cultural Center. In addition, the Judd Goldman Adaptive Sailing Program provides instruction for the physically challenged in Burnham Harbor. For more information call

3301 S. Laramie Avenue, Cicero
Tel: 773-242 1121.
Off-Track Betting Facilities
177 N. State Street
Tel: 312-419 8787;
233 W. Jackson Boulevard
Tel: 312-427 2300.
Auto Racing
Raceway Park, 130th Street and Ashland Avenue, Calumet Park
Tel: 708–385 4035.

the Chicago Park District's **Marine Department**, tel: 312-747 0737.

Swimming
The Chicago Park District has 32 beaches along Lake Michigan as well as numerous indoor and outdoor pools. The beaches are open from June 15 to Labor Day, from 9am–9.30pm. Lifeguards are on duty. Tel: 312-742 7529.

Tennis
Chicago Park District has indoor and outdoor tennis courts. Lessons are available at many locations.

Beach Volleyball
You can sign up for summer volleyball at several beaches.

Further Reading

American Apocalypse: The Great Fire and The Myth of Chicago by Ross Miller, University of Chicago Press (1990). A look at the rebuilding of Chicago following the fire that destroyed most of the city.
Chicago Architecture 1872–1922, edited by John Zukowsky, Prestel-Verlag, Munich, in association with the Art Institute of Chicago.
The Plan of Chicago: 1909–1979, Art Institute of Chicago (1979), ed. John Zukowsky.
Chicago's Famous Buildings, Third Edition, University of Chicago Press (1980) ed. Ira J. Bach.
Boss: Richard J. Daley of Chicago by Mike Royko, New York (1971). The story of Mayor Richard J. Daley by the renowned late Tribune columnist.
Chicago Days: 150 Defining Moments in the Life of a Great City by the staff of the Chicago Tribune, edited by Stevenson Swanson, Contemporary Books (1997). Pictures and stories of defining events of Chicago.
City on The Make by Nelson Algren, (originally published in 1951), with introduction by Studs Terkel, University of Chicago (1987).
Biking on Bike Trails Between Chicago & Milwaukee by Peter Blommer, Blommer Books (1998).
Sister Carrie by Theodore Dreiser, edited by Robert Coltrane and Neda M. Westlake, University of Pennsylvania (1998). Originally published in 1900, this controversial account of a small-town girl's encounter with the big city was banned for 12 years but later recognized as having an important influence on 20th century literature.
The Wicked City: Chicago from Kenna to Capone by Curt Johnson, R. Craig Sautter, contributor, and Roger Ebert, introduction (1998).

The wheeler-dealers of Chicago from 1880–1950.
Twenty Years at Hull-House: With Autobiographical Notes by Jane Addams, Ruth Sidel, Norah Hamilton, Penguin Twentieth Century Classics (1998). A story of hope and courage.
There Are No Children Here by Alex Kotlowitz, Anchor (1992). A powerful account of two young boys growing up in the crime-ridden Chicago projects.
    The gritty crime novels of **Sarah Paretsky**, which feature tough, wise-cracking private eye V.I. Warshawski, are all set in Chicago.

Other Insight Guides

The widely-acclaimed Insight Guide series includes 190 titles covering every continent. There are also more than 100 Pocket Guides and 60 Compact Guides. The 40-plus titles covering the United States include:
Insight Guide: Crossing America. Documents three routes by car, vividly portraying the people and places you'll encounter on the way.
Insight Guide: New York City. Not only covers all the sights worth seeing but also includes some great features, such as the encounters that happen during a typical night-time police patrol.
Pocket Guide: Boston. Contains personal recommendations from a local host, plus detailed itineraries and full-size fold-out map.
Pocket Guide: Atlanta. The practical, personalized guide to the city of the 1996 Olympics. Detailed itineraries and full-size fold-out map.
Insight Compact Guide: Florida. A great example of these perfect on-the-spot guides. It packs an amazing amount of information into a portable format, with text, photo-graphs and maps carefully cross-referenced.

ART & PHOTO CREDITS

Chuck Berman 10/11, 21, 50/51, 57, 58, 60, 62, 64, 75, 86, 96/97, 98, 107, 108, 113, 118, 119, 121, 124/125, 126/127, 128/129, 139, 140L, 145, 164, 165, 168, 169, 170, 171, 172, 173, 174, 175, 176/177, 178, 184, 188/189, 190, 191, 192, 193, 195, 196, 197, 202/203, 205, 207, 210, 212, 213, 214/215, 216, 217, 228, 240/241, 243, 249, 255
C & S Chattopadhyay 1, 12/13
Chicago Botanic Garden 240
Chicago Historical Society 20, 22, 23, 24, 25, 27, 28, 29, 30, 31, 32, 33L, 33R, 34, 40, 41, 44, 45
Chicago Sun-Times 18, 26, 36/37, 39, 42, 43, 47, 48, 49, 66, 67, 76, 78R, 79, 230
Jerry Dennis 92, 156
Firestone/Sipa-Press/Rex Features 69
Wolfgang Fritz 130
Glyn Genin/APA 2/3, 2B, 4/5, 4BL, 4BR, 5B, 48, 49, 54, 55, 56, 59, 61, 83, 99, 101, 102, 103, 140R, 141, 143T, 145T, 147T, 148T, 155, 157T, 159, 159T, 167, 169T, 170T, 181T, 183T, 186, 192T, 193T, 195T, 197T, 206, 207T, 210T, 221T, 223T, 225, 226, 227, 234T, 235, 237, 237T, 239, 245T, 246, 251T
Luke Golobitsch 16/17, 88L, 100, 104/105, 142, 230/231, 232, 238, 250, 251, 254, 256
Blaine Harrington 122, 136/137
Ray F Hillstrom Jr. 70, 71, 82, 249T, 253T
Robert Holmes 144, 147, 181, 194, 224, 227T
The Image Bank 112
Fernando Jones 89R
Cathy Kleiman, Lincoln Park Zoo Society 185

Milwaukee Visitors & Convention Bureau 253
NASA 148
Marc PoKempner 6/7, 8/9, 14, 109, 204
Eddy Posthuma de Boer 52/53, 72/73, 143, 152/153
James Quinn 74, 77, 80, 88R, 90, 91, 111, 114/115, 247
Rex Features 223
Sten M Rosenlund 65
James P Rowan 110, 123, 146, 183, 185T, 247T, 248
Ron Schramm 116, 120, 162/163, 179, 211
Six Flags Great America 252
Sporting Pictures (UK) 106
Topham 19, 35, 46
Harry Walker 63, 89L, 182, 198, 199, 219, 221L, 221R, 229
Margaret Wright 138, 154, 157, 209, 234, 236

Cartographic Editor **Zoë Goodwin**
Production **Stuart A Everitt**
Design Consultants
Carlotta Junger, Graham Mitchener
Picture Research **Hilary Genin,**
Monica Allende

Picture Spreads

Pages 94/95
Top Row, left to right: Ron Schramm, Ron Schramm, Glyn Genin, Glyn Genin
Centre Row, left to right: Glyn Genin, Ron Schramm, Glyn Genin
Bottom Row, left to right: James P Rowan, Glyn Genin

Pages 150/151
Top Row, left to right: Kathleen Culbert-Aguilar/The Art Institute of Chicago/Gift of Mrs J Ward Thorne, Helen Birch Bartlett Memorial Collection/The Art Insitute of Chicago
Bottom Row, left to right: George F Harding Collection/The Art Institute of Chicago, Glyn Genin, Christopher Gallager/Bequest of Arthur Rubloff/The Art Institute of Chicago

Pages 160/161
Top Row, left to right: Jerry Dennis, Blaine Harrington, Ron Schramm
Centre Row, left to right: Jerry Dennis, Rex Features
Bottom Row, left to right: Ron Schramm, Ron Schramm

Pages 200/201
Top Row, left to right: James P Rowan, Ray F Hillstrom Jr., Ray F Hillstrom Jr., Robert Holmes
Bottom Row, left to right: James P Rowan, Glyn Genin, Ray F Hillstrom Jr., Ray F Hillstrom Jr.

Map Production Gar Bowes Design
© 1999 Apa Publications GmbH & Co.
Verlag KG (Singapore branch)

Index

Numbers in italics refer to photographs

A
B
C
D
E
F
G
H
I
a
b
c
d
f
g
h
i
j
k
l

The World of Insight Guides

400 books in three complementary series cover every major destination in every continent.